WORLD HISTORY

Observations and Assessments from Creation to Today

James P. Stobaugh

First printing: March 2012

Master Books®, P.O. Box 726, Green Forest, AR 72638

Master Books® is a division of the New Leaf Publishing Group, Inc.

ISBN-13: 978-0-89051-648-5
Library of Congress Catalog Number: 2011945531

Cover design by Diana Bogardus.
Interior design by Terry White.

Please consider requesting that a copy of this volume be purchased by your local library system.

Printed in the United States of America

Please visit our website for other great titles:
www.masterbooks.net

For information regarding author interviews, please contact the publicity department at (870) 438-5288

Master Books®
A Division of New Leaf Publishing Group
www.masterbooks.net

This book is dedicated to this new generation of young believers whose fervor and dedication to the purposes of the Lord shall yet bring a great revival. Stand tall, young people, and serve our Lord with alacrity and courage!

Using Your Student Textbook

How this course has been developed:

1. **Chapters:** This course has 34 chapters (representing 34 weeks of study).

2. **Lessons:** Each chapter has five lessons each, taking approximately 20 to 30 minutes each. There will be a short reading followed by critical thinking questions. Some questions require a specific answer from the text, while others are more open-ended, leading the student to think "outside the box."

3. **Weekly exams:** The final lesson of the week is the exam covering the week's chapter.

4. **Student responsibility:** Responsibility to complete this course is on the student. Students are to complete the readings every day, handing their responses to a parent or teacher for evaluation. Independence is strongly encouraged in this course, which was designed for the student to practice independent learning.

5. **Grading:** Turn in your assignments daily or weekly to your parent/teacher.

Thoughout this book you will find the following components:

1. **Narrative Background:** background on the period.

2. **Critical Thinking Questions:** questions based roughly on Bloom's Taxonomy.

3. **Concepts/Generalizations:** terms, concepts, and theories to be learned.

4. **History Maker:** a person(s) who clearly changed the course of history.

5. **Historiographies or Historical Debate:** an examination of historical theories surrounding a period or topic.

6. **World View Formation:** An overview of historical understandings of who God is. There is also a subsection where we examine important thinkers of the period/topic.

7. **History & World View Overview:** an overview of world views.

What the student will need each day:

1. **Notepad:** for writing assignments.

2. **Pen/pencil:** for the answers and essays.

About the Author

James P. Stobaugh and his wife, Karen, have homeschooled their four children since 1985. They have a growing ministry, For Such a Time As This Ministries, committed to challenging this generation to change its world for Christ.

Dr. Stobaugh is an ordained pastor, a certified secondary teacher, and an SAT coach. His academic credentials include: BA, cum laude Vanderbilt University; Teacher Certification, Peabody College for Teachers; MA, Rutgers University; MDiv, Princeton Theological Seminary; Merrill Fellow, Harvard University; DMin Gordon Conwell Seminary.

Dr. Stobaugh has written articles for magazines: *Leadership, Presbyterian Survey, Princeton Spire, Ministries Today,* and *Pulpit Digest.* Dr. Stobaugh's books include the *SAT Preparation Course for the Christian Student,* the *ACT Preparation Course for the Christian Student,* as well as *American History, British History,* and *World History* high school curriculum.

Contents

Preface

History is meant to be a light that illuminates the present and directs attention toward the possibilities of the future. However, history is only ancient, dusty chronicles if one does not honestly study and asses these written records of events, as well as the events themselves. History is a social science¾a branch of knowledge that uses specific methods and tools to achieve its goals.

Historians examine archival footprints. Some of these are written records: diaries, letters, oral histories, recordings, inscriptions, biographies, and many others. At times history seems merely to be a list of kings, of wars, and of other significant things. As a result, it can seem like only the study of a bunch of dead people. Who cares? Like Huck Finn, we quip, "After supper the widow Douglas got out her book and learned me about Moses and the bulrushes, and I was in a sweat to find out all about him; but by and by she let it out that Moses had been dead a considerable long time; so then I didn't care no more about him, because I don't take no stock in dead people" (Twain, Mark. The Adventures of Huckleberry Finn).

But history is alive, and full of interesting, glorious, and useful things! And it is terribly relevant to all of us.

There are lots of different histories. The Earth, the world of nature, and the universe all have pasts, but they have no histories, per se. Histories have to do with real, alive (or once alive) people. Only human societies have histories, based on collective memories from which they reconstruct their pasts.

Not all attempts to reconstruct the past have resulted in histories. My Uncle George (not a real uncle but just a family friend), grand wizard of the Ku Klux Klan, had an entirely different view of African history than I, a father of three African-American children. Uncle George had a delusional "history" that was very much like a Nazi propaganda film, but it was not a "history." It was a "past" made up of venal images, obscured remembrances, and visceral prejudices that stewed in his poor, conflicted mind.

My history was big enough to love Uncle George—may he rest in peace—and I did, as did my three children. And in my life, we were brought together into an eternal peace. Perhaps that is the best thing one can say about world history; it brings everyone together in one shared history.

To be a true history, an account of the past must not only retell what happened but must also relate events and people to each other. It must inquire into causes and effects. It must

The United Nations Office at Geneva, Switzerland

try to discern falsehood in the old records, such as attempts of historical figures to make them look better than they really were. It must also present the evidence on which its findings are based.

It is clear that all our information in regard to past events and conditions must be derived from evidence of some kind, and certain evidences are better than others.

To that end, I do not expect students to be completely neutral about historical sources. And yet, scholarly historical inquiry demands that we implement the following principles:

1. Historians must evaluate the veracity of sources. There must be a hierarchy of historical sources. Primary source material, for instance, is usually the best source of information.

2. Historians must be committed to telling both sides of the historical story. They may choose to lobby for one view over the other, but they must fairly examine all theories.

3. Historians must avoid stereotypes and archetypes. They must overcome personal prejudices and dispassionately view history in ruthlessly objective terms.

4. Historians must be committed to the truth no matter where their scholarship leads them. At times historians will discover unflattering information about their nation/state.

5. Finally, historians understand that real, abiding, and eternal history is ultimately made only by people who obey God at all costs.

After everything is said and done, historians are only studying the past. They cannot really change the past. Theories about the past come and go, and change with each generation; however, the past is past. Historians will debate about history, but they can never alter it. Only God can change history, and God alone.

When persons are reborn in Christ, their present, future, and, yes, even their past is changed. History is literarily rewritten. They are new creations. That bad choice, that sin, that catastrophe is placed under the blood of the Lamb, and everything starts fresh and new; a new history for new people.

This happened in my own life. 150 years ago my great-great-great-grandfather, whose passion was to kill Yankees, was a slave owner in Eastern Tennessee. With that inheritance, like most white Southerners who grew up in the

Bungalow in Bora Bora

1960s, I grew to mistrust African-Americans. Like so many people captured by their history and culture, present and future became my past. However, when I was a senior in high school, I was saved. Jesus Christ became my Lord and Savior. My attitudes changed. It took time, but prejudices disappeared. Ultimately, I married my New Jersey wife, Karen, and we adopted three African-American children—whose ancestors, by the way, may have been owned by my great-great-great-uncle!

Three of my children are African-American. Imagine! Quite literally, my history was rewritten. It has been changed irrevocably by my decision to invite Jesus Christ to be Savior of my life. In a real sense, family prejudice and death existing for generations ended in my generation. The destructive historical cycle that was part of my history has ended. No one, nothing can do that but the Lord. History has been rewritten!

My prayer is that if you do not know this God who can change history—even your history—this history text might encourage you to invite Jesus Christ into your heart as Savior.

View from the top of St. Peters Basilica in the Vatican city. Large parts of central Rome are visible.

Chapter 1

MESOPOTAMIA

First Thoughts . . .

Authorities in the field of history do not all agree about the definition of civilization. Most accept the view that "a civilization is a culture which has attained a degree of complexity usually characterized by urban life." In other words, a civilization is a culture capable of sustaining the social, political, and religious needs of a densely populated society. The Mesopotamian region, beginning with the Sumerians, created a system of writing to keep records, monumental architecture in place of simple buildings, and art that was worthy of its people. All these characteristics of civilization first appeared in Mesopotamia.

Chapter Learning Objectives . . .

In chapter 1 we will learn that Mesopotamia is probably the location of the Garden of Eden. Next, we will examine the rise of the Sumerian civilization. We will study how subsequent nations conquered and enlarged the Mesopotamian footprint. Along the way we will examine Mesopotamian gods and contrast them with the God of the Jews.

As a result of this chapter you should be able to:

1. Discuss at least three important contributions that the Sumerian civilization made to the Western world.

2. Contrast Mesopotamian gods and goddesses with the Jewish God.

3. Write a short report on the life of Daniel.

4. Analyze the Mesopotamian civilizations.

5. Describe an ordinary day in the life of a 14 to 18-year-old Mesopotamian youth.

THE STORY OF MESOPOTAMIA

The story of Mesopotamia is the story of the very genesis of civilization. There is some debate about where people stopped merely herding their livestock and started farming and building cities and therefore creating a civilization. However, there are some strong arguments that it began in Mesopotamia. Mesopotamia, which means "between the rivers," lies between the Tigris and Euphrates rivers. It is located in the general vicinity of the present national states of Iraq and Syria. There is strong evidence that Mesopotamia is in fact Eden, where God placed the first man, Adam, and the first woman, Eve (Genesis 1).

Mesopotamia's oldest known communities date from 7000 BC, although that date is much debated. Most biblical scholars argue for a more recent date (c. 4000 BC).

Several civilizations prospered in the region until, in the sixth century BC, it became part of the Persian Empire, the largest empire in the world up to then (see Daniel 5).

The first city-state (an autonomous, self-contained urban center, surrounded by a dependent agricultural area) in the region was made up of the Sumerian cities Eridu and Uruk, among others. Abram emigrated from the Sumerian city of Ur.

Sumerians developed a system of writing by imprinting on clay tablets using a stylus. A form of printing was a similar first: they carved negative images on a stone cylinder usually from two to six centimeters long. These were repeatedly rolled over fresh clay to produce positive inscriptions. As forerunners of finger rings used to imprint wax seals in later times, they were used to identify possessions, to seal written tablets, and to protect other valuables. Sumerians also invented the wheel and therefore improved transportation endeavors and building programs.

Other contiguous people groups took note of these wonderful things. They were not slow to follow. About 2330 BC, Sumeria was conquered by Sargon I, king of the Akkadians. The Gutians, tribespeople from the eastern hills, ended Akkadian rule about 2200 BC, and, a few years later,

The tomb of Cyrus the Greatin Pasargad, Iran.

the Sumerian Ur arose to rule much of Mesopotamia. Finally, Hammurabi of Babylon (who reigned about 1792–1750 BC) conquered the whole Mesopotamia area. The Hittites conquered much of the area, but the Persians actually dominated the entire region of Mesopotamia.

Mesopotamian peoples produced highly decorated pottery and clothing. They also invented musical instruments such as the harp and lyre, which were used to accompany the recital of their many epic literary works (e.g., the Epic of Gilgamesh). They developed the concept of the library, assiduously collecting and cataloguing their mass of literary works. These works were the basis of some vigorous public and private debates.

Furthermore, scholars are convinced that the Sumerians in particular had a form of assembly for making key political decisions using a consensual approach. They held courts to make legal judgments. They were the first people to develop a code of law, and therefore used precedent to determine later court cases. That they also developed some understanding of economics is attested to by evidence of price-setting agreements and openly advocated urban planning. The word *suburb* is mentioned for the first time in a Sumerian text.

The Sumerians used gold, silver, tin, lead, copper, and bronze in jewelry making and in the construction of buildings. They were not, however, able to develop iron weaponry—a shortcoming that ultimately hindered them militarily when invading armies brandished iron swords and chariots.

In general, Mesopotamian women had very few rights. However, they were free to go to the marketplaces, and to attend to legal matters for their absent husbands. They were even able to own their own property, borrow and lend, and engage in business for themselves. High-status women, such as priestesses and members of royal families, learned to read and to write. Finally, several Sumerian deities were women figures, which increased the status of women considerably.

The earliest writing in Mesopotamia was a picture writing invented by the Sumerians, who wrote on clay tablets using long reeds. The script the Sumerians invented was a type of writing called cuneiform. This picture language, similar to but more abstract than Egyptian hieroglyphics, eventually developed into a syllabic alphabet under the Persians. In other words, this is the language/writing that Daniel, Esther, and other Jewish exiles would have used.

Individual words were represented by crude pictorial symbols that resembled in some way the object being represented. This complicated writing system dominated Mesopotamia until the century before the birth of Christ. The Persians greatly simplified cuneiform until it resembled something closer to an alphabet.

They wrote on clay tablets with long reeds while the clay was still wet. The fresh clay hardened and a permanent record was created. The original Mesopotamian writings were crude pictures of the objects being named, but the difficulty of drawing on fresh clay eventually produced the wedges and hooks unique to cuneiform. This writing would be formed by laying the length of the reed along the wet clay and moving the end nearest the hand from one side to another to form the hooks. As with all cultures, writing greatly changed Mesopotamian social structure and the civilization's relationship to its own history. Writing allowed laws to be written (e.g., Hammurabi Code) and so to assume a static and independent character. Also, history became more detailed and incorporated much more of local cultures' histories (Richard Hooker).

Ancient cuneiform writing in Ur, southern Iraq. Photo by Unclefester89, 2005 (PD-US).

In October 539 BC, with the Jews in exile, the Persian king Cyrus took Babylon, the ancient capital of an empire covering modern Iraq, Syria, Lebanon, and Israel. Babylon was, by that time, the ancient world's capital of scholarship and science. The subject provinces soon recognized Cyrus as their legitimate ruler. Since he was already the ruler of modern Turkey and Iran, it is not an exaggeration to say that the capture of Babylon meant the birth of the first true world empire. The Persian Empire was to last for more than two centuries, until it was conquered by the Macedonian Greek king Alexander the Great. Cyrus allowed the Jews (who were exiled in Babylonia) to return home.

For our purposes, the release of the exilic Jewish community was most important. The Jewish exile began with the destruction of Jerusalem and the transportation of Jewish survivors (notably Daniel and his friends) to Babylon by King Nebuchadnezzar in 586 BC. The majority of Jews remained in Babylonia even after the reestablishment of Jerusalem by Nehemiah.

Assignment

Discuss at least three important contributions that the Sumerian civilization made to the Western world.

View over the reconstructed city of Babylon, Iraq, by the U.S. Navy, 2005.

MESOPOTAMIA

Sumerian religions were polytheistic. The gods played a crucial role in the Sumerians' lives, both as a nation and as individuals. Most Sumerians, for instance, had a personal god or gods with whom they forged a special relationship. They were "good luck charms." The people looked to them for protection and assistance in all things, while also blaming them when things went wrong. These gods continued to be worshiped right through to the late Babylonian period.

The Sumerian pantheon was called the Anunnaki, although another name, the Igigi, was also used. These gods appeared to be polarities; thus, the first evidence of dualism entered world views. There were, in other words, good gods—the Anunnaki—and bad gods—the Igigi.

Originally, Marduk was the city god of Babylon, but in 1800 BC, he became the supreme god of the Mesopotamian pantheon. In fact, he was the god of the Palestinian provinces—and many think he was the god that Elijah confronted on Mt. Carmel (1 Kings 18). As such, he was recognized by the gods of the cities that were subjected by the Babylonian kings. According to myth, Marduk defended the other gods against the diabolical monster Tiamat. After he had killed it, he brought order to the cosmos, built the Esagila, and created mankind. This is clearly seen in the Gilgamesh Epic. In the poem Enûma Elish it is stated that all other gods are just manifestations of Marduk

Marduk and other gods and goddesses were worshiped at Ziggurats or temples. In fact, one, named Etemenanki, the foundation of heaven on earth, is considered by most scholars to be the tower of Babel of Genesis 11.

The reconstructed facade of the Neo-Sumerian Great Ziggurat of Ur, near Nasiriyah, Iraq, by Hardnfast, 2005.

When the Babylonians celebrated New Year (the so-called Akitu festival), they remembered how Marduk had created order in the universe. The heart of this cosmos was Babylon, and the Esagila shrine was, therefore, the center of the universe. The Babylonian Marduk was embraced by the Persian invaders.

The gods bound people together in their social groups and were believed to have provided what they needed to survive. The Sumerians developed stories and festivals to explain and solicit help for their everyday lives. Priests reminded the people every new year that the gods determined their futures for the coming year. The priests were responsible for the sacrifices and cultic rituals that were essential for the help of the gods. In addition, property belonged to the gods, so priests administered it. This made the priests valuable and important figures in their communities.

Mesopotamian gods were impersonal with their human charges. What a contrast this was to the Judeo-Christian God that Daniel and his friends served!

Assignment

Contrast Mesopotamian gods and goddesses with the Jewish God.

German late medieval depiction of the construction of the tower, by Meister der Weltenchronik, c1370s.

HISTORY MAKER: DANIEL

Daniel is one of those pivotal men of history who was able to make a great impact on history without having any official influence or power. One of the four great prophets, although he is not once spoken of in the Old Testament as a prophet, Daniel was born in Jerusalem about 623 BC during the reign of Josiah. At the first deportation of the Jews by Nebuchadnezzar (the kingdom of Israel had come to an end nearly a century before), Daniel and other noble youths were carried off to Babylon. As was the custom, the young elite of a conquered nation were taken to the mother country where they were raised in the ways of the empire. The hope was that the Jewish exiles would become good Babylonian citizens. Daniel was obliged to enter into the service of the king of Babylon, and in accordance with the custom of the age received the Chaldean name of Belteshazzar. His training in the schools of the wise men in Babylon was to fit him for service to the empire. Daniel, however, while he was willing to serve his new masters in an official capacity, had no intention of embracing Babylonian religion or culture. In fact, Daniel was distinguished during this period for his piety and his strict observance of the Mosaic Law. He gained the confidence and esteem of those who were over him. In other words, he was willing to prosper in Babylon, but he would never be a Babylonian. His habit of attention gained during his education in Jerusalem enabled him to soon master the wisdom and learning

Daniel in the Lions' Den by Currier & Ives, c1893.

of the Chaldeans, and even to excel his captors. He soon became known for his skill in the interpretation of dreams, a very important role in the superstitious Babylonian court. Daniel's commitment to the worship of God inevitably put him in conflict with his superiors. His fidelity to God exposed him to persecution, and he was cast into a den of lions but was miraculously delivered; after which Darius issued a decree enjoining reverence for "the God of Daniel" (Daniel 6:26). He probably died at Susa, about 85 years of age. Ezekiel, with whom he was a contemporary, mentions him as a pattern of righteousness (Ezekiel 14:14, 20).

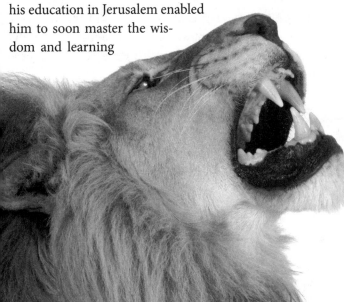

Assignment

Write a short report on the life of Daniel. How is your life similar to and different from the life of Daniel?

DAILY LIFE

Most Mesopotamians (Sumerians, Babylonians, Persians, etc.) were farmers. There were skilled craftsmen too—potters, builders, and traders. As Mesopotamian kings conquered other nations they returned with slaves, one of the most famous of whom was Daniel.

Most Mesopotamians wore a garment that was a flounced skirt. The skirts varied in length. The upper part of the body was often left bare. Women's skirts appear to be less elaborate but more colorful when compared to the men's. Sumerian noble women dressed in colorful clothes and head dresses. Their jewelry was made from gold, silver, and bright stones.

The rich lived in large, elaborate homes with spacious courtyards. Most homes were clustered around the Ziggurat temple. While most homes were single dwellings, they often shared an exterior wall with another home, much like contemporary condominiums.

Since wood was scarce, families built their homes with sun-dried brick. Inevitably, there was a small family courtyard. The courtyard, or first floor, in each house was very important. It often contained a playground, a vegetable garden, and a chicken coop. Most homes were designed with three stories of living space. The first living space was the courtyard. Stairs led up to the second and third floors, and then to the roof. Mesopotamians were skillful architects who could construct sturdy multi-level houses.

Roofs were flat and became everyone's summer bedroom.

Babylon, like all cities, had rich sections of town and poorer sections of town. Normally, the better houses were built closer to the royal palaces and the temples. Generally speaking, though, all families lived in single dwellings.

Women in ancient Mesopotamia were not equal to men, but they did have more rights than women in other ancient cultures. They bought and sold goods, owned property, and owned their own businesses. Upper-class women,

like members of the royal family and those who gave their life to the temple as priestesses, could learn how to read and write. Some women even had civil government jobs.

Only the very rich went to school, and the schools were run by the temple priests.

Life revolved around the two rivers, the Tigris and Euphrates. Since there were so few natural resources, Mesopotamians relied on overland and river trade. Goods were traded with cultures all over Asia Minor and Northern Africa.

Babylonian, and especially Persian, soldiers were second to none in the ancient world They conquered all of the known world at the time, except for Greece. Every Mesopotamian king kept a large standing army.

Assignment

Describe an ordinary day in the life of a 14 to18-year-old Mesopotamian youth.

FOUNDATIONS OF WORLD VIEWS

First Thoughts . . .

A world view is the way a person sees, understands, and responds to life from the philosophical position he or she embraces as his or her own. World view is a framework that ties everything together and allows people to understand society, the world, and their place in it. A world view helps people make critical decisions that shape our future. A study of world views is at the heart of world history.

Chapter Learning Objectives . . .

Chapter 2 will begin with two important historical figures, two lawgivers, Moses and Hammurabi. Next we will discuss the concept of world view. We will employ a paradigm popular in the university to describe different world views: Theism, Deism, Romanticism, Naturalism, Realism, Absurdism, and Existentialism. Finally, we will study mighty King Nebuchadnezzar, conqueror of Judah.

As a result of this chapter you should be able to:

1. Evaluate present controversy over the public display of the Ten Commandments..
2. Compare Hammurabi's Code with the Ten Commandments.
3. Examine Jesus' statements about the Ten Commandments.
4. Analyze the importance of Hammurabi's Code to history.
5. Evaluate the possible problems and potential advantages that Hammurabi's Code brought to Babylon.
6. Discuss the meaning and importance of world view discernment.
7. Research ways the Bible depicts Nebuchadnezzar.

MOSES

Moses, author of the Pentateuch, prophet, and lawgiver, was born in Goshen, a part of the exilic Hebrew community in Egypt. At that time the Hebrews, who lived in Egypt, were oppressed by Pharaoh. When Pharaoh ordered, as a form of birth control, that all Hebrew male infants be put to death, Moses' mother placed her baby in a basket woven from papyrus reeds and set it afloat on the Nile River in view of his sister, Miriam (Exodus 2:4; Numbers 26:59).

Moses was rescued by Pharaoh's daughter, who adopted Moses and brought him up as her son. As an adult, Moses killed an Egyptian who had murdered a Hebrew, and then fled from Egypt into the wilderness where he was a shepherd until he was 80 years of age. Just when Moses must have been thinking about retirement, God called him back to Egypt to deliver Israel from bondage. Later, on the way to the Promised Land, Moses received the stone tablets on which God had engraved these Ten Commandments: "I am the Lord your God, who brought you out of Egypt, out of the land of slavery. You shall have no other gods before me.

"You shall not make for yourself an image in the form of anything in heaven above or on the earth beneath or in the waters below. You shall not bow down to them or worship them; for I, the LORD your God, am a jealous God, punishing the children for the sin of the parents to the third and fourth generation of those who hate me, but showing love to a thousand generations of those who love me and keep my commandments. You shall not misuse the name of the LORD your God, for the Lord will not hold anyone guiltless who

Statue of Moses by Ignazio Jacometti on the base of the Colonna dell'Immacolata, Rome Italy, date unknown

Moses receiving the law by F. W. McCleave, c1877 (PD-US).

misuses his name. Remember the Sabbath day by keeping it holy. Six days you shall labor and do all your work, but the seventh day is a Sabbath to the LORD your God. On it you shall not do any work, neither you, nor your son or daughter, nor your male or female servant, nor your animals, nor any foreigner residing in your towns. For in six days the LORD made the heavens and the earth, the sea, and all that is in them, but he rested on the seventh day. Therefore the LORD blessed the Sabbath day and made it holy. Honor your father and your mother, so that you may live long in the land the LORD your God is giving you. You shall not murder. You shall not commit adultery. You shall not steal. You shall not give false testimony against your neighbor. You shall not covet your neighbor's house. You shall not covet your neighbor's wife, or his male or female servant, his ox or donkey, or anything that belongs to your neighbor" (Exodus 20).

Assignment

Approximately 1,400 years after God gave Moses the Ten Commandments, Jesus summed them up when He was confronted by the religious leaders of the day:

"Teacher, which is the greatest commandment in the Law?" Jesus replied: "'Love the Lord your God with all your heart and with all your soul and with all your mind.' This is the first and greatest commandment. And the second is like it: 'Love your neighbor as yourself.' All the Law and the Prophets hang on these two commandments" (Matthew 22:36–40).

Why did Jesus summarize the Ten Commandments in this way?

HAMMURABI

Hammurabi (1800 BC)

The foundation of all law making in Babylonia, from about the middle of the 23rd century BC until the fall of the empire to the Persians, was the code of Hammurabi, the first king of all Babylonia. He expelled invaders from his dominions, cemented the union of north and south Babylonia, made Babylon the capital, and thus consolidated an empire that endured for almost 20 centuries. The code that he compiled is the oldest known in history, older by nearly a thousand years than the Ten Commandments. Hammurabi, who was probably Amraphel (Genesis 14:1), a contemporary of Abraham, is regarded as having certainly contributed through his laws to Western legal traditions. King Hammurabi of Babylonia, the greatest ruler in the first Babylonian Empire, extended his empire northward from the Persian Gulf through the Tigris and Euphrates river valleys and westward to the coast of the Mediterranean Sea. What is even more important is that throughout his long reign he personally supervised public project building and set up a civil service. Hammurabi is primarily remembered for the Hammurabi Code—his codification of the laws governing Babylonian life.

Law Code of Hammurabi Stele, inscribed on a basalt stele (c. 1790 BC) in the Akkadian language in the cuneiform script. These laws stand as one of the first written codes of law in recorded history.

Excerpts from the Hammurabi Code:

1. If anyone ensnare another, putting a ban upon him, but he cannot prove it, then he that ensnared him shall be put to death.

2. If anyone bring an accusation against a man, and the accused go to the river and leap into the river, if he sink in the river his accuser shall take possession of his house. But if the river prove that the accused is not guilty, and he escape unhurt, then he who had brought the accusation shall be put to death, while he who leaped into the river shall take possession of the house that had belonged to his accuser.

3. If anyone bring an accusation of any crime before the elders, and does not prove what he has charged, he shall, if it be a capital offense charged, be put to death.

4. If he satisfies the elders to impose a fine of grain or money, he shall receive the fine that the action produces.

5. If a judge try a case, reach a decision, and present his judgment in writing; if later error shall appear in his decision, and it be through his own fault, then he shall pay 12 times the fine set by him in the case, and he shall be publicly removed from the judge's bench, and never again shall he sit there to render judgment.

6. If anyone steals the property of a temple or of the court, he shall be put to death, and also the one who receives the stolen thing from him shall be put to death.

7. If anyone buy from the son or the slave of another man, without witnesses or a contract, silver or gold, a male or female slave, an ox or a sheep, an ass or anything, or if he take it in charge, he is considered a thief and shall be put to death.

8. If anyone steals cattle or sheep or an ass or a pig or a goat, if it belongs to a god or to the court, the thief shall pay thirtyfold; if it belongs to a freed man of the king he

shall pay tenfold; if the thief has nothing with which to pay he shall be put to death.

9. If anyone lose an article, and find it in the possession of another: if the person in whose possession the thing is found say "A merchant sold it to me, I paid for it before witnesses," and if the owner of the thing say, "I will bring witnesses who know my property," then shall the purchaser bring the merchant who sold it to him, and the witnesses before whom he bought it, and the owner shall bring witnesses who can identify his property. The judge shall examine their testimony—both of the witnesses before whom the price was paid, and of the witnesses who identify the lost article on oath. The merchant is then proved to be a thief and shall be put to death. The owner of the lost article receives his property, and he who bought it receives the money he paid from the estate of the merchant.

10. If the purchaser does not bring the merchant and the witnesses before whom he bought the article, but its owner bring witnesses who identify it, then the buyer is the thief and shall be put to death, and the owner receives the lost article.

Prologue of the Code of Hammurabi (the 305 first inscripted squares on the stele). Some gaps in the list of benefits bestowed on cities recently annexed by Hammurabi may prove the tablet is older than the celebrated basalt stele (also in the Louvre). Clay, early 18th century.

Assignment

The notion that laws might supersede the authority of an autocratic leader was a novel idea. What possible problems and potential advantages did Hammurabi's Code bring to Babylon?

WAR OF THE WORLD VIEWS

History is not merely the story of wars and politics; it is also a story of ideals and world views. Columbus, Powhatan, and other history players were not primarily motivated by political and military gain. At their core, they were like we are—people motivated by their human relationships, religious beliefs, and cultural needs.

What is a "world view"? A world view is a way that a person understands, relates to, and responds from a philosophical position that he embraces as his own. World view is a framework that ties everything together, that allows us to understand society, the world, and our place in it.

Fathers of Philosophy

From our study of Greek history we know that there are basically two world view roots: One originated with Aristotle, who argued that the empirical world is primary. Thus, if one wants to advance knowledge one has to learn more about the world. Another root originated with Plato, who argued that the unseen world is primary. In Plato's case, that meant that if one wished to understand the world he studied the gods. In our case, we agree with Plato to the extent that we believe that God—who cannot be seen, measured—is in fact more real than the world.

Both Plato and Aristotle were impacted by Socrates. Socrates was one of the most influential but mysterious figures in Western philosophy. He wrote nothing, yet he had a profound influence on someone who did: Plato. Plato carefully recorded most of his dialogues.

Unlike earlier philosophers, Socrates' main concern was with ethics. There was nothing remotely pragmatic about Socrates, who was the consummate idealist. Until his day, philosophers invested most of their time explaining the natural world. In fact, the natural world often intruded into the abstract world of ideas and reality. Socrates kept both worlds completely separate.

To Socrates, the natural laws governing the rotation of the earth were merely uninteresting speculation of no earthly good. Socrates was more interested in such meaty concepts as "virtue" and "justice."

Taking issue with the Sophists, Socrates believed that ethics, specifically virtue, must be learned and practiced like any trade. One was not born virtuous; one developed virtue as he would a good habit. It could be practiced only by experts. There was, then, nothing pragmatic about the pursuit of virtue. It was systematic; it was intentional. Virtue was acquired and maintained by open and free dialogue. For the first time, the importance of human language was advanced by a philosopher (to reappear at the end of the 20th century in postmodern philosophy).

There was no more important philosopher in Western culture than Socrates' disciple Plato. Plato, like Socrates, regarded ethics as the highest branch of knowledge. Plato stressed the intellectual basis of virtue, identifying virtue with wisdom. Plato believed that the world was made of forms (such as a rock) and ideas (such as virtue). The ability of human beings to appreciate forms made a person virtuous. Knowledge came from the gods; opinion was from man. Virtuous activity, then, was dependent upon knowledge of the forms.

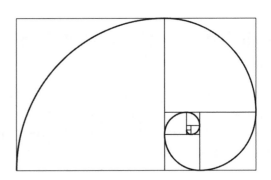

Fibonacci Spiral

To Plato, knowledge and virtue were inseparable. To Aristotle, they were unconnected. Aristotle was not on a search for absolute truth. He was not even certain it existed. Truth, beauty, and goodness were to be observed and quantified from human behavior and the senses, but they were not the legal tender of the land. Goodness in particular was not an absolute, and in Aristotle's opinion it was much abused. Goodness was an average between two absolutes.

Aristotle said that mankind should strike a balance between passion and temperance, between extremes of all sorts. He said that good people should seek the "Golden Mean" defined as a course of life that was never extreme.

Finally, while Plato argued that reality lay in knowledge of the gods, Aristotle argued that reality lay in empirical, measurable knowledge. To Aristotle, reality was tied to purpose and to action. For these reasons, Aristotle became known as the father of modern science. Aristotle's most enduring impact occurred in the area of metaphysics—philosophical speculation about the nature, substance, and structure of reality. It is not physics—concerned with the visible or natural world. Metaphysics is concerned with explaining the nonphysical world. Aristotle, then, advanced the discussion about God, the human soul, and the nature of space and time. What makes this particularly interesting is Aristotle's penchant for delving into the metaphysical by talking about the gods in human terms.

Aristotle said, "All men by nature desire to know," and it is by the senses that the gods were known–or not. Faith had nothing to do with it. In other words, Aristotle, for the first time, discussed the gods as if they were quantified entities. He spoke about them as if they were not present. The Hebrews had done this earlier (Genesis 3), but Aristotle was probably not aware of Moses' text.

While some Christian thinkers such as Augustine and Aquinas employed Aristotelian logic in their discussions about God, they never speculated about His existence as Aristotle did. They used Aristotle's techniques only to understand more about God.

Most of you have not heard of this particular world view paradigm. It is called a cultural world view paradigm (as contrasted to a sociopolitical paradigm). Both are useful. Both are accurate. However, most Americans obtain their world views from culture, not from scholarship and education.

While sociopolitical descriptions of world views are completely accurate, they are not used by American universities or the media at all. When have you hear the term "cosmic humanist" used on television? In a movie? Very few people use this terminology in the real world. Therefore, if Christians wish to be involved in apologetics they must use a language that non-Christians can understand. Chesterton once lamented that Evangelical Christians are like Americans who visit France. Chesterton generalized that Americans, by and large, speak their words slower, articulate their words more carefully, and speak fewer words to complete a thought. However, what they should do, Chesterton argues, is to speak French in France! If we believers want the world to hear us, we need to speak their language.

Seven Major World Views

Here is a short sketch of the seven major world views with examples:

Theism: God is personally involved with humankind. Theism argues that the universe is a purposive, divinely created entity. It argues that all human life is sacred and all persons are of equal dignity. They are, in other words, created in the image of God. History is linear and moves toward a final goal. Nature is controlled by God and is an orderly system. Humanity is neither the center of nature nor the universe, but is the steward of creation. Righteousness will triumph in a decisive conquest of evil. Earthly life does not exhaust human existence but looks ahead to the resurrection of the dead and to a final, comprehensive judgment of humanity (adapted from Carl F. H. Henry, *Toward a Recovery of Christian Belief*). This was the only viable world view until the Renaissance. Examples: Homer, Virgil, C. S. Lewis, A. J. Cronin, Tolkien.

2 **Deism:** God was present but is no longer present. The world is like a clock wound up by God many years ago, but He is now absent. The clock (i.e., the world) is present; God is absent. Still, though, Deism embraced a Judeo-Christian morality. God's absence, for instance, in no way mitigated His importance to original creation. He was also omnipotent but not omniscient. His absence was His decision. He was in no way forced to be absent from the world. He chose to assume that role so that Socratic empiricism and rationalism could reign as sovereign king. Speculative Theism replaced revelatory biblical Theism. Once the living God was abandoned, Jesus Christ and the Bible became cognitive orphans (Carl F. H. Henry). Examples: Albert Einstein, Voltaire.

3 **Romanticism:** Romanticism, and its American version, Transcendentalism, posited that God was nature and "it" was good. The more natural things were, the better. Nature was inherently good. Nature alone was the ultimate reality. In other words, nature was the Romantic god. Man was essentially a complex animal, too complex to be controlled by absolute, codified truth (as one would find in the Bible). Human intuition replaced the Holy Spirit. Depending upon the demands on individual lives, truth and good were relative and changing. Romanticism, however, like Deism, had not completely abandoned Judeo-Christian morality. Truth and the good, although changing, were nonetheless relatively durable. Examples: James Fenimore Cooper, Goethe.

4 **Naturalism:** If God exists, He is pretty wimpish. Only the laws of nature have any force. God is either uninterested or downright mean. All reality was reducible to impersonal processes and energy events (Carl F. H. Henry). All life, including human life, was transient. Its final destination was death. Truth and good, therefore, were also transient. They were culture-conditioned distinctions that the human race projected upon the cosmos and upon history (Carl F. H. Henry). This maturation, as it were, of the human race necessitated a deliberate rejection of all transcendentally final authority. Examples: Epicurus, Ernest Nagel.

5 **Realism:** Akin to Naturalism is Realism. Reality is, to a Realist, a world with no purpose, no meaning, no order. Realism insists that personality has no ultimate status in the universe, but is logically inconsistent when it affirms an ethically imperative social agenda congruent with universal human rights and dignity. Realism, then, throws around terms like "dignity" and "human rights" and "power." What Realists mean, however, is that these concepts are real when they fulfill a social agenda that enhances human dominance over the universal. Thus, Realism believes in a world where bad things happen all the time to good people. Why not? There is no God, no ontological controlling force for good. The world is a place where the only reality is that which we can experience, but it must be experience that we can measure or replicate. Certainly pain and misery fit that category. If an experience is a unique occurrence (e.g., a miracle) it is not real. Examples: Plato, Amit Goswami.

6 **Absurdism:** A modern movement where there is neither a god nor any reason to have one. Everything is disorganized, anarchy rules. There is a compete abandonment of explaining the cosmos and therefore an abandonment of being in relationship with the deity. It is not that Absurdists are unsure about who creates everything or is in control of everything. Absurdists simply do not care one way or the other. Examples: Albert Camus, Kurt Vonnegut, Jr.

7 **Existentialism:** The submergence of God in overwhelming data and in experience is the first step toward putting God out to die. Truth is open to debate. Everything is relative. A very pessimistic view. Examples: Franz Kafka, Jean-Paul Sartre.

Assignment

A. Match each quote with a world view.

A. Existentialism	Feelings are everything.
B. Deism	My god is the rising sun; my goddess, the rising moon.
C. Naturalism	It is true because I said it is true.
D. Romanticism	God was here—He set up our great country—but He is gone now.
E. Realism	Only the world around us has any force.

B. True or False

1.	Most Americans today are Theists.
2.	Most Americans today are Christian Theists.
3.	Postmoderns love to play with scientific gadgets but are inherently suspicious of their efficacy.
4.	The decade of the 1960s was a triumph of Existentialism.
5.	One reason Americans are so open to the Gospel is because our culture has become dysfunctional.
6.	A perfect example of postmoderns would be Clint Eastwood.
7.	*Toy Story* is a perfect example of postmodernism.
8.	The best way to convert a Romantic is to hand him a dead squirrel.
9.	John Wayne movies are generally Theistic movies.
10.	The *Star Wars* movies are Theistic in tone and substance.
11.	The Beatles moved from nostalgic Romanticism to nihilistic Absurdism.
12.	For most of history, Theism has been the dominant world view.

NEBUCHADNEZZAR

Nebuchadnezzar (c. 630–561 BC) was the greatest king of the Chaldean dynasty of Babylonia. He ascended the throne on his father's death, just after winning Syria from the Egyptians (605 BC). He attacked Judah, captured Jerusalem, and deported important citizens to Babylon. He paved roads, rebuilt temples, and dug canals. He also built the Hanging Gardens of Babylon.

Nebuchadnezzar by William Blake, 1795 (PD-Art).

During Nebuchadnezzar's 57-year reign, the Babylonian Empire reached its greatest glory. However, there were some setbacks. In 601 BC, Nebuchadnezzar attempted the invasion of Egypt but was repulsed by heavy losses. Overall, though, his reign was a prosperous and peaceful one.

One trademark of Nebuchadnezzar was the temples he built in many of the cities of his kingdom. Babylon was greatly enlarged. The city covered some 500 acres and was protected by massive double fortifications. The Euphrates River, which bisected it, was spanned by a bridge. In the great palace were the magnificent Hanging Gardens.

Many feel, partly based on the biblical witness, that Nebuchadnezzar eventually went insane. In any event, the last years of Nebuchadnezzar's life were filled with family discord. He left no strong successor: his son was overthrown after reigning only two years. Babylon, however, survived and was visited by the Greek historian Herodotus, who described its marvels this way:

Excerpts from the Greek historian Herodotus:

The city of Babylon is situated on a large plain. It is square in shape, and each side is 14 miles long, so that the complete circuit is 56 miles. It is built like no other city known to the Greeks. A wide, deep moat full of water runs round it, and inside the moat is a wall 330 feet high and 86 feet thick. I must tell you where the earth was used when it was taken from the moat, and how the wall was built. As they were digging the moat they formed the mud which was brought out of the excavations into bricks, and when they had molded a sufficient number of bricks, they baked them in kilns. With these bricks they built the banks of the moat, and after that the wall itself, using hot bitumen for mortar and inserting reed-mats every thirty rows to strengthen it. Along the edges on top of the wall they put one-roomed buildings facing each other, with sufficient space between them for a four-horse

Bust of Herodotus, second century AD. Roman copy after a Greek original. On display along the portico of the Stoa of Attalus in Athens (CC BY-SA 3.0).

chariot to turn round. There are a hundred gates in the wall, all made of bronze with posts and lintels of the same material. The Euphrates, a wide, swift, and deep river which rises in Armenia and flows into the Persian Gulf, runs through the city, dividing it into two parts. The wall runs down to the river on both sides, and the ends are joined by fortifications of baked bricks along each bank of the river. The city itself contains many houses three or four stories high, and all the streets are straight, some running parallel to the river and some at right angles to it. At the end of each street which runs down to the river there is a gate made of bronze in the wall to give access to the river.

These walls form the city's outer defense. Inside them there is another wall, narrower than the first but almost as strong. In each half of the city there is a fortified building; on one side of the river there is the royal palace with its great defensive wall, and on the other is the temple of Bel, the Babylonian Zeus. This is an enclosure a quarter of a mile square, with bronze gates, and was still in existence when I visited Babylon. In the middle of the enclosure is a solid square tower with its sides more than two hundred yards long. On top of it there is another tower and another on top of that, and so on up to eight stages. The staircase to the upper stories runs spirally round the outside, and about halfway up there is a platform with seats where people going up can rest. On the top story there is a large temple in which there is a great couch covered with fine draperies, with a table made of gold alongside it.

There is another temple in the sacred enclosure at Babylon. It is at ground level, and contains a large seated figure of Bel, made of gold. The base of the statue, the throne on which it sits, and the great table alongside are also golden. The Babylonians told me it took more than 18 tons of gold to make them.

As the river divides the city in two, anyone who wanted to cross from one part to the other had at first to go by boat, and this must have caused a good deal in inconvenience. Queen Nitocris, however, found an answer to this. When she was altering the course of the Euphrates upstream from Babylon so as to improve the defenses of the city, she made use of these operations to bridge the river and add to her own fame. She had long blocks of stone cut, and when they were ready and the basin for the river had been dug, she diverted its waters into the basin.

Gateway into Nebuchadnezzar's palace. Photo by American Colony (Jerusalem), Photo Dept., 1932.

While this was filling, the old river bed became dry, and Nitocris used bricks baked in the same way as had been done for the walls to build embankments on either side of the river where it ran through the city, and ramps leading to them from the gates that opened on to the river. At the same time she used the stone blocks which had been prepared to build piers for a bridge at the city center, binding the stones together with iron and lead. On these piers she laid squared timbers over which the inhabitants were allowed to cross during the day. At night, however, the timbers were removed to stop people crossing in the dark and committing burglaries.

Assignment

Write a report describing how the Bible depicts Nebuchadnezzar.

Glazed tiles symbolizing a lion in three-dimensional shape from the gates of ancient Babylon. The Lion was a symbol of Babylon, and represents Ishtar, the goddess of fertility, love, and war.

Chapter 3

THE JEWISH EXILE

First Thoughts . . .

Nebuchadnezzar, the greatest of Babylonian kings, destroys Israel and takes 10,000 of the most important Jewish leaders back to Babylon. The destruction of the temple and the exile to Babylon represents a tremendous shock to the Jewish people. It may be hard to imagine today what it must have meant back then, because we really have no basis of comparison. Before the Exile, Judaism meant living with the constant presence of God, which was always accessible at the temple. Miracles occurred near the temple daily and could be witnessed by anyone. For example, whichever way the wind was blowing, the smoke of the sacrifices always went straight to heaven (aish.com). No wonder they wept by the rivers of Babylon. However, while the Babylonians could be very cruel in their conquests, their attitude toward the exiled Jewish community is "live and let live." Life in Babylonia turned out not to be too awful. In fact, by the time Nehemiah is ready to return with a remnant, a majority of Jews prefer to stay in Babylon.

Chapter Learning Objectives . . .

Chapter 3 begins by looking at a general history of Israel and ties that into the story of the Jewish exile. The temptation for Jewish exiles in Babylon to be absorbed into a foreign culture is overwhelming, due in part to the Persian religion Zoroastrianism, which we will examine closely. Eventually, a remnant of faithful Jews returns home with Nehemiah, with permission from the Persian king Cyrus the Great to rebuild the Temple and the Holy City of Jerusalem. We will end this chapter by looking at the history of this most holy of religious cities.

As a result of this chapter you should be able to:

1. Discuss how the covenant theme was a significant part of early Jewish history.
2. Evaluate the reasons a majority of Jewish exiles remained in Babylon.
3. Identify ways Christians today can survive and even prosper without being absorbed by the culture surrounding them.
4. Compare and contrast Zoroastrianism with Judaism.
5. Define "syncretism" and reframe it as a problem Christians face all the time.

THE HISTORY OF ISRAEL

The history of Israel is tied to the history of Judaism. History is of the utmost importance in Judaism. Whereas the sacred texts of most ancient religions focus on legends and philosophy, the focus of the Old Testament is on historical narrative. Most Jewish holidays are intended to connect modern Jews with their historical ancestors and traditions.

The biblical book of Genesis begins with the one true all-powerful God creating the world out of chaos in six days, adding human beings on the sixth day. Mankind repeatedly turns away from God and to immorality until God destroys the earth with a flood. God then makes a covenant (a sacred, irrevocable agreement) with Noah that He will never again destroy the entire earth with a flood.

Abram (later renamed Abraham), who is considered the founder of the Jewish religion, begins his journey from Samaria to the Holy Land (Gen. 11).

The faith of Abraham and his descendants (called the patriarchs) was simple, and centered on a covenant between Abraham and God. Religious practice consisted of sacrifice and prayer at a sacred altar. Circumcision was the defining mark of the religious community. Its **eschatology** was the promise of land and many descendents.

During the time of Joseph's leadership in Egypt, a severe famine caused the Hebrew tribes to migrate to Egypt, where they were enslaved. God rescued them from bondage by afflicting the Egyptians with successive plagues then drowning the Egyptian army in the Red Sea to allow the Hebrews to escape (Exodus). At Mount Sinai, God established the nation of Israel (named for Abraham's grandson Jacob) as His own and, through the Ten Commandments, gave them the terms of His covenant with them. He then sustained the Israelites through their 40-year journey in the wilderness before leading them into Canaan, the land promised to Abraham. Central to all these events was Moses, who fulfilled many leadership roles, including religious, political, legislative, and military.

Sacrifice of Isaac by Rembrandt, 1635 (PD-US).

The conquest of Canaan is narrated in the biblical book of Joshua, with miraculous events (walls fell at a shout, the sun stood still) rivaling those of the Exodus. After the conquest of Canaan, Israel was led by leaders called "judges," during which time the Israelites are described as repeatedly falling into apostasy.

Ultimately, Israel wanted a king, like the other nations had. The prophet and last judge, Samuel, reluctantly crowned Saul as Israel's first king. Samuel and his loyal Jewish followers saw this as a rejection of God's kingship (1 Sam. 8–12).

Saul's reign was marred by conflicts with the prophet Samuel, who held ongoing authority over the kingship. King David, Saul's successor, solved these problems by combining religious and political authority in one person (David and his descendents) and in one place (the city of Jerusalem). David was succeeded by his son Solomon, whose history is recorded in 1 Kings 1–11 and 2 Chronicles 1–9. During Solomon's long reign of 40 years, Israel attained its greatest influence. In a single year he collected tribute amounting to 666 talents of gold (1 Kings 10:13). As soon as he had settled himself in his kingdom and arranged the affairs of his extensive empire, he formed an alliance with Egypt by marrying a daughter of Pharaoh. Eventually, he had 700 wives and 300 concubines representing many religions. Solomon's reign became clouded as he fell into idolatry due to the influence of many of his wives (1 Kings 11:3). After Solo-mon's reign the nation split into two kingdoms: Israel (in the north) and Judah (in the south). Israel was conquered by the Assyrian ruler Shalmaneser V in the eighth century BC The kingdom of Judah was conquered by a Babylonian army in the early sixth century BC The Judaic elite were exiled to Babylon, but later at least a part of them returned to their homeland, led by prophets Ezra and Nehemiah, after the subsequent conquest of Babylonia by the Persians.

Death of King Saul by Elie Marcuse, 1848 (PD-US).

King David in Prayer by Pieter Fransz de Grebber, c1635 (PD-Art).

Assignment

Discuss how the covenant theme was a significant part of early Jewish history.

THE JEWISH EXILE

After conquering Jerusalem in 597 BC, the Chaldeans, a people group in the Babylonian Empire whose most famous member was Nebuchadnezzar, following standard Mesopotamian practice, deported the Jews to Babylonia. Approximately 10,000 people were forced to relocate to the city of Babylon, the capital of the Chaldean Empire. Among this group were Daniel and his young friends. In 586 BC Judah itself ceased to be an independent kingdom, and the earlier deportees found themselves without a homeland and without a nation. This period in Jewish history, called the Exile, ended in 538 when the Persians overthrew the Chaldeans.

Nebuchadnezzar, the king of the Chaldeans, deported only the most prominent citizens of Judah: professionals, priests, craftsmen, and the wealthy. The "people of the land" (*am-hares*) were allowed to stay. They were called "Samaritans." It is clear that the wealthy and professional Jews in Babylon regarded themselves as the true Jewish people.

The Exile was unexplainable. Hebrew history was built on the promise of God to protect the Hebrews and use them for His purposes in human history. Their defeat and the loss of the land promised to them by God was a devastating blow. But some creative Jews in Babylon, Daniel among them, managed to "remake" themselves without changing their God-centered world view. They prospered in Babylonia without becoming Babylonian. However, the majority of the Jewish exiles blended into Babylonian society so completely that they could not be identified as being different from Babylonian people.

When Cyrus the Persian conquered Mesopotamia, he allowed the Jews to return home. This was no ordinary event, though. Cyrus sent them home specifically to worship their God. Cyrus conquered Mesopotamia and the entire Middle East for religious reasons. Unlike any conqueror before him, Cyrus set out to conquer the entire world. Before Cyrus and the Persians, conquest was largely

Tomb of Cyrus II of Persia at Pasargadae by fr:Utilisateur:Mbenoist, 2001 (CC BY-SA 3.0).

a strategic affair; one guaranteed territorial safety by conquering potential enemies. But Cyrus wanted the whole world and he wanted it for religious reasons. He was a religious evangelist.

Barely a century earlier, the Persians were a small tribe of nomads living north of Mesopotamia. In the middle of the seventh century BC, a prophet, Zoroaster (also called Zarathustra), appeared among the Persians and preached a new religion called Zoroastrianism. This religion would become the religious system of the Persians. The Zoroastrians believed that the universe was dualistic, that it was made up of two distinct parts: One was good and light: the other evil and dark. Cosmic history was simply the epic battle between these two spiritual forces; at the end of time, a climactic battle would decide once and for all which of the two would dominate the universe. Human beings, in everything they did, participated in this struggle; all the gods and all the religions were part of this epic, almost eternal battle.

Ancient bas-reliefs of Persepolis, Iran

Cyrus believed that the final battle was approaching, and that Persia would bring about the triumph of good. To this end, he sought to conquer all peoples and create the stage for the final triumph of Persia. Convinced that the God of the Jews was good, Cyrus wanted to reestablish the Jewish religion in Palestine.

The salient feature to keep in mind, however, is that Cyrus sent the Jews home for religious purposes only. Judah was reestablished only so Yahweh could be worshipped, and the Jews were sent to Judah for the express purpose of worshiping Yahweh. They were not allowed to rebuild a political state.

Before the Exile, Judah and Israel were merely kingdoms; now Judah was a theological state. The symbol of this new state dedicated to God was the temple of Solomon, which had been burned to the ground by Nebuchadnezzar in 586 BC. Under the direction of Zerubbabel and later Ezra, the temple was rebuilt and the walls of the city rebuilt by Nehemiah.

For another 200 years Persia dominated all of the Middle East and Egypt, and nearly conquered Greece. During all this time Palestine was a tribute state of Persia. However, in the late fourth century BC, another man finally did conquer the known Western world: Alexander of Macedon.

Assignment

A. When we read the book of Nehemiah, it's easy to imagine that the majority of Jewish exiles returned to Jerusalem with Nehemiah and Ezra. In fact, though, the majority of Jewish exiles remained in Babylon. Why?

B. Daniel and Esther were called to survive and to prosper in an inhospitable land. Each was a captive of a repressive regime and was asked to be a leader in that regime. Like Daniel and Esther, how can Christians today survive and even prosper without being absorbed by the culture surrounding them?

Ruins of Babylon by American Colony (Jerusalem). Photo Dept., photographer. 1932 (PD-US).

ZOROASTRIANISM

Cyrus the Great was a fervent follower of Zoroastrianism, the religion founded by Zoroaster (Zarathustra) in Persia (present-day Iran). Once the official religion of the Persian Empire, it has been replaced by Islam. Zoroastrians today number fewer than 200,000. But during the Exile, because Zoroastrianism shared some beliefs with Judaism, it no doubt drew many Jewish exiles into its fold, creating "syncretism," a combining of beliefs from one or more religions.

For one thing, Zoroastrianism was a monotheistic faith. It also embraced beliefs concerning God and Satan, the soul, heaven and hell, the virgin birth of a savior, slaughter of the innocents, resurrection, the final judgment—all of which paralleled Judaism.

In Zoroastrianism, the single god Ahura Mazda is supreme. This god's communication to humans is expressed through a number of proverbs called "Bounteous Immortals." Within the Gathas, the original Zoroastrian sacred text, these Immortals are sometimes described as concepts, and are sometimes personified.

Also, there is a cosmic dualism between the all-powerful god Ahura Mazda, the only deity deemed worthy of being worshipped, and the evil spirit of violence and death, Angra Mainyu, who opposes Ahura Mazda.

The resulting cosmic conflict involves the entire universe, including humans, who are required to choose which god to follow. Evil and the Spirit of Evil will be completely destroyed at the end of time.

There is also an afterlife. After death, a soul is allowed three days to meditate on his or her past life. The soul is then judged and if the good works and deeds outweigh the bad, the soul is taken into heaven. Otherwise, the soul is led to hell.

Here is a summary of the beliefs of Zoroastrianism:

- The present world is where good and evil are mixed. People's good works are seen as gradually transforming

Zoroaster holds the celestial sphere in Raphael's School of Athens by Raffaello Sanzio, 1509 (PD-Art).

the world toward its heavenly ideal.

- In the future, a final state will occur when good and evil will be separated.

- Eventually, everything will be purified. Even the occupants of hell will be released.

- A savior will be born of a virgin, but of the lineage of the Prophet Zoroaster who will raise the dead and judge everyone in a final judgment

Assignment

Compare and contrast Zoroastrianism and Judaism.

JERUSALEM

In the biblical account, when first mentioned, Jerusalem (known as "Salem") is ruled by Melchizedek, an ally of Abraham. Later, in the time of Joshua, Jerusalem was in territory allocated to the tribe of Benjamin (Joshua 18:28), but it continued to be under the independent control of the Jebusites until it was conquered by David and made into the capital of the united Kingdom of Israel.

King David reigned until 970 BC. He was succeeded by his son Solomon, who built the Holy Temple on Mount Moriah. Solomon's Temple was the repository for the Ark of the Covenant. For more than 450 years, until the Babylonian conquest in 587 BC, Jerusalem was the political capital of Israel. Upon Solomon's death (c. 930 BC), the ten northern tribes split to form the Kingdom of Israel. Under the leadership of the house of David and Solomon, Jerusalem remained the capital of the Kingdom of Judah.

When the Assyrians conquered the Kingdom of Israel in 722 BC, Jerusalem was strengthened by a great influx of refugees from the Northern Kingdom. The First Temple Period ended around 586 BC, as the Babylonians conquered Judah and Jerusalem and laid waste to Solomon's Temple. In 538 BC, after 50 years of Babylonian captivity, Persia's King Cyrus the Great invited the Jews to return to Judah to rebuild the Temple.

Meeting of Abraham and Melchizedek by Dieric Bouts the Elder, c1464 (PD-Art).

Assignment

Summarize the history of Jerusalem.

Panoramic view of Jerusalem, Israel , 2011.

Visit of the Queen of Sheba to King Solomon, Gates of Paradise, Florence, Italy.

EGYPT

First Thoughts . . .

Perhaps no civilization has captured the imagination more than Egypt. We will travel back in time to a place that has left its imprint and impact on humanity forever. We will discover anew the civilization of Egypt, whose quest for immortality has mystified generations. At no other period of known history has a civilization left behind so many interesting riddles. Why did these people build pyramids? What did they write about the afterlife?

Chapter Learning Objectives . . .

Chapter 4 begins with an overview of Egyptian history up to the conquest of the Romans. Along the way we will discuss why and how the pyramids were built. We will study in-depth historical figures such as Cleopatra.

As a result of this chapter you should be able to:

1. Compare the rise of the Egyptian civilization with the rise of the Sumerian civilization.
2. Give an overview of the way pyramids were made.
3. Describe three of the most important Egyptian pharaohs.
4. Discuss why Cleopatra got involved in the Roman Civil War (after the assassination of Julius Caesar).
5. Explore the most enduring legacy of Egyptian history.

ANCIENT EGYPT

Egypt is located at the crossroads of the African and Asian continents. Thus, from the beginning, it had strategic importance to both continents.

In ancient times, the boundaries of Egypt were the Mediterranean Sea to the north and Aswan to the south. Its eastern and western boundaries were deserts. The Nile River, the most important geographic feature of the area, runs the length of the country, flowing from south to north.

Egypt was once mostly temperate and full of large, fertile, well-watered delta land. It was essentially one big oasis. Eventually, though, climate changes dried up most of this land, except the Nile River basin.

Ancient Egypt was divided into two regions: Upper Egypt and Lower Egypt. Lower (northern) Egypt consisted of the delta made by the Nile River as it empties into the Mediterranean Sea. Upper Egypt was the long, narrow strip of ancient Egypt located south of the Delta.

Evidence indicates that people began settling along the Lower Nile Delta about 5000 BC. Before that, most of, the people in Egypt had been shepherds. When much of Egypt became a desert, the Nile River continued to flood as it had every summer for thousands of years, leaving rich deposits of soil along its banks. In this fertile delta, a new civilization arose as former shepherds came to farm the land.

Eventually small cities grew, and then there were two nations. These were called Upper and Lower Egypt. Menes, the king of Lower Egypt, eventually conquered everything and formed a dynasty. Approximately 3000 BC, Menes joined Upper and Lower Egypt into one kingdom, of which Memphis was the capital. In this period, called the Old Kingdom, hieroglyphics—Egyptian writing—was developed and written on papyrus scrolls.

Egypt became a highly centralized state, united by a god-king and an imperial bureaucracy. The king was in essence a god on earth, and the chief mediator between

humanity and the higher gods of the heavens. Around 2650 BC, the king ordered construction of pyramids, specialized burial chambers from which it was believed their souls would ascend to the heavens and reside with the gods. At that point in history, eternal life was considered the exclusive privilege of the king.

Beneath the king were his priests, the nobles of the court, the local notables in the nomes (provinces), the scribes, and other staff of the bureaucracy. A small part-time army was retained, but Egypt's vast deserts helped protect the country from outsiders. The remaining 80 percent of the population were serfs—slaves, really. They spent three months of the year farming the Nile Delta. The rest of the year they were conscripted by the State for various building projects. The theory that Jewish slaves constructed the pyramids is not supported by history or archaeology. The pyramids were built mostly by local farmers.

The god-kings of the Old Kingdom had spent so lavishly on their burial chambers that the economy was severly strained. Furthermore, the nobles and the priests were wrestling for control of the kingdom. The central government at Memphis collapsed circa 2180 BC. The local notables staged civil war for the throne. There was a time of famine and disease.

The illusion of an all-powerful god-king ruling timelessly over Egypt was shattered. People no longer felt that the king alone was entitled to eternal life or protection of the gods. "The Democratization of the Afterlife" began during this phase, in which all those who submitted to such venerable deities as Aset (Isis) and Wesir (Osiris) could be

The Weighing of the Heart ritual, shown in the Book of the Dead of Sesostris. Photo by Manfred Werner - Tsui (CC BY-SA 3.0).

granted eternal life. In other words, the common people had access to the gods and, to a lesser degree, access to the throne (www.unrv.com).

Assignment

Compare the rise of the Egyptian civilization with the rise of the Sumerian civilization.

Seafront of the Nile River, Cairo, Egypt.

PYRAMIDS AND KINGDOMS

During the Middle Kingdom period, for the first time, high officials came from people outside of the royal family. The pyramids began to be smaller and less solid. The ancient Egyptians built more than 90 royal pyramids, from about 2650 BC until about 1550 BC. During that time, the pyramid form evolved from a series of stepped terraces that resembled a battleship to the better-known, sloped pyramidal shape we see today. Pyramids, of course, were simply large tombs which stored the remains of important people. Generally speaking, the larger the pyramid was, the more important the entombed person had been. Egyptian religious leaders argued that this was the best way to send off deceased people to their afterlife. Inside the tombs/pyramids were stored important items needed on the journey to the afterlife.

Building a pyramid was a great engineering feat. It required a lot of planning to build such a large and complicated structure. Normally a tertiary director or project manager coordinated the whole project. He would gather a team of engineers and thousands of workers/ slaves to help him. No one knows how many workers it took to build a pyramid, but presumably it took a lot.

The first task for the engineers was to estimate the amount of stone needed, then to have the stone cut from local quarries. Large sandstone blocks were used for the interior, with limestone on the exterior. Limestone was especially suited for the task. Limestone in its natural state is pliable and soft but hardens up on exposure to air. As soon as the limestone was quarried, it was laid out in the desert to cure and harden in the hot, dry air.

As soon as a block was cut, it was pushed out using large, smooth beams rolling on rocks to the work site. Often the biggest problem for the workers was not starting the process—it was stopping the process! Going downhill, the blocks could easily accelerate out of control, so they had to be controlled by ropes held around stout anchor poles bedded in the ground. The blocks could also be pulled up a

Pyramids in Giza

gentle rise with ease by a team of oxen. Workers built upward from each new base, similar to the way construction crews build skyscrapers today.

In 2160 BC, Egypt's capital was moved from Memphis to Herakleopolis in northern Middle Egypt—Upper Egypt, where it was controlled by Theban rulers.

The ascendancy of Thebes as the center of Egyptian political life was a signal that the sun god Amon-Ra was the primary god in Egyptian life. For the first time in Egypt's history, a form of monotheism was practiced.

During the rule of the kings of the ninth and tenth dynasties (2134–2040 BC), Thebes emerged as the administrative center of royal power. The Theban kings successfully challenged the Herakleopolitan pharaohs, winning complete control of Egypt. It remained that way until the reign of Akhenaton (1353–1335 BC).

In 1279–1213 BC, Ramses II began ambitious building projects, including his mortuary temple, the Ramesseum (on the West Bank near Luxor). Many scholars believe that he used the exilic, captive Hebrews as laborers. It was probably from Ramses II that Moses, had freed the Israelites. The Theban princes established themselves as the new rulers of

Egypt around 1570 BC.

The most important institution was the clergy. The Thebans attributed their success to their chief god Amun. The Egyptians, already a deeply religious people, became all the more so after the Hyksos were repelled. Amun, the Theban god of Winds, was associated with Re, the Memphis solar god of the Old Kingdom. This new Amen-Re was regarded as an all-powerful creator and warrior deity, the patron of the New Kingdom. The Theban priests of Amen-Re became the powers behind the throne as they confirmed the right of the king to rule. The priesthood also came to exercise considerable influence over the New Kingdom's burgeoning economy.

In an effort to wrest political and religious authority from the priesthood and return it to the Monarchy, a king by the name of Amenhotep revolted. Amenhotep denied the existence of Amen-Re and all other gods. According to him, the only true god was Aten, the sun disk, and Amenhotep was Aten's high priest. Amenhotep renamed himself Akhenaten ("servant of Aten"). He closed all the temples and constructed a new capital around his solar monotheism. Not only the priests but the people at large were scandalized. Once Amenhotep died, the Theban priests again took control. The cults of the old gods were restored, and it would be centuries before monotheism was again inflicted upon the population.

Bolstered by a strong military and a feeling of religious patriotism, the Egyptians of the New Kingdom successfully repelled an invasion of the Sea Peoples. The Sea Peoples were a mysterious race of marauders who had managed to destabilize other parts of the Mediterranean. The New Kingdom finally abandoned the practice of pyramid building. Instead they buried kings in rock-cut tombs. It was in such a tomb that the famous mummified body of Tutankhamun (death mask, left) was discovered.

Egypt reached the height of power in the New Kingdom that it would never recover. Around 1089 BC, the Theban princes took full control of the south of the country, leaving the monarchy with the north. The country was divided, and the monarchy of the north was weak. Kings from Libya and then from Nubia took over parts of Egypt. Foreign-ruled Egypt came into conflict with the new power in the ancient world—Assyria. The Assyrians destroyed Memphis and placed puppet rulers in parts of Egypt.

The Egyptians gradually regained control of their country from all foreign influences, but their international power and overseas empire was ruined. The kings could retain control only by hiring large numbers of mercenaries, who were increasingly coming from Greece.

At this time Assyria fell to Babylon, which in turn fell to Persia. Persia then subjected Egypt to foreign control again. Xerxes was considered a cruel occupier, and when the Persian Empire was overthrown, the Egyptians welcomed their new liberator, though he was also a foreigner. His name was Alexander the Great.

Assignment

Give an overview of the way pyramids were built.

GREEK AND ROMAN CONQUEST

Alexander the Great took Egypt from the Persians in 332 BC. During the first part of 331 BC, he began his most lasting contribution to civilization—the construction of the cultural epicenter of the Western world—the city of Alexandria. On the natural harbor near Rhacotis he built the fortified port city Alexandria. Alexander then connected the island of Pharos, located in the center of the bay, to the mainland with a 1,300-meter causeway, the Heptastadion. Thus two great harbors were created for his city, and towering over it all was the Pharos Lighthouse, one of the Seven Wonders of the Ancient World.

Unfortunately, Alexander did not stay long enough to see the completion of a single building in his new city. Instead, he set out on his conquest of Asia. He never returned, due to his death in Babylon at the age of 38.

Following Alexander's death, his generals divided the empire, each setting up his own kingdom. One of them, Ptolemy, took Egypt as his share and made Alexandria its capital.

It was under the Ptolemaic Dynasty that Alexandria truly became the cultural and economic center of the ancient world. Ptolemy and his descendants adopted Egyptian religions. While these newly discovered "gods" and "goddesses" had a distinctly Greek flavor, they were the same deities that Ramses II had worshiped centuries before.

This was quite literally a golden age for the citizens of Alexandria, and for Egypt as a whole. Although Alexander didn't live to see his city's glory, Alexandria nevertheless became the racial melting pot he is said to have wanted for his capital city. Ptolemy decided early on that Alexandria would not be just another port capital, but the home of a new age in Greek culture. The Greeks had a long tradition of enlightened rulers, and the Ptolemies would be no exception.

Ptolemy invited scholars and artists from all over the known world to live in Alexandria and foster the learning culture of that city. The arrival of many of these learned people, and later the successors they found among the citizens of their new home, resulted in one of the most famous historic images of its day: the Library at Alexandria, which served as the center of Western civilization for two centuries.

The eventual fate of the library is unknown. A significant portion of it is said to have been destroyed during Julius Caesar's war against Roman general Pompey, though how significant this portion was, or even its size, is not certain. At any rate, the library no longer existed at the time of the Islamic Conquest in the seventh century AD.

It was under the Ptolemaic Dynasty that Alexandria truly became the cultural and economic center of the ancient world. Egypt was ruled from Alexandria by Ptolemy's descendants until the death of Cleopatra VII in 30 BC. Little by little, however, the glory days of the early Ptolemies came to an end as Egypt increasingly came under the influence of Rome (www.touregypt.net).

Assignment

Describe three of the most important Egyptian pharaohs.

Statue of Roman emperor Julius Caesar

CLEOPATRA

In 51 BC, Ptolemy Auletes died and left his kingdom in his will to his 18-year-old daughter, Cleopatra, and her younger brother, Ptolemy XIII, who was 12 at the time. Cleopatra was born in 69 BC in Alexandria, Egypt. She had two older sisters, Cleopatra VI and Berenice IV, as well as a younger sister, Arsinoe IV. There were two younger brothers as well, Ptolemy XIII and Ptolemy XIV. It is thought that Cleopatra VI may have died as a child and Auletes had Berenice beheaded. At Ptolemy Auletes' death, Pompey, a Roman leader, was left in charge of the children. During the two centuries that preceded Ptolemy Auletes' death, the Ptolemys were allied with the Romans.

British actress Lillie Langtry as Cleopatra, LOC, 1891.

The Ptolemys' strength was failing and the Roman Empire was rising. City after city was falling to Roman power, and the Ptolemies could do nothing but create a pact with them. During the later rule of the Ptolemys, the Romans gained more and more control over Egypt.

According to Egyptian law, Cleopatra was married to her younger brother, Ptolemy XIII, when he was 12. However she soon dropped his name from any official documents. She also had her own portrait and name on coins of that time, ignoring her brother's.

When Cleopatra became co-regent, her world was crumbling around her. She did what she felt was necessary to try to save Alexandria, whatever the price. In her estimation, that meant becoming a consort of Julius Caesar, and, after his death, of Mark Antony.

In 48 BC Caesar arrived in Alexandria. He brought with him 3,200 legionaries and 800 cavalry. He also brought 12 other soldiers who bore the insignia of the Roman government, carrying a bundle of rods with an ax whose blade projected out. Caesar made Cleopatra the sole ruler of Egypt.

During July of the year 46 BC, Caesar returned to Rome. He was given many honors and a ten-year dictatorship. These celebrations lasted from September to October, and he brought Cleopatra over, along with her entourage. The conservative Republicans were extremely offended when he established Cleopatra in his home.

During the time that followed, Cleopatra watched carefully to see who would be the next power in Rome. She was invited by Mark Antony to Tarsus in 41 BC. Cleopatra and Antony spent the winter of 41–40 in Alexandria.

In the spring of 40 BC, Mark Antony left Cleopatra and returned home. He did not see her for four years. When he

Roman soldiers enter Cleopatra's chamber as she lay dying by Bartolomeo Pinelli, 1821 (PD-Art).

returned he married her. In 32–31 BC, Antony finally divorced his wife. This forced the Western part of the world to recognize his marriage to Cleopatra.

Octavian's navy severely defeated Antony in Actium, Greece, on September 2, 31 BC. Octavian's admiral, Agrippa, planned and carried out the defeat. In less than a year, Antony unenthusiastically defended Alexandria against the advancing army of Octavian. After the defeat, Antony committed suicide by falling on his own sword in 30 BC.

After Antony's death, Cleopatra was taken to Octavian, where her role in Octavian's triumph was carefully explained to her. He had no interest in any relationship, negotiation, or reconciliation with the queen of Egypt. She would be displayed as a slave in the cities she had ruled over.

She decided she would not live that way, so she had an asp, which was an Egyptian cobra, brought to her hidden in a basket of figs. She died on August 12, 30 BC at the age of 39. The Egyptian religion declared that death by snakebite would secure immortality. With this, she achieved her dying wish, not to be forgotten.

Her death marked the end of the Egyptian monarchs. The Roman emperors came into rule in Egypt. Cleopatra was the last pharaoh (www.touregypt.net).

Assignment

Why did Cleopatra get involved in the Roman Civil War (after the assassination of Julius Caesar)?

Chapter 5

EGYPTIAN LIFE

First Thoughts . . .

From the beginning, the Egyptian religion, lifestyle, and world view developed from living in close proximity to the mighty Nile River. Communities of hunter-gatherers made the Nile River the center of community life. The drying up of the Sahara increasingly confined them to the river area. No problem. Soon these communities became sufficiently stable to be united in a single political entity. Egyptian culture was born.

Chapter Learning Objectives . . .

In chapter 5, we will examine some of the philosophies that both created, and were influenced by, the Egyptian river culture that emerged in prehistory. Next, we will examine more closely the religions and everyday life of Egyptian society. We will finish by examining the Jewish expatriate community and its exodus from Egyptian hegemony.

As a result of this chapter you should be able to:

1. Speculate on the dangers of individualism to a Christian walk.

2. React to Pyrrho's belief that "things are equally indifferent, immeasurable, and inarbitrable."

3. Contrast the Egyptian views of the afterlife with Christian views of the afterlife.

4. Describe life in an ancient Egyptian family.

5. List the attributes of God that were manifested in His deliverance of the Israelites from Egypt.

6. Contrast the God of Jews and Christians with the Egyptian god Amon-Ra.

PHILOSOPHERS AND WORLD VIEWS

Cynicism (350 BC)

Cynicism took root in the Egyptian intelligentsia with vigor. Inevitably prosperity brings a philosophical price tag: cynicism. Cynics are often ultra-conservatives who yearn for the "good old days" when thinkers were less impressionable in their demeanor. Such was the case during the Greek Enlightenment, which saw the rise of the cynic Diogenes. For the first time, philosophers began to talk in earnest about the individual. Diogenes, a sort of 300 BC bohemian, dressed and lived in countercultural fashion. He was weird! Whereas Socrates talked about living an avant-garde lifestyle, Diogenes actually lived it. Diogenes argued that his Greek peers spent too much time pursuing material things that were at best unnecessary for life and at worst a profound distraction. A story is told that Alexander the Great once approached Diogenes and asked him what he could do to reward Diogenes. Diogenes, who happened to be relaxing in the sun, responded to the most powerful political figure in the world, "Stop blocking my sun."

It is disputed whether Diogenes left anything in writing. If he did, the texts he composed have since been lost. In Cynicism, living and writing are two components of ethical practice, but Diogenes was much like Socrates. He regarded the superiority of verbal interaction over the written account. Diogenes scolded one of his followers who asked to borrow one of Diogenes' writing tablets: "You are a simpleton; you do not choose painted figs, but real ones; and yet you pass over the true training and would apply yourself to written rules" (Diogenes Laertius, *Lives of Eminent Philosophers*, book 6, chapter 48).

Diogenes by John William Waterhouse, 1882 (PD-US).

Skepticism (300 BC)

Skepticism, like cynicism, was a reactionary philosophy. It was formulated by the Pyrrhonists, a school of Greek philosophy that derived its name from its founder, Pyrrho of Elis. Pyrrho, whose primary concern was ethics, maintained that human beings could know nothing of the real nature of things, and that consequently the wise person would give up trying to do so. This philosophy anticipates 21st-century Absurdism.

The philosopher Pyrrho in stormy lake by Petrarca-Meister, 1st quarter of 16th century (PD-US).

A disciple of Pyrrho wrote:

Pyrrho himself left nothing in writing, but his pupil Timon says that whoever wants to be happy must consider these three questions: First, how are things by nature? Second, what attitude should we adopt toward them? Third, what will be the outcome for those who have such an attitude? According to Timon, Pyrrho declared that things are equally indifferent, immeasurable, and inarbitrable. For this reason neither our sensations nor our opinions tell us truths or falsehoods. Therefore for this reason we should not put our trust in them one bit, but should be unopinionated, uncommitted, and unwavering, saying concerning each individual thing that it no more is than is not, or both is and is not, or neither is nor is not.

Assignment

A. Individualism—a by-product of Cynicism—was the watchword for the self-indulgent 1960s. What are the dangers of individualism (or privatism) to a Christian walk?

B. React to Pyrrho's idea that "things are equally indifferent, unmeasurable, and inarbitrable."

EGYPTIAN RELIGION

Religion guided every aspect of Egyptian life. Egyptian religion was based on polytheism, or the worship of many deities, except during the reign of Akhenaten, when the god Amon-Ra predominated. The Egyptians had as many as 2,000 gods and goddesses. Some, such as Amun, were worshipped throughout the whole country, while others had only a local following. Normally gods and goddesses were represented as part human and part animal.

Judgment scene from the Book of the Dead. Photo by Jon Bodsworth (PD-US).

For example, Horus, the sky god, had the head of a hawk and the body of a human. In fact, ancient Egyptians considered animals such as the bull, the cat, and the crocodile to be holy. Their two chief gods were Amon-Ra and Osiris. Amon-Ra was believed to be the sun god and the lord of the universe. Osiris was the god of the underworld. Stories about him revolved around the idea of immortality. He was the god who made a peaceful afterlife

Detail of an old Egyptian marble representation of Amon-Ra.

possible. The Egyptian "Book of the Dead" contains the major ideas and beliefs of the ancient Egyptian religion. Because their religion stressed an afterlife, Egyptians devoted much time and wealth to preparing for survival in the next world.

The Egyptians had many tales about how the world began. According to one legend, it started with an ocean in darkness. Then a mound of dry land rose up and the sun god Re appeared. He created light and all things. Another version has the sun god emerging from a sacred blue lotus that grew out of the mud, while a third version has him appearing as a scarab beetle on the eastern horizon (www.history101.net/Egypt).

Temples, considered dwelling places for the gods, were everywhere. Each city had a temple built for its own god. The temple was designed to be a cosmic center in which men had communication with the gods. As the priests became more powerful, tombs became a part of great temples. The priests' duty was to care for the gods and attend to their needs. The priests had many duties such as funeral rites, teaching school, supervising the artists and works, and advising people on problems (www.history101.net/Egypt).

The Egyptians saw death as a transitional stage in the progress from life on earth to a better life in the next world. They believed they could reach their full potential only after death. Each person was thought to have three souls, the "ka," the "ba," and the "akh." For these to function properly, it was considered essential for the body to survive intact. That is the reason Egyptians invested so much energy in mummifying a corpse.

When a person died, the priests recited prayers, and a final attempt was made to revive the deceased. The body was then washed and purified in a special shelter called an "ibu." The body was then taken to the "wabet," which was the embalmer's workshop. A cut was made in the left side, and all the organs were removed and stored in containers known as "canopic" jars. The body was then packed with a salt called "natron" for a period of 40 days. After the 40 days had passed, the insides were filled with linen or sawdust, resin, and natron. The body was wrapped in bandages with jewelry and amulets between the layers. A portrait mask was placed over the head of the deceased by the Chief Embalmer, who wore a jackal mask to represent Anubis. The wrapped body, or mummy, was put into a coffin (www.history101.net/Egypt).

After a period of about 70 days, in which the mummification process took place, the mummy was placed in a decorated coffin. Furniture, carved statues, games, food, and other items useful to the next life were prepared to be

Philae Temples on the Agilkia island, dedicated to the god Osiris.

buried with the mummy. The last ritual performed by the priest on the mummy was called the "Opening of the Mouth." This ceremony was to magically give the deceased the ability to speak and eat again, and to have full use of his body. After the mummy was placed in a stone sarcophagus, the tomb was sealed.

Assignment

Contrast Egyptian views of the afterlife with Christian views of the afterlife.

EGYPTIAN PEOPLE

The geography of Egypt is deeply important in understanding why the Egyptians built their lives around the Nile River. Both before and during the use of canal irrigation in Egypt, the Nile Valley could be separated into two parts, the River Basin or the flat alluvial (or black land soil), and the Red Land or red desert land. The River Basin of the Nile was in sharp contrast to the rest of the land of Egypt and was rich with wildlife and waterfowl, depending on the waxing and waning cycles of the Nile. In contrast, the Red Desert was a flat, dry area that was devoid of most life and water during all seasons. Both geographies influenced emerging Egyptian life.

Agricultural crops were not the mainstay of the ancient Egyptian diet. Rather, the Nile supplied a constant influx of fish that was cultivated year round.

The life of an ancient Egyptian was short and difficult. Newborn children were not likely to survive their first year. The infant mortality rate was extremely high, possibly around 60–70 percent, and the mortality rate for women in childbirth was also extremely high. Many, if not most, Egyptian women died in childbirth before their 30th birthday. Children, then, were seen as a special blessing from the gods if they survived their first year (www.ancientegypt.com).

At approximately age five, boys and girls were separated in their learning experiences. Boys from wealthy families went to school. Boys from poor families began helping with the men's jobs in the fields or whatever other occupations their fathers happened to hold (e.g., carpenter). A boy's education lasted until he was between 12 and 16, at which time he was considered to be an adult who could begin to work for himself.

The earliest age for men to marry was 16, but normally they were between 17 and 20 years of age when they took their first wife. Men could have several wives, but, in fact, very few did. It was too expensive to have more than one. As a result, this was usually done only by the very wealthy.

Most men continued to work until they died. No one retired. The average life span was approximately 30 years of age for a poor working man, 25 for a poor woman. Making it past the age of 40 was rare.

Girls' lives were much different from boys'. Girls' lives were centered in the home and the family. At age four, girls would begin to learn from their mothers how to maintain a household. They learned how to sew, prepare food, and keep house. The hours spent doing domestic chores were much longer than the educational hours of boys. Cloth had to be woven and then sewn into clothing, the fields planted and tended, food prepared, and countless other household chores performed. Girls were expected to marry around age 12 or 13, although there is evidence of girls marrying as young as 8 or 9 years of age. Widows were to be taken care of by their sons. If a woman had no sons, she was to be taken care of by her daughter and son-in-law, but this was rare and occurred only if the daughter had become part of a wealthier family. It was more likely that widows would be forced to live as beggars (www.ancientegypt.com; see also www.msnu.edu).

Assignment

Describe what your life would be like if you lived in an average ancient Egyptian family.

EGYPT AND THE HEBREWS

Because of a famine, Jacob, joining his son Joseph, brought his family to the Goshen district of Egypt. Joseph was second in command of all Egypt. Over time, the children of Israel living in Egypt multiplied. Pharaoh feared the Israelites were becoming too influential and powerful. He started to oppress and enslave them as a way of weakening them. The Israelites were forced to cut stones in the quarries, build cities, erect monuments, and construct roads. Despite this oppression, the Israelites continued to multiply. So Pharaoh decreed that all male newborns of Jewish mothers be killed.

Jacob's great-grandson Amram, who married Yocheved, had a daughter named Miriam and a son named Aaron. Yocheved then gave birth to a third child. To save him from being killed by Pharaoh's soldiers, she placed him in a basket that she hid among the reeds at the edge of the Nile River. When Pharaoh's daughter came to bathe in the Nile, she discovered the baby. She called the baby Moses, meaning "drawn from the water," and decided to adopt him as her son. She hired Moses' birth mother to be his nurse.

After Moses encountered God on Mount Horeb and became Israel's leader, he approached his Egyptian brother, Pharaoh Ramses II, with these words: "The God of Israel said, 'Let My people go, that they may serve me.'" Pharaoh did not believe in the God of the Israelites, and he refused to let the Jewish slaves go free. Moses warned him that God would punish both him and his people with plagues.

First, the waters of the land of Egypt turned into blood. Second, the entire

Moses, artist unknown, c1887 (PD-US).

land was covered by the plague of frogs. The third plague had gnats crawling forth from the dust to cover all of Egypt. Despite the plagues, Pharaoh refused to let the Israelites go.

The fourth plague consisted of swarms of flies all over the country. After this plague, Pharaoh promised to let the Jews go on condition that they would not go too far. Moses prayed and the flies disappeared, but as soon as they had gone, Pharaoh again changed his mind and decided not to let the Jews go free. Then God sent the fifth plague—a fatal pestilence that killed most of the domestic animals of the Egyptians. In the sixth plague, boils burst forth upon man and beast throughout Egypt.

Then Moses announced to Pharaoh that the seventh plague—a violent hailstorm—would kill everything that was outside and not sheltered. Pharaoh started to relent and agreed to let the Jewish men

Moses Fountain, Albany, N.Y., c1904

go free, but he insisted that the Jewish women and children and all their possessions remain in Egypt. Moses could not accept his offer. With the eighth plague, swarms of locusts devoured everything green that had escaped the hail and previous plagues. The ninth plague was a blanket of darkness that enveloped all of Egypt except for Goshen, where the children of Israel lived. The tenth and final plague began at midnight on the 15th of Nissan, when all firstborn sons in the land of Egypt began dying, including the firstborn of Pharaoh.

Finally, Pharaoh called for Moses and Aaron and told them: "Arise, go out from among my people, both you and the children of Israel; and go, serve God as you have said, and go, and bless me also."

The Jews departed Egypt in haste.

After three days, Pharaoh regretted that he had permitted the Israelites to leave. With his army Pharaoh pursued his former slaves. He reached them near the banks of the Red Sea. Moses led the Israelites onward until they came to the very borders of the Red Sea. Then God spoke to Moses: "Lift up your rod, stretch out your hand over the sea and divide it; and the children shall go into the midst of the sea on dry ground." Moses did as God ordered. Then a strong east wind blew all night, and the waters of the Red Sea divided. The Israelites marched along a dry path through the Red Sea until they reached the opposite side in safety. The Egyptians continued their pursuit, but the waters of the Red Sea drowned Pharaoh's army (www.touregypt.net).

Colossi of Ramses II (Moses' stepbrother) in front of Luxor Temple in Luxor (Thebes), Egypt.

Assignment

List the attributes of the Hebrews' God manifested in His deliverance of His people from Egypt.

Chapter 6

GREECE

First Thoughts . . .

The great Greek historian Edith Hamilton, speaking about Greece, said, "Civilization . . . is a matter of imponderables, of delight in the things of the mind, of love of beauty, of honor, grace, courtesy, delicate feeling. Where imponderables are things of first importance, there is the height of civilization, and if, at the same time, the power of art exists unimpaired, human life has reached a level seldom attained and very seldom surpassed." To Hamilton, to all mankind, Greece was the height of imponderables. What was then produced of art and thought has never been surpassed and very rarely equaled, and its stamp is still evident on all the art and all the thought of the Western world.

Chapter Learning Objectives . . .

In chapter 6, we will revisit Greek history. Along the way we will watch the rise of city-states and will stop and examine two very closely: Sparta and Athens. Finally, we will enjoy a day in the life of an Athenian.

As a result of this chapter you should be able to:

1. Give examples of how the mountainous terrain of the Greek Peninsula affected the way Greek civilization evolved.

2. Explain why the city-states emerged as the main political entities in Greece.

3. Evaluate where you would rather live: ancient Athens or Sparta.

4. Pretend that you are offering to guide a future traveler through your town or city or rural area.

5. In light of your understanding of Greek culture and history, interpret 1 Corinthians 15.

GROWTH OF GREEK CIVILIZATION

Five hundred years before Christ in a little town on the far western border of the settled and civilized world, a strange new power was at work. Something had awakened in the minds and spirits of the men there which was so to influence the world that the slow passage of long time, of century upon century and the shattering changes they brought, would be powerless to wear away that deep impress.

—Edith Hamilton, *The Greek Way*

Greece is the southernmost region on the European continent. Its mild, almost tropical climate attests to this fact. At the same time, this potential paradise is a land covered by mountains, surrounded on all sides except the north by water, and dotted with numerous islands. This geographical contradiction is one of the anachronisms that are Greece.

The Aegean Sea and the many natural harbors along the coastlines allowed the Greeks to prosper in seafaring commerce and to develop an eclectic culture that drew contacts outside Greece. In other words, from the beginning, Greek culture and civilization had a cosmopolitan/international air.

The Greek world encompassed many settlements around the Mediterranean and Black Seas and, during the height of the Macedonian Empire (Alexander the Great), reached as far east as India.

Never has a civilization been so influenced by its geography. The mountains, which served as natural barriers and boundaries, dictated the political and economic character of Greece. Agriculture was possible, even desirable in limited, isolated pockets, but there was no room for vast wheat or barley fields such as those of Egypt's delta. Therefore, the Greek economy, from its genesis, was diversified and interdependent.

The geography also dictated that the Greeks live in independent, isolated communities. Eventually these communities were organized into city-states. The inhospitable

View from the Aegean Sea, Greece

landscape obligated the Greeks to look beyond their borders to the sea and to their adjoining Mediterranean communities to subsidize the paltry agrarian options open to them.

Geography also encouraged the Greek people to be vigorous and intuitive, even whimsical—characteristics reflected in their gods.

The Greeks introduced the idea that the universe was orderly, that man's senses were valid, and, as a consequence, that man's proper purpose was to live his own life to the fullest. Egyptian gods were partly anthropomorphic; Greek gods were supermen.

The ancient Greeks did not have a religion per se; they did not go to Sunday school and church as we do. They did not have the Ten Commandments or any other moral system to follow. Besides, hardly any self-respecting Greek really thought that mythological gods and goddesses were alive, at least not the way we think of our Judeo-Christian God. The Greeks assumed that their gods cared little, if at all, for mankind. While it is true that Greek society had its gods, it did not place great importance on mystical beliefs. Indeed, what gods it did revere (rather than worship) were much different from the God whom Christians worship. Christians believe the biblical teaching that man is created "in God's image"; the Greeks created gods in the image of man. Their gods were neither omnipotent nor omnipresent. Edith Hamilton stated, "Before Greece, all religion was magical." She further illustrated that mystical beliefs were based on fear of the unknown, whereas the Greeks "changed a world that was full of fear into a world full of beauty." Hamilton continued, "The Greeks were the first intellectuals. In a world where the irrational had played the chief role, they came forward as the protagonists of the mind." Thus, the Greeks introduced the idea that the universe was orderly, that man's senses were valid, and, as a consequence, that man's proper purpose was to live his own life to the fullest. Man's chief end, however, was certainly not to please the gods. It was to enjoy the aesthetics.

Assignment

Give examples of how the mountainous terrain of the Greek Peninsula affected the way Greek civilization evolved.

Mount Olympus in Greece. In the foreground is the small town of Litohoro.

GROWTH OF GREEK CIVILIZATION

The word *Greek*, according to Aristotle, came from the word *Graikoi*, which was the prehistoric name of the Hellenes. The people we call Greeks, who lived in a country called Greece, actually called themselves Hellenves, who lived in a country called Hellas.

Given the isolation created by Greece's geography, villages started to band together to form strong trading and political centers. These groups of villages were called city-states. The first-city states, or at least urban centers, appeared around 3000 BC. Evidence of these has been found all over modern-day Greece, in some northeastern Aegean islands, the Cycladic islands, Crete, and the Greek mainland.

During the Minoan Period in Crete, an island close to Greece, in approximately 2000 BC, a more sed-

The palace of Knossos (Crete, Greece): part of the northern entrance, reconstructed by the British archaeologist Sir Arthur Evans. Photo by Marc Ryckaert, 2009 (CC BY-SA 3.0).

entary society developed with a culture specific to that region. The first writing was invented, and communication opened up between the Cretan Minoans and people from the eastern Mediterranean countries. This led to an exchange of culture and ideas that not only became established as part of Minoan culture but that also spread to other fledgling city-states and Mediterranean cultures. The Minoans developed the first mercantile navy fleet, and used it to import sundry merchandise.

Around 1500 BC, Crete Island, including its Minoan civilization, was devastated by a volcano. The Mycenaeans, based on the Greek mainland, took advantage of this collapse of Minoan culture and established themselves as the leading force throughout the Aegean area. Their cities in Mycenae, Thebes, and Athens became the bureaucratic

centers of their vast kingdom. During this period the Mycenaean civilization was a ruthless, aggressive city-state. The society was based essentially upon warfare, so its elite class consisted of warlords. Their culture thrived for around 400 years. The cities of the warlords were large and powerful, art and agriculture flourished, and there was great prosperity.

This continued until around 1200 BC, by which time the power of the Mycenaen kings was declining. By the 12th century BC, their dominance had collapsed, due in part to an invasion by the Dorian tribes from the north of Greece.

Next, there was a long period of cultural and economic stagnation that lasted from around 1150 to 900 BC. This so-called Dark Age ended with the emergence of the Greek renaissance, known as the Geometric Period (9th–8th

The island of Crete. The western and central parts appear surrounded by quicksilver in this astronaut photograph taken from the International Space Station. This phenomenon is known as sunglint, caused by light reflecting off of the sea surface directly toward the observer. Photographed by the ISS Expedition 28 crew, 2011 (NASA).

centuries BC). The great Greek city-states were formed and, as in all subsequent renaissance times, the Geometric Period witnessed the development of literature and arts. Homeric epics and the Greek alphabet were both created during this time of enlightenment. The Archaic Period that followed during the 7th–6th centuries BC included fundamental political and social changes. The Greek city-states established colonies at all points of the compass: North Africa to the south, the Black Sea to the north, and Spain to the west.

This was the start of what has come to be known as the Classical Period. By the 5th–4th centuries BC, Athens dominated both politically and culturally in what is called the Golden Age of Pericles, only to lose this dominance at the end of the Peloponnesian War in 404 BC. The fourth century BC saw the development of Macedonians as a new force in the Greek world. Philip II, king of Macedonia, and his son Alexander played leading roles. In 388 BC, 18-year-old Alexander led the Macedonian cavalry to victory at the Battle of Chaeronea. After the assassination of King Philip II in 336 BC during an expedition to free the Greek states of Asia Minor from the Persians, unrest grew between Greeks and Macedonians in Thebes.

Alexander conquered Thebes and, as a warning to other Greeks, destroyed the city, leaving only its temples standing. Greeks and Macedonians again joined forces under Alexander and went on to conquer Persia, Egypt, and regions as far as the Indus River. Alexander the Great's tremendous empire radically changed the political and cultural situation in the then-known world.

After his early death at age 33, his vast empire was divided among his generals. Although the political entity that he created did not continue, his legacy was a uniform economic and cultural world that stretched from the Strait of Gibraltar to the Indus River. In the succeeding Hellenistic Age (3rd–1st centuries BC), the Greek city-states had lost their position of power and prestige, although they did remain self-governing and independent of one another.

This, however, was soon to change: In 146 BC, Greece was conquered by the Romans and was subsequently absorbed by the expanding Roman Empire.

Assignment

Why did the city-states emerge as the main political entities in Greece?

Philip II of King of Macedon, Ny Carlsberg Glyptotek.
Photo by Gunnar Bach Pedersen, 2006 (PD-US).

SPARTA

The largest of these city-states was the militaristic Sparta, which controlled more than 3,000 square miles of surrounding territory. The most famous of these city-states, which controlled most of the Mediterranean world, was the cultural apogee, Athens. There were others, but these two, by far, were the most famous and influential.

All the Greek city-states began as monarchies. However, by 800 BC most monarchies were replaced by representative democracies, the first of their kind. These were not democracies as we think of the term today–only propertied citizens could vote–but there was no suzerainty like one would find in Babylon either.

This was a period of aggressive colonization. The Greeks, pressured by growing populations around the city-states, actively searched for unpopulated or thinly populated areas to colonize in Greece and the Aegean Sea realm. The Greek city-state influence appeared on the Italian and Sicilian shores, and set up trade centers in the Middle East and Egypt. At the same time, as Greek culture spread across the Mediterranean, the city-states—particularly Athens—became wealthy and powerful.

However, there was as yet no military, political, or cultural center of the Greek world. Different city-states developed separate cultures. The greatest flowering of culture occurred on the city-states of Asia Minor, and especially Miletus. Greek philosophy began in these city-states and soon spread around the Greek world. Corinth and later Argos became great centers of literature. The most important of the city-states, as stated, were Athens and Sparta. Sparta, after defeating Athens in the Peloponnesian Wars, eventually dominated the political scene, and would remain so until Alexander the Great conquered Greece in the 4th century BC.

Sparta dominated more land mass than any other Greek city. The military and the city-state became the center of Spartan existence. Spartans existed for the sake of the state, not vice versa. For instance, the state determined whether children, both male and female, were strong when they were born; weak infants were left in the hills to die of exposure. Infanticide was a common practice in the Greek world, but Sparta institutionalized it as a state decision rather than a family decision. The male children who survived were sent to military school at the age of seven.

These schools taught discipline and survival skills. There is a story about a Spartan boy who, in order to conceal a fox that he had stolen, hid it beneath his cloak and allowed the fox to gnaw him rather than let the theft be revealed. He died of the wounds. If he had been discovered, the disgrace would not have been in the stealing, but in allowing it to be detected. The boy's action illustrated the main purpose of the Spartan educational system, which was to produce men capable of showing such bravery as soldiers. Military strength was felt to be essential to Sparta for its very survival. At age 20, after 13 years of training, the Spartan became a soldier—his highest calling. The Spartan soldier spent his life with his fellow soldiers. He married, but he did not live with his family.

Hoplites, depicted on an Attic vase dated to 510–500 BC. Photo by Jastrow (PD-US).

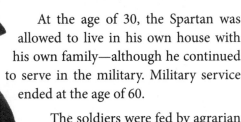

At the age of 30, the Spartan was allowed to live in his own house with his own family—although he continued to serve in the military. Military service ended at the age of 60.

The soldiers were fed by agrarian peasants, called helots. These servants of the state had no duties except to produce food and other useful products for the state.

One reason that Greek armies were so successful is that their armies consisted of Hoplites. The Hoplites were the military elite, shock troops of the seventh century BC. Hoplites were soldiers who worked together, formed a team, and created what was called a Phalanx. Earlier, a looser and more individual battle style prevailed. This style of battle is described in the *Iliad*. The Hoplite was ineffective if he fought alone. He was armed in such a way that he could only fight effectively in formation, with his shield firmly fixed on his left to protect his own left side and his neighbor's right. This style of fighting was ideally suited for mountainous terrain.

All this required adequate training, commitment to the team, and larger numbers. The Hoplites were normally volunteers who could afford to fit themselves out with the appropriate armor and weapons. It was, then, so far as the term is applicable, an army of the wealthier middle class.

Thus, the Hoplites developed into more than a military cadre: they became a social class. This caused the ruling nobles to lose some influence in the city-state. The citizen-soldier, the class which now provided the dominant force on the battlefield, was less easy to exclude from public life.

Athens

It is hard to believe that so different a culture existed in a city-state only 100 miles away from Sparta. Athens had been occupied since 3000 BC, but not until the height of Mycenaean rule (1400–1200 BC), did the city begin to create the buildings commonly associated with it. Originally situated on the rocky hill known as the Acropolis, the city began to spread southward. As Athens expanded physically, so did the government. For one thing, the city embraced a form of representative democracy. More people were involved in the day-to-day operations of government than at any previous time in the history of the world.

For this and other reasons, the arts were stimulated and encouraged. By 600 BC, Athens was filled with beautiful works of sculpture and architecture. This renaissance spread to the entire Mediterranean world. The expansion of Athenian culture continued until it was halted by the Persians in 480 BC. The Persians ransacked the city, burning temples and homes. It wasn't until 449 BC that peace with Persia was attained and the destroyed temples and buildings were reconstructed. From 400 BC forward, the city of Athens began to look like the classical city we all know. During that time in Athens, the Agora, the area below the citadel, became the center of civic life. The Agora was the meeting place where the Athenians could speak of civic and public affairs. Every free male had a voice and a vote in Athenian government. On each side of the Agora was an important center of Athenian life. The Areopagus, on one side, was where the high court sat. The Pnyx, on the other side, was where the Athenian Assembly convened.

Assignment

Would you rather live in ancient Athens or Sparta? Why?

Leonidas statue at Sparta city in Greece

A DAY IN OLD ATHENS: A SPECULATIVE ESSAY

Excerpt from *A Day in Old Athens*, by William Stearns Davis, 1914:

The morning crowds bound for Athens.—it is very early in the morning. The sun has just pushed above the long ridge of Hymettus, sending a slanting red bar of light across the Attic plain, and touching the opposite slopes of Ægaleos with livid fire. Already, however, life is stirring outside the city. Long since, little market boats have rowed across the narrow strait from Salamis, bringing the island farmers' produce and other farmers from the plain and the mountain slopes have started for market. In the ruddy light the marble temples on the lofty Acropolis rising ahead of these hurrying rustics are standing out clearly; the spear and helmet of the great brazen statue of the Athena Promachos are flashing from the noble citadel, as a kind of day beacon, beckoning onward toward the city. From the Peiræus, the harbor town, a confused hymn of mariners lading and unlading vessels is even now rising, but we cannot turn ourselves thither. Our route is to follow the farmers bound for market.

The most direct road from the Peiræus to Athens is hidden indeed, for it leads between the towering ramparts of the "Long Walls," two mighty barriers which run parallel almost four miles from the inland city to the harbor, giving a guarded passage in wartime and making Athens safe against starvation from any land blockade; but there is an outside road leading also to Athens from the western farmsteads, and this we can conveniently follow. Upon this route the crowd which one meets is certainly not aristocratic, but it is nonetheless Athenian. Here goes a drover, clad in skins, his legs wound with woolen bands in lieu of stockings; before him and his wolf-like dog shambles a flock of black sheep or less manageable goats, bleating and baaing as they are propelled toward market. After him there may come an unkempt, long-bearded farmer flogging on a pack ass or a mule attached to a clumsy cart with solid wheels, and laden with all kinds of market produce. The roadway, be it said, is not good, and all carters have their troubles; therefore, there is a deal of gesticulating and

Panoramic view of the Acropolis. (Above) Heracles and Athena, 480–470 BC. From Vulci (PD-US).

profane invocation of Hermes and all other gods of traffic; for, early as it is, the market place is already filling, and every delay promises a loss. There are still other companions bound toward the city: countrymen bearing cages of poultry; others engaged in the uncertain calling of driving pigs; swarthy Oriental sailors, with rings in their ears, bearing bales of Phoenician goods from the Peiræus; respectable country gentlemen, walking gravely in their best white mantles and striving to avoid the mud and contamination; and perhaps also a small company of soldiers, just back from foreign service, passes, clattering shields and spear staves.

The crowds grow denser as everybody approaches the frequented "Peiræus Gate," for nearly all of Attica which lies within easy reach of Athens has business in the Market Place every morning. On passing the gate a fairly straight way leads through the city to the market, but progress for the multitude becomes slow. If it is one of the main thoroughfares, it is now very likely to be almost blocked with people. There are few late risers at Athens; the Council of Five Hundred, the huge Jury Courts, and the Public Assembly are appointed to gather at sunrise. The plays in the theater, which, however, are given only on certain festivals, begin likewise at sunrise. The philosophers say that "the man who would accomplish great things must be up while yet it is dark." Athenians, therefore, are always awake and stirring at an hour when men of later ages and more cold and foggy climes will be painfully yawning ere getting out of bed.

The Market Place attracts the great masses, but by no means all; hither and thither bevies of sturdy slave girls, carrying graceful pitchers on their heads, are hurrying towards the fountains which gush cool water at most of the street corners. Theirs is a highly necessary task, for few or no houses have their own water supply; and around each fountain one can see half a dozen by no means slatternly maidens, splashing and flirting the water one at another, while they wait their turn with the pitchers, and laugh and exchange banter with the passing farmers' lads. Many in the street crowds are rosy-cheeked schoolboys, walking decorously, if they are lads of good breeding, and blushing modestly when they are greeted by their fathers' acquaintances. They do not loiter on the way. Close behind, carrying their writing tablets, follow the faithful "pedagogues," the body-servants appointed to conduct them to school, give them informal instruction, and, if need be, correct their faults in no painless manner. Besides the water maids and the schoolboys, from the innumerable house doors now opening the respective masters are stepping forth —followed by one, two, or several serving varlets, as many as their wealth affords. All these join in the crowd entering from the country. "Athenian democracy" always implies a goodly amount of hustling and pushing. No wonder the ways are a busy sight!

Progress is slower near the Market Place because of the extreme narrowness of the streets. They are only fifteen feet wide or even less—intolerable alleys a later age would call them—and dirty to boot. Sometimes they are muddy, more often extremely dusty. Worse still, they are contaminated by great accumulations of filth; for the city is without an efficient sewer system or regular scavengers. Even as the crowd elbows along, a house door will frequently open, an ill-favored slave boy show his head, and with the yell, "Out of the way!" slap a bucket of dirty water into the street. There are many things to offend the nose as well as the eyes of men of a later race. It is fortunate indeed that the Athenians are otherwise a healthy folk, or they would seem liable to perpetual pestilence; even so, great plagues have in past years harried the city.

The first entrance to Athens will thus bring to a stranger, full of the city's fame and expectant of meeting objects of beauty at every turn, almost instant disappointment. The narrow, dirty, ill-paved streets are also very crooked. One can readily be lost in a labyrinth of filthy little lanes the moment one quits the few main thoroughfares. High over head, to be sure, the red crags of the Acropolis may be towering, crowned with the red, gold, and white tinted marble of the temples, but all around seems only monotonous squalor. The houses seem one continuous series of blank walls; mostly of one, occasionally of two stories, and with flat roofs. These walls are usually spread over with some dirty gray or perhaps yellow stucco. For most houses, the only break in the street walls are the simple doors, all jealously barred and admitting no glance within. There are usually no street windows, if the house is only one story high. If it has two stories, a few narrow slits above the way may hint that here are the apartments for the slaves or women. There are no street numbers. There are often no street names. "So-and-so lives in such-and-such a quarter, near the Temple of Heracles"; that will enable you to find a householder, after a few tactful questions from the neighbors; and after all, Athens is a relatively small city: now thinning, now gaining, but the main stream always working toward the Market Place.

Roman agora and Library of Hadrian Augustus at Athens, Greece

Assignment

Pretend that you are offering to guide a future traveler through your town or city or rural area. What would you highlight?

Chapter 7

LIFE IN ATHENS: PART ONE

First Thoughts . . .

Historian William Stearns Davis writes, "To three ancient nations the men of the 20th century owe an incalculable debt. To the Jews we owe most of our notions of religion; to the Romans we owe traditions and examples in law, administration, and the general management of human affairs which still keep their influence and value; and finally, to the Greeks we owe nearly all our ideas as to the fundamentals of art, literature, and philosophy, in fact, of almost the whole of our intellectual life." These Greeks lived in many city-states, with Sparta and Athens being central. Sparta was a great military nation most famous for its warrior prowess, but it created not a single great poet, and certainly never a philosopher or sculptor. The civilized life of Greece, during the centuries when she was accomplishing the most, was peculiarly located in Athens. Sophocles, Plato, and Herodotus developed their genius in Athens. They were the ripe products of a society that, in its excellences and weaknesses, presented some of the most interesting pictures and examples in the world. However, to understand the Athenian civilization and genius, it is not enough to know its wars, laws, and politicians. In this chapter we will see Athens as an average Athenian saw it and lived in it from day to day.

Chapter Learning Objectives . . .

In chapter 7, we will examine Athenian families—moms, dads, and their children. We will examine ancillary institutions such as slavery. We will look closely at the lives of Greek women. Finally, we will examine Greek education.

As a result of this chapter you should be able to:

1. Discuss what life was like for Greek women.
2. Analyze why infanticide was practiced by some Greek families.
3. Speculate why slavery was tolerated and even encouraged.
4. Discuss Athenian family life and education.
5. Describe a typical Athenian citizen.

ATHENIAN WOMEN

Athenian women, like most women in the ancient world, had few educational or political rights, but they had tremendous power in the household itself. In a typical Athenian home, the wife of the master/owner reigned supreme.

An Athenian girl was brought up with the distinct expectation of matrimony. No one talked about "romance" or "love." The young woman actually had very little to say about the choice of her future mate. Marriage was contracted primarily to provide children to keep up the state and to perpetuate legally recognized families. That a girl should have any will of her own in the matter was seldom considered. Quite probably she would not have seen her husband until the wedding day. Normally, Athenian women were married at about age 15.

If a young man (who would marry at about age 30) was independent in life, the negotiations would be with him directly. If he was still dependent on a paternal allowance, the two sets of parents would usually arrange matters themselves, and demand only the formal consent of the prospective bridegroom. He would probably accept promptly the bride whom his father had selected. If he refused, he risked a stormy encounter with his parents, and would finally capitulate. He had perhaps never seen "her," and could only hope for the best; and after all, she was so young that, according to his friends, he could train her to be very useful and obedient if he would only take pains. The parents, or, failing them, the guardians, adjusted the dowry—the lump sum which the bride would bring with her toward the new establishment. Many maxims enjoin "marry only your equal in fortune." The poor man who wed an heiress would not really be his own master; the dread of losing the big dowry would keep him in perpetual bondage to her whims. The dowry was a great protection to the bride. If her husband were to divorce her (as by law he might), the dowry would have to be repaid to her guardians with 18 percent interest.

The Caryatids (sculpted female figure serving as architectrual support), Athens.

As William Stearns Davis explains in *A Day in Old Athens* (1914):

Assuredly the Athenian house mother cannot match her husband in discussing philosophy or foreign politics, but she has her own home problems and confronts them well. A dozen or twenty servants must be kept busy. From her, all the young children must get their first education and the girls probably everything they are taught until they are married. Even if she does not meet many men, she will strive valiantly to keep the good opinion of her husband. Her husband has turned over to her the entire management of the household. This means that if he is an easygoing man, she soon understands his home business far better than he does himself, and really has him quite at her mercy. Between caring for her husband's wants, nursing the sick slaves, acting as arbitress in their inevitable disputes, keeping a constant watch upon the storeroom, and finally in attending to the manufacture of nearly all the family clothing, she is not likely to rust in busy idleness, or sit complaining of her lot. At the many great public festivals she is always at least an onlooker and often she marches proudly in the magnificent processions. She is allowed to attend the tragedies in the theater. Probably, too, the family will own a country farm, and spend a part of the year thereon. Here she will be allowed a delightful freedom of movement, impossible in the closely built city. All in all, then, she will complain of too much enforced activity rather than of too much idleness.

Section of the *Augustan Altar of Peace*. Photo by Manfred Heyde, 2009 (CC BY-SA 3.0).

Assignment

Greek women could not vote, did not own property, and, generally speaking, did not have any rights at all. Yet, in the Athenian democracy, they seemed, by and large, to be very contented with their station in life. Why?

FAMILY LIFE

Besides the oversight of the slaves, the Athenian mother also spent a great deal of time in care of her children. Children, especially boys, were valued above all gifts. A childless home was one of the greatest of calamities to Athenians. It meant a solitary old age, and still worse, the dying out of the family and the worship of the family gods.

One especially inhumane practice existed in Ancient Greece: Some parents left injured, weak, or otherwise "imperfect" infants in desolate places to die. This is painfully illustrated in Sophocles' *Oedipus Rex*. Public opinion, as well as the law, allowed a father (especially if he had one or two children already) to kill an infant. After the birth of a child, there was always a time when family members waited nervously to see what the father would do.

The first seven years of a Greek boy's life were spent with his nanny and his mother. Prior to that time, the father ignored his son. Later, the father assumed a proprietary interest—choosing his son's future mate and occupation. An Athenian daughter was tutored by her mother and generally ignored by her father (although clearly there were exceptions).

Assignment

Why do you think some fathers purposely murdered their newborn children?

Present-day ruins of Dionysus theatre, Athens, Greece.

SLAVERY IN ATHENS

While Athenians did not have vast numbers of slaves like the Romans did later, slavery was very much a part of Athenian life. Slaves were everywhere—they ran households, worked in industries, planted crops, and supported armies. In fact, some scholars believe there were more male slaves in Athens than male free men.

In a culture that so fervently supported democracy, there is no record of any Greek citizen opposing slavery. It was accepted as a necessary part of Greek life. Aristotle argued, "The lower sort of mankind are by nature slaves, and it is better for all inferiors that they should be under the rule of a master. The use made of slaves and of tame animals is not very different; for both by their bodies minister to the needs of life."

There were many different ways in which a person could have become a slave in ancient Greece. They might have been born into slavery. They might have been taken prisoner in a military campaign. Some newborn children were abandoned by their parents and then claimed by a family. Finally, if a family needed money, they might sell one of the children into slavery. Female children, in particular, might be abandoned and sold by their parents. Fathers worried about the dowry that would be required when their daughters were married.

Slaves were treated differently in ancient Greece depending upon what their purpose was. Household slaves were often treated almost as part of the family. The woman of the house normally always supervised slaves. Most wealthy Greek households had as many as 10–20 slaves.

Slaves that worked outside often had horrible living conditions. They might live under the basest conditions.

Slaves had to marry whomever their masters wished. They could not use their own names but were assigned names by their master. Slaves usually did not live long because of the grueling work and dangerous conditions of their work.

Slaves were everywhere and did all sorts of different work. The Athenian police force was made up mainly of slaves.

Slaves cost about $180 in today's money.

Assignment

In a democracy such as Athens, why was slavery tolerated or even encouraged?

EDUCATION

Formal education was a right of every Athenian male citizen, but it was not required. Political leaders understood that Athenian democracy was dependent upon an educated population. Practically all Athenians were at least literate.

In contrast with American education, Athenian education emphasized character before knowledge. There were free public schools, usually run by a "master teacher" and conducted in open-air courts. Public schools intentionally sought to make boys self-sufficient, patriotic, religious, and, in general, unselfish, loyal Athenian citizens. No such thing existed as a values-free Athenian education.

This was serious business. Around 590 BC, a law was passed forbidding schools in Athens to open before daybreak, or to be kept open after dark! Can you imagine?

Athenian schools were numerous, because they were small. To teach children of the poorer classes, it was enough to have a small room and a few stools; but no expense was spared for wealthier patrons. As in America today, there were sections of Athens that had better schools than other sections. People paid more to live in these places. Public schools were often the perceived advantage that every Athenian sought.

Students were compelled to memorize long passages from writings of the great poets. This was purely whole-book, essay-based education. Homer's *Iliad* and *Odyssey* were the main textbooks.

One interesting aspect of Athenian education was that all boys were required to learn to sing and to recite poetry.

As their sons grew older, wealthier parents retained famous philosophers to teach rhetoric to their children. For example, King Philip II retained Aristotle to teach his son Alexander. Also, before Alexander, elite Athenians were taught by Plato, who had been teaching his philosophy out at the groves of the Academy, or joining some of his rivals in theoretical wisdom.

Odysseus Overcome by Demodocus' Song, by Francesco Hayez, c1813 (PD-US).

By age 18, most young Athenian men completed their regular education, at which time they entered military school for two additional years. At age 20, they graduated.

Assignment

Athenian education emphasized moral education. Students were taught to read and to write, but they were also taught principles of good citizenship. Given the present state of education in America's public schools, explain the dangers of separating the values of society from its educational system.

Chapter 8

LIFE IN ATHENS: PART TWO

First Thoughts . . .

Greece is a country surrounded by water, so the sea has always played an important role in its economy, particularly in Athens. Enterprising Athenians were skillful seafarers who tapped into existing markets and created new ones at coastal sites across the Mediterranean Sea. By the seventh and sixth centuries BC, Greek colonies and settlements stretched all the way from western Asia Minor to southern Italy, Sicily, North Africa, and even to the coasts of southern France and Spain. Science, especially in the area of medicine, assured the success of these commercial enterprises. Likewise, the Greek army and navy, the most formidable of their era, assured the safety and continued success of Athenian citizens and businessmen.

Chapter Learning Objectives . . .

In chapter 8, we will examine Greek medicine and Athenian commercial enterprises. Then we will examine the Greek military—army and navy—and its effective policing of the Mediterranean world.

As a result of this chapter you should be able to:

1. Discuss why Greek religion and medicine were naturally connected.

2. Speculate as to why such a connection seems comparatively absent from American medicine.

3. Compare ancient Athenian business to contemporary business.

4. Explain why Greek armies were so successful.

5. Explain what a "trireme" was and why it was such an effective instrument of warfare.

6. Evaluate why a peace-loving Athenian democracy was so skillful in conducting warfare.

MEDICINE

Disease was a serious problem for the Greeks, as for all other people in the ancient and medieval worlds. One out of three babies died before they were a year old. Half of all children died before age 10. Most people who survived childhood died before their 50th birthday.

Naturally, then, Greeks were quite interested in using scientific observation and logic to figure out what caused diseases. The result was that Greek doctors worked out a logical system for understanding disease. Their medical findings have been recorded and compiled in the *Hippocratic Writings*, named for the first and foremost of these doctors, **Hippocrates**. Medicine was a good career: "A physician is worth more than several other men put together, for he can cut out arrows and spread healing herbs," says a character in Homer's *Iliad*.

Doctors believed that people were made out of four substances, or "humors": blood, black bile, yellow bile, and phlegm. Healthy people had the right amount of each humor, but if a person had too much of one humor, he would be unbalanced and become sick. For instance, too much blood would cause a fever, so bloodletting became the dominant "remedy," often with grave consequences. This misguided practice continued for two or three centuries!

A slight but significant witness to the general good health of the Greeks is the rarity of any mention in their literature of such a common ill as toothache. Greek medicine and surgery, as it appeared in Homeric writings, was simply a certain amount of practical knowledge gained by rough experience, largely supplemented by primitive superstition. Medicine and surgery won a real place among the practical sciences. As one historian explained, "The sick man stands at least a tolerable chance of rational treatment, and of not being murdered by wizards and fanatical exorcists."

Healing, however, was not perceived as a science separated from religion. Certain gods were devoted to the healing arts, and the temple was also the hospital. A patient slept overnight in the temple, and the gods, in theory, visited him

Statue of the father of Medicine, Hippocrates, at the place where he died, city of Larissa, Greece.

in a dream, revealing a course of treatment that would lead to recovery. No doubt there was a lot of chicanery involved, and surely many patients did not get better. However, there are documented cases of many being healed, perhaps due to the hope they received or to a positive attitude. The value of mental therapeutics was, and still is, recognized as beneficial to healing.

However, not all medicine was left to the priests and the gods. Attached to the temple were skilled physicians who "interpreted" a patient's dream and offered opportunities for prolonged residence with treatment by baths, purgation, dieting, mineral waters, sea baths, all kinds of mild gymnastics, etc. "Suffice it to say, the sonorous connection of religion and science was abundantly evident in the medicinal interventions available in Athens" (William Stearns Davis).

Assignment

Why, in Greek thought, were religion and medicine naturally connected? Why do you think such a connection is not as greatly respected in American medicine?

BUSINESS AND TRADE

From the start, the Greek economy was inextricably tied to the sea. Greeks sailed all over the Mediterranean Sea. The primary industry was fishing. Fishermen sold their fish in markets. Other Greeks were traders who bought things at one port and sold them at another port, and made some profit for themselves along the way. Later, as Greek city-states became more sedentary, some farmers started a vigorous sheep, goat, and cattle industry.

Each Greek city-state minted its own coins. Greek traders began to use these coins in their business transactions.

Athenian greatness was largely due to the fact that Athens was the richest and greatest commercial city of Greece, with only Corinth as a formidable rival.

Manufacturing was more or less **a cottage industry,** but Athenian seaports made the distribution of products and the gathering of natural resources relatively easy. However, a major proportion of Greek manufactured wares were not exported, but were sold directly by the manufacturer to the consumer.

Athens had few natural resources to export—only olive oil, fish, and natural marble rock—but imports such as iron ore and other vital resources flowed into Athenian seaports from colonies and other overseas markets.

An important factor in the commerce of Athens was the "money-changer" or "banker."

Since there was no single fixed standard of coinage in Greece, a banking industry was critical to the cosmopolitan commercial industry that flourished in Athens.

One particularly successful business—pottery—emerged in Athens. Athenian pottery became famous all over the civilized world for its artistic character and durability. Many pieces still exist today.

Assignment

In Greece, a vocation in business was perceived as inferior to one in the arts. In America, big business seems to control everything—art, business, health care, and even religion. Why?

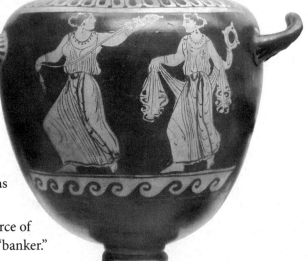

THE ATHENIAN ARMY

When it came to military matters, Athenians were not on a par with Spartans, but they loved Athens and were willing to fight and die for her. Theirs was the first citizen army in world history. Not that Athens did not value the career militarist; the citizens seemed always at war, or getting ready for war, and the career army and navy man was valued. But, at the same time, the "GI Joe" in the Athenian military was the ordinary craftsman, ordinary freed man. Every physically fit citizen was liable to military service from his 18th to his 60th year. What is so unique at that point in world history is the civilian aspect of the Athenian army. While there was a career officer class, Athenian armies were mustered in and mustered out according to each national threat that emerged and dissipated.

The organization of the Athenian army was brilliant in its simplicity; each of the 10 Athenian tribes sent its own special battalion. A unit of the Athenian citizen army, like practically all Greek armies, was comprised of heavily armed infantry soldiers—the **hoplites**. Hoplites had javelins, and sometimes slings and bows. They carried small but deadly swords. They were the heart of the Athenian army and the reason it was so successful.

The use of hoplites was an ingenious way to have an effective fighting force without maintaining a standing army. Tactics were simple and easily learned. Hoplites formed long, parallel lines, close to each other. Every hoplite carried a large round shield that covered his own left side and the right side of the man to his left. A **phalanx** was, therefore, very densely packed and could not easily turn to the left or the right. It was highly effective and guaranteed Greek military victory for a century and a half.

Greek cavalry units used no saddles and no stirrups. As Davis explains, "They were merely mounted on thin horse pads, and it was very hard to grip the horse with the knees tightly enough to keep from being upset ignominiously while wielding the spear. The best use for the cavalry perhaps was for the riders to take a sheaf of javelins, ride up and discharge them at the foe as skirmishers, then fall back behind the hoplites; though after the battle the horsemen would have plenty to do in the retreat or the pursuit."

The Greeks had neither flags nor standards, and gave no medals for valor. There were no division signs or emblems. Every citizen was expected to do his duty with valor and ingenuity. The notion that one soldier was isolated from all others for recognition was not considered.

What was fundamental Greek strategy? First, Greek generals selected a broad stretch of level ground for the struggle, since stony, hilly, or uneven ground would never do for the maneuvering of hoplites. The two opposing armies exchanged derisive shouts and catcalls. Almost never did fighting occur at night. When the general was ready, the phalanx advanced on the run. At first the phalanx pushed into the middle of the enemy. In fact, it appeared that the Greeks would surely be destroyed. Then, from within the phalanx emerged fierce Greek swordsmen. This Greek killing machine descended on their enemies like a mighty storm. At battle's end, huge numbers of enemy casualties would clutter the ground. A Greek army could defeat a foe 100 times its size. The Phalanx would continue to advance, enlarge, and move like a massive, deadly reaper across the field.

Assignment

Why were Greek armies so successful?

THE ATHENIAN NAVY

At the heart of the Athenian economy was the sea, which was protected by the Athenian navy. The Athenian navy was vital to national interests, and derived its name *trireme* from its three banks of oars on each side, manned by one man per oar. The early trireme was fast and agile, and became the dominant warship in the Mediterranean Sea wars. the heart of the Athenian navy was the **trireme**.

The trireme was a class of warship used by the ancient civilizations of the Mediterranean, especially the Phoenicians. Triremes played a vital role in the creation of the Athenian maritime empire. The ancient Greek navy was one of the most powerful of its time.

Triremes were built for speed and mobility. They were 120 feet long and were powered by 170 rowers. They were built low to the ground, so the lowest lines of rowers were just 18 inches above the waterline. The ships were quite narrow, which meant that they were not built to handle open ocean. Battles, therefore, occurred close to shore or in narrow straits.

Most of the crew officers were Athenian citizens. The rowers were not slaves, as many assume, but were paid rowers. Besides the rowers, a trireme's crew included 14 spearmen and 4 archers. These were the "marines" of the Greek navy.

The most famous victory for the Athenian triremes was at the Battle of Salamis. King Xerxes, accompanied by 200,000 soldiers, approached Athens by land. The Greeks hoped to stop the movement of the Persians into the Balkan Peninsula by stationing their navy at the Thermopylae inlet. King Leonidas of Sparta, along with 4,000 Peloponnesians and Central Greeks and 300 of his Spartans, defended the mountain pass of Thermopylae. They stayed in close communication with the naval barricade to their east.

As the Persians approached, a storm came up and destroyed several of their ships.

Meanwhile, the Persian land force met **Leonidas** at Thermopylae. At first it looked as if Leonidas could hold out indefinitely, but then a traitor informed the Persian generals of another pass through the mountains. When Leonidas realized he could no longer hold his position, he dismissed the 4,000 Greek troops. He and his 300 Spartans stayed behind.

The Athenian general Themistocles then lured the Persian navy into the straits of Euboea, where the naval battle of **Artemisium** occurred. They fought for three days, the Greeks assuming a semicircular position. Both sides received and inflicted heavy losses. However, the tactical advantage was gained by the Persians when Themistocles retreated after receiving word that Leonidas had lost the ground of Thermopylae. Retreating into the Strait of Salamis, Themistocles arranged his ships to be ready for a quick attack on the Persians. When the front line of the Persian fleet entered the strait, it was demolished by the heavier and quicker Greek triremes. Xerxes was forced to retreat from Greece.

Assignment

What was the trireme and why was it such an effective instrument of warfare?

The Odeon of Herodes Atticus, theatre in Athens, Greece.

LIFE IN ATHENS: PART TWO

GREEK WARS

First Thoughts . . .

In ancient Greece, a new system of warfare evolved; weaponry, tactics, ideas, and formations changed. Modified by Philip II and mainly by Alexander the Great after the Macedonians conquered Greece, this new age of warfare lasted until the rise of the Roman Empire, when the legion formation became the general method of battle. Ironically, this new battle system ultimately caused the demise of the Greek military, because it resulted in Greeks conquering other Greeks during the Peloponnesian War. Yet nothing could quell Greek culture—Alexander the Great made sure of that.

Chapter Learning Objectives . . .

In chapter 9, we will enter into the heart of Greek culture as we examine Greek religion. Then we will examine the Persian Wars and the Peloponnesian War. Finally, we will ride with Alexander the Great as he conquers the known world.

As a result of this chapter you should be able to:

1. Contrast Greek religion and ethics with those of Hebrew contemporaries in Palestine.
2. Evaluate why the Greeks won the Persian Wars.
3. Evaluate why the Spartans won the Peloponnesian War.
4. Pretend that you live in AD 55 Athens, and share the gospel with a potential Greek convert.
5. Discuss what legacy Alexander the Great left to the world.

RELIGION

Greek religion was a typical form of early paganism, which means it was polytheistic, consisting of the worship of many gods. The gods had a job to do, though. The Greeks believed that the gods would offer protection and guide their city-states. This was the same expectation shared by other ancient civilizations. Greeks believed that they had to worship and please the gods to have good fortune, so they participated in ceremonies and sacrifices in order to curry the favor of their gods. To that end, temples were erected as places to offer sacrifices to the gods.

The Greeks also firmly believed that this life was not the only reality in which the soul lives, but after this lifetime, a whole new and different one awaited them. Adherents didn't believe in personal salvation, per se, which no doubt troubled many of them, but their Greek traditions required that they live a humble life in proper abeyance to their gods and goddesses.

Greek religion made no claims of universality, so its people did not try to convert others. They had no priests, sacred texts, or moral code (e.g., Hammurabi Code; Ten Commandments) backed by religious beliefs. Greek religion was essentially a body of myths designed to explain natural phenomena and to highlight desirable character traits that good Greek citizens were expected to exhibit. Each city-state had its favorite gods and goddesses, a tradition that cemented the body of citizens into a loyal community. The gods and goddesses, however, were more like modern college mascots than omniscient deities. The gods were admired and feared, being distinguished from man by their immortality. The gods, who controlled natural and social forces, supposedly resided on Mount Olympus.

Ancient bust of the greek god Zeus in British Museum

Although the Greeks heavily depended on their gods to uphold their society, they also relied on an oracle. Oracles primarily offered guidance and advice. While in one sense, oracles were glorified fortune tellers, in another sense, they were greatly admired and feared. Delphi's oracle was particularly revered. Oracles controlled many human decisions about peace, war, migration, crime, and punishment.

Greeks showed appreciation to their deities through animal sacrifice. Many temples and shrines, erected as places of worship, were also places to show respect and to offer sacrifices. It is obvious that the Greeks placed a lot of pride in their temples and shrines, for extensive time was taken to rebuild, preserve, and beautify them. Prayers and hymns accompanied sacrifices, and sometimes performances and other ritual acts, such as dances or early forms of drama, followed.

The concept of an afterlife was extremely important to the Greeks. They believed that their souls were carried on to another dimension and lived on after death. However, they did not believe in reincarnation: The thought of a dead body's receiving new life was abhorrent to them. They believed that a body dissolved into the elements and could never be recovered. The Greeks' fear of bodily resurrection was one of the reasons the apostle Paul confronted the Greek believers at the church in Corinth (1 Corinthians 15).

Assignment

The Greeks kept their formal religion (but not their morality) separate from their daily lives. They relied on their religion for cultic rituals and religious superstitions, but for issues concerning everyday life, they consulted oracles and philosophers. Contrast the Greek way of life with that of their Hebrew contemporaries in Palestine.

PERSIAN WARS

The Persian Wars were a defining moment in Greek history. The Athenians, who would dominate Greece culturally and politically, assured their hegemony in the Greek civilization for two centuries.

The Persian Wars were actually initiated by the Greeks. In 498 BC, the Athenians conquered and burned Sardis, which was the capital of Lydia, owned by the Persian Empire. Other Greek cities in Asia Minor joined the revolt. Persian King Darius I (521–486 BC) had regained control over the rebellious Greek city-states and was determined to move them farther down the Greek peninsula.

The Persians and the Greeks met at **Marathon**, close to Athens, and the Persians were soundly defeated. This was an important battle in Greek history. Had the Athenians lost, Greece would have eventually come under the control of the Persians, and Greece's subsequent cultural and artistic contributions to the world would have been quite different—perhaps even nonexistent.

At that point, the Athenians thought of themselves as the center of Greek culture and Greek power. That pride was the foundation on which much of their cultural prowess was built. The first great dramas, for instance, were the dramas of **Aeschylus**; their principal subject was the celebration of Athenian greatness. The great building projects of the latter half of the fifth century were motivated by the desire to display Athenian wealth, greatness, and power.

The Persians, however, weren't finished with Greece. While Marathon stands as one of the greatest of Greek military accomplishments, it was really more of an irritation to the Persians. When **Xerxes** (486–465 BC) became king, he sought revenge. This time the Persians meant business. In 481 BC, Xerxes gathered an army of 200,000 troops and 600 ships. There would be no mercy.

The Athenians knew the Persians would be back. Athenian leader Themistocles began a navy-building project of epic proportions. By 481 BC, Athens had a navy of 200 ships.

Themistocles understood that victory would come if the Greeks defeated the Persian navy, because the Persian army could succeed only with the support of its naval fleet. He also understood that it was the stormy season on the Aegean Sea, which surrounded Greece. In fact, many of Xerxes' boats were destroyed at sea.

While King Leonidas and his 300 Spartans delayed the Persians at Thermopylae, Themistocles and his Greek navy waited. Finally, the Greeks met the Persians off the island of Salamis. The Athenians destroyed most of the Persian fleet. The Persian army retreated.

It is difficult to assess all the consequences of the Greek victory over the Persians. While the Spartans were principally responsible for the land victory, the Athenian fleet was probably the most important component of that victory. The alliances that Athens would make following the retreat of the Persians, the so-called Delian League, made Athens the premier Greek city-state. This power would make Athens the cultural center of the Greek world, but it would also make the Spartans increasingly suspicious of Athenian intentions.

Assignment

In spite of the fact that the Persians substantively outnumbered the Greeks, the Greeks won the Persian Wars. Why?

PELOPONNESIAN WARS

The war that pitted Athens and the Athenian empire against Sparta, Thebes, Corinth, and other members of the **Peloponnesian Confederacy** (431–404 BC) ended Athenian hegemony over the Greek world forever.

The underlying cause of the war was Sparta's fear of the growth of power in Athens. At the same time, Sparta was waiting for an opportunity to knock Athens down a notch or two. Sparta issued an ultimatum that would have practically destroyed Athenian power. When the Athenian ruler Pericles refused the ultimatum, Sparta declared war.

Sparta expected to defeat Athens quickly. In numbers as well as discipline and combat effectiveness of troops, Athens was decidedly inferior to the Spartan-Theban forces. The defect in this strategy was that Athens could not be starved into surrender. Her fleet made sure Athens would not be beaten so quickly. Pericles, knowing that his city's walls were impregnable and that his navy would be able to ensure the food supply, opted for a defensive strategy of attrition. As it turned out, both Sparta and Athens were wrong.

Ultimately a plague turned the tide. Athens was devastated by a plague imported from Egypt. In fact, **Pericles** himself died. Athens sued for peace in 430, but Sparta refused. Then, the tables turned again. Athens won several sea battles and it looked as though Sparta would lose after all.

This was an unprecedented disgrace for Sparta. This time Sparta sued for peace, which Athens foolishly refused. In 424 BC, all Athenian offensive plans failed.

Athenian hopes now rested on taking up an even more bold offensive to cut Spartan and Corinthian supplies from Sicily. In 416 BC, the campaign at first gained momentum. Syracuse was under siege on land and at sea, but Athenian attempts to take the city were thwarted. The Athenian fleet was blocked at the harbor and then defeated in battle.

Sparta now had a strong fleet with additional reinforcements from the west. Athens had lost its best sailors and had nearly exhausted its treasury. With the grain supply from Sicily and from Egypt completely under Spartan control (with some help from Persia), Athens was totally dependent on food from Crimea through the Hellespont. There the Athenian commanders Thrasybulus and Thrasylus defeated the Spartan Mindarus at Cynossema in September of 411 BC. Once more, Sparta requested peace, but Athenian leadership refused again.

In autumn of 408 BC, the Spartan navy closed the last avenue of Athenian grain supply. After six months of starvation and no prospect for relief, Athens surrendered on generous terms offered by Sparta. Athens' city walls and those connecting Athens to Piraeus were torn down and the empire dissolved. Ancient Athens was no more.

Assignment

Why did the Spartans ultimately win the Peloponnesian War?

Bust of the greek statesman Pericles at the British Museum

ALEXANDER THE GREAT

Alexander the Great, the king of Macedonia and conqueror of the known world, was one of the greatest military geniuses of all times.

Alexander was born in 356 BC in Macedonia. He was son of Philip II, king of Macedonia, whom Alexander greatly admired.

When Alexander was 13, his father hired Greek philosopher Aristotle to be Alexander's tutor. During the next three years Aristotle taught Alexander rhetoric, literature, and science. From the beginning, Alexander showed great promise.

He was also a natural soldier. Two years later, in 338 BC, Philip gave Alexander a position as a commanding officer among his nation's senior generals during the Macedonian army's invasion of Greece. The Macedonians won the campaign, thanks to Alexander's generalship.

Soon his father Phillip II was assassinated. Alexander III, later called "the Great," was now king of Macedonia. He promptly conquered all of Greece. In 334 BC, he traveled to Persia where he defeated a Persian army. He defeated another Persian army, this one led by King Darius III, who managed to escape. Alexander then took Syria and Phoenicia, cutting off the Persian fleet from its ports.

In 332 BC, he completed a seven-month siege of Tyre, considered his greatest military achievement, and then took Egypt, where he founded perhaps the greatest ancient city. By that time, Alexander was claiming to be a god, and no one would contest the issue with him!

In control of the entire eastern Mediterranean coast, in 331 BC, Alexander defeated Darius in a decisive battle, though Darius again escaped. Next, Alexander conquered Babylon itself, and the great Persian Empire was finished. By 326 BC, he reached India, where he stopped. He fell ill at Babylon and died at age 33. He was buried in Alexandria, Egypt.

Alexander the Great did many amazing things during his conquest of most of the known world. However, he also experienced much sadness during his life. His father was mostly absent from his life. Family members betrayed him. Alexander was purported to be an alcoholic. He killed friends while he was drunk. At one point, he killed a childhood friend while drunk, and then, realizing what he had done, would have killed himself if his bodyguards had not stopped him. Alexander's supreme and lasting importance to the world was the extension of Greek culture. For the first time, the entire known western world was united under one government. This increased trade and cultural syncretism.

Assignment

When others had failed, why was Alexander so successful?

Statue of Alexander the Great at Thessaloniki, a city in Greece.

 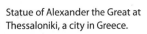

Relief of Alexander the Great at Thessaloniki, a city in Greece.

GREEK WARS

Chapter 10

PHILOSOPHERS AND WORLD VIEWS

First Thoughts . . .

In a real way, the culture war that is raging across America began thousands of years ago in the writings and thoughts of Greek philosophers. Philosopher Alfred Whitehead noted, "Western philosophy is just a series of footnotes to Plato." Indeed. To a large degree the decision that Burger King® makes in ad campaigns more or less reflects a world view decision that is a derivation of Platonic philosophy. Does one emphasize the "spiritual" value of a Whopper or the "sensual" value of a Whopper? These two questions have set the perimeters of world view discussion since before Christ was born. How did it begin? Greek philosophers did something no one, other than the Hebrew prophets, had done: they broke away from a mythological approach to explaining the world, and for the first time used reason and evidence to discuss ontology (i.e., the beginning of things). Initially concerned with explaining the entire cosmos, Greek philosophers strived to identify its single underlying principle. This changed the world forever.

Chapter Learning Objectives . . .

In chapter 10, we will look closely at Herodotus, who set standards for historians in all ages. Next, we will discuss several philosophers, beginning with the Ionians, and compare their philosophies to Christian orthodoxy. We will finish by discussing Greek ethics, particularly Aristotle's "Golden Mean."

As a result of this chapter you should be able to:

1. Analyze Herodotus' teachings.
2. Discuss the Ionian philosophers and their connection with modern philosophy.
3. Analyze Pythagoras and his philosophy.
4. Compare Socrates' views with Christian orthodoxy.
5. Evaluate Aristotle's "Golden Mean."

HISTORY MAKER: HERODOTUS

Herodotus wrote *The Histories* at approximately the same time that Moses was writing the Pentateuch—the first five books of the Bible. In fact, Herodotus' writings confirm the historical veracity of Moses' writings. Some of the stories are quite similar. Is this coincidence or do they both refer to the same people and events, which would provide evidence indicating that the Bible and *The Histories* are true? The fact that they were written at about the same time and the stories in each of the books are similar is unquestionable proof that the Bible is accurate.

Herodotus, who lived during the fifth century BC, was the first writer to so unify the record of facts as to raise historical narrative to the level of literature. His real claim to fame, in this writer's opinion, is his confirmation of Old Testament facts.

Statue of philosopher Herodotus at Parliment in Vienna.

Some scholars have claimed that many of the Old Testament records are not true. However, Herodotus offered evidence that supported the Bible. For instance, both the Bible and Herodotus refer to Joseph's living in Egypt. The biblical account goes on to describe how the wife of an Egyptian leader, Potiphar, tried to seduce the young Joseph (Gen. 39:7–10). Herodotus tells of an Egyptian ruler who, for the sake of performing an experiment, searched at length for a married woman who had been faithful to her husband.

Herodotus mentions that whereas the Egyptian women transported burdens upon their shoulders, the men carried them upon their heads. This is the very opposite of the custom in many countries. This is described by both Herodotus and the Bible. Finally, when Joseph, who had become second in command throughout Egypt, received his estranged brothers into his house, they were given water with which to wash their feet (Gen. 43:24). Herodotus recorded a story of an Egyptian ruler who had a golden foot-pan in which his guests were provided water to wash their feet.

Another example is Herodotus' and the Bible's similar descriptions of the Assyrian king Sennacherib's siege of Jerusalem (2 Kings 18:13; Isa. 36:1).

Ancient Babylon was known as "the jewel of the kingdoms, the glory of the Babylonians' pride" (Isa. 13:19), "the boast of the whole earth" (Jer. 51:41). Herodotus described Babylon in a similar way. Jeremiah alluded to Babylon's massive fortifications (Jer. 51:53, 58). Herodotus' record specifies that the city was enclosed by great walls 350 high and 75 feet thick.

Herodotus' writings, then, are important extra-biblical confirmations of biblical events.

Assignment

Highlight several biblical references confirmed by Herodotus' teachings.

PRE-SOCRATIC PHILOSOPHY

The Persian Wars were a defining moment in Greek history. The Athenians, who would dominate Greece culturally and politically, assured their hegemony in the Greek civilization for two centuries.

The Ionian School (580 BC)

Ionians' early fascination with the physical world anticipated later discussions in Western philosophy. Western philosophy grew out of discussions about ultimate things, or things that seemed really important. Thales, Anaximander, and Anaminenes, Greek philosophers living in the ancient Greek province of Ionia, saw their vocation in that light. They speculated on **penultimate truth**. There was no demarcation between philosophy and the physical sciences. They argued that all things were created from an unknown, intangible, invisible, ubiquitous substance called "**apeiron.**" This strange substance was indestructible and unlimited. It was made finite in the sense that mankind alone could observe the portion that was on the earth. The Ionian School anticipated the modern notion of an unbounded universe created by nameless physical forces unrelated to any deity, much less to a benevolent, loving God.

Passage

I. Of all things that are, the most ancient is God, for he is uncreated.

II. The most beautiful is Cosmos, because it is God's action.

III. The largest is space, because it holds all things.

IV. The swiftest is mind, because it speeds everywhere

V. The strongest is necessity, for it matters all.

VI. The wisest is time, because he brings everything to light.

VII. The things you offer to your parents you must wait to get from your children.

VIII. There is no difference between life and death.

IX. Know thyself.

X. Someone asked him which is older, day or night, and he replied, "Night is the older by one day."

XI. Someone asked him who is the happiest man and he replied, "The one who has healthy body, resourceful mind, and a docile nature" (Thales).

Assignment

The Ionian philosophers piqued the interest of generations of philosophers and invited later thinkers to merge the visible and invisible worlds without reference to a personal, omniscient God. They were the first philosophers to suggest that material substance explains natural phenomena. It was a mere hop, skip, and jump to the panoply that atheist Carl Sagan developed in the last part of the 20th century. Why?

SCHOOLS OF THOUGHT

The Phythagoreans (530 B.C.)

Pythagoras was the first philosopher to require some standard of behavior from his followers. One can imagine what a novel and important step this was—that a religion would require a commitment from its adherents.

Pythagoras, a great philosopher and mathematician, started the first "organized religion." The Phythagoreans adhered to a sort of moral code that anticipated the ethical codes of later religions (e.g., Hammurabi's Code and the Ten Commandments). His ethics, admittedly, seem facile and nugatory by modern standards. The Pythagoreans Brotherhood, for instance, was not allowed to eat beans. Furthermore, believing that the universe was composed of mathematical formulas and geometric shapes, Pythagoras formed the first "scientific religion" whose followers believed that reality was ordered by natural, immutable laws. The degree to which people understood these laws determined their ability to control their fate.

The following is an excerpt from the *Doxographists*:

And again from another starting-point, Pythagoras, son of Muesarchos, who was the first to call this matter by the name of philosophy, assumed as first principles the numbers and the symmetries existing in them, which he calls harmonies, and the elements compounded of both, that are called geometrical. And again he includes the monad and the undefined dyad among the first principles; and for him one of the first principles tends toward the creative and form-giving cause, which is intelligence, that is god, and the other tends toward the passive and material cause, which is the visible universe. And he says that the starting-point of number is the decade; for all Greeks and all barbarians count as far as ten, and when they get as far as this they return to the monad. And again, he says, the power of the ten is in the four and the tetrad. And the reason is this: if anyone returning from the monad adds the numbers in a series as far as the four, he will fill out the number ten (i.e., 1 + 2 + 3 + 4=10); but if he goes beyond the number of the tetrad, he will exceed the ten.

The Eleatic School (500 BC)

The Eleatic School argued that reality was indivisible and endless. Perhaps no pre-Socratic philosophical movement had as much influence on Western thought than that of the Eleatic School. Its main proponent, Parmenides, argued that reality was indivisible and endless. There was no beginning or ending to time, either. All things were the same. From the beginning of time, everything existed that was to exist and that which existed changed in form, but not in substance. Thus, change was impossible. Something might change in form—ice to water to steam—but it was the same in substance. Also, once a thing moved in one direction it continued to move in that direction until time and circumstances stopped it. This viewpoint, carried to its logical conclusion, had a profound effect on Western thought. For one thing, the basis for the whole Theory of Relativity proposed by

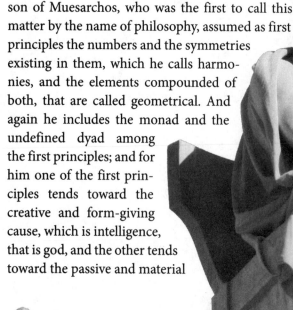

Statue of Socrates (ancient Greek philosopher) in front of the Academy of Athens, Greece.

Albert Einstein was similar to that of Parmenides. Likewise, philosophers such as David Hume, in his rejection of the miraculous, espoused an Eleatic view of reality.

An imaginary conversation between Socrates and Parmenides:

"And would you make an idea of man apart from us and from all other human creatures, or of fire and water?" Socrates says. "I am often undecided, Parmenides, as to whether I ought to include them or not."

"And would you feel equally undecided, Socrates, about things of which the mention may provoke a smile? I mean such things as hair, mud, dirt, or anything else which is vile and paltry; would you suppose that each of these has an idea distinct from the actual objects with which we come into contact, or not?"

"Certainly not," said Socrates, "visible things like these are such as they appear to us, and I am afraid that there would be an absurdity in assuming any idea of them, although I sometimes get disturbed, and begin to think that there is nothing without an idea; but then again, when I have taken up this position, I run away, because I am afraid that I may fall into a bottomless pit of nonsense, and perish; and so I return to the ideas of which I was just now speaking, and occupy myself with them."

"Yes, Socrates," said Parmenides, "that is because you are still young; the time will come, if I am not mistaken, when philosophy will have a firmer grasp of you, and then you will not despise even the meanest things; at your age, you are too much disposed to regard opinions of men. But I should like to know whether you mean that there are certain ideas of which all other things partake, and from which they derive their names; that similar, for example, become similar, because they partake of similarity; and great things become great, because they partake of greatness; and that just and beautiful things become just and beautiful, because they partake of justice and beauty? Then each individual partakes either of the whole of the idea or else of a part of the idea? Can there be any other mode of participation?"

"There cannot be," Socrates said. "Then do you think that the whole idea is one, and yet, being one, is in each one of the many? Why not, Parmenides? Because one and the same thing will exist as a whole at the same time in many separate individuals, and will therefore be in a state of separation from itself" (Parmenides, by Plato).

Socrates (469 BC)

Socrates was one of the most influential but mysterious figures in Western philosophy. He wrote nothing, yet he had a profound influence on someone who did: Plato. Plato carefully recorded most of his dialogues. Unlike earlier philosophers, Socrates' main concern was with ethics. There was nothing remotely pragmatic about Socrates, who was the consummate idealist. Until his day, philosophers invested most of their time explaining the natural world. In fact, the natural world often intruded into the abstract world of ideas and reality. Socrates kept both worlds completely separate. To Socrates, the natural laws governing the rotation of the earth were merely uninteresting speculation of no earthly good. Socrates was more interested in such meaty concepts as "virtue" and "justice." Taking issue with the Sophists, Socrates believed that ethics, specifically virtue, must be learned and practiced like any trade. One was not born virtuous; one developed virtue as he would a good habit. It could be practiced only by experts. There was, then, nothing pragmatic about the pursuit of virtue. It was systematic; it was intentional. Virtue was acquired and maintained by open and free dialogue. For the first time, the importance of human language was advanced by a philosopher (to reappear at the end of the 20th century in postmodern philosophy).

Socrates speaking in Plato's *Phaedo*:

I would have you look to yourselves; that is a service which you may always be doing to me and mine as well as to yourselves. And you need not make professions; for if you take no thought for yourselves, and walk not according to the precepts which I have given you, now for the first time, the warmth of your professions will be of no avail.

Assignment

A. Phythagoras, as stated earlier, was the first philosopher to require some standard of behavior from his followers. What would a religion be like that did not require any behavioral change in its adherents?

B. Discuss how the Theory of Relativity was Eleatic in origin and composition.

C. Socrates argued that one was not born virtuous, but that he or she could determine to work hard to develop virtue and eventually become virtuous through practice and ongoing open discussion. How is this view contradictory to Christian orthodoxy?

PLATO AND ARISTOTLE

Plato (428 B.C.)

There was no more important philosopher in Western culture than Socrates' disciple Plato. Plato, like Socrates, regarded ethics as the highest branch of knowledge. Plato stressed the intellectual basis of virtue, identifying virtue with wisdom. Plato believed that the world was made of forms (such as a rock) and ideas (such as virtue). The ability of human beings to appreciate forms made a person virtuous. Knowledge came from the gods; opinion was from man. Virtuous activity, then, was dependent upon knowledge of the forms.

A passage from Plato's *Allegory of the Cave*:

And now, I said, let me show in a figure how far our nature is enlightened or unenlightened: Behold! Human beings living in an underground den, which has a mouth open towards the light and reaching all along the den; here they have been from their childhood, and have their legs and necks chained so that they cannot move, and can only see before them, being prevented by the chains from turning round their heads. Above and behind them a fire is blazing at a distance, and between the fire and the prisoners there is a raised way; and you will see, if you look, a low wall built along the way, like the screen which marionette players have in front of them, over which they show the puppets. I see.

And do you see, I said, men passing along the wall carrying all sorts of vessels, and statues and figures of animals made of wood and stone and various materials, which appear over the wall? Some of them are talking, others silent.

You have shown me a strange image, and they are strange prisoners.

Like ourselves, I replied; and they see only their own shadows, or the shadows of one another, which the fire throws on the opposite wall of the cave?

Plato (left) and Aristotle (right), a detail of *The School of Athens*, a fresco by Raphael., 1509 (PD-Art).

True, he said; how could they see anything but the shadows if they were never allowed to move their heads?

And of the objects which are being carried in like manner they would only see the shadows?

First Chaos came, and then broad-bosomed Earth,
The everlasting seat of all that is,
And Love.

In other words, after Chaos, the Earth and Love, these two, came into being. Also Parmenides sings of Generation: "First in the train of gods, he fashioned Love."

The veriest coward would become an inspired hero, equal to the bravest, at such a time; Love would inspire him. That courage which, as Homer says, the god breathes into the souls of some heroes, Love of his own nature infuses into the lover. . . . And greatly as the gods honour the virtue of love, still the return of love on the part of the beloved to the lover is more admired and valued and rewarded by them, for the lover is more divine; because he is inspired by God. Now Achilles was quite aware, for he had been told by his mother, that he might avoid death and return home, and live to a good old age, if he abstained from slaying Hektor. Nevertheless he gave his life to revenge his friend, and dared to die, not only in his defense, but after he was dead. Wherefore the gods honoured him even above Alcestis, and sent him to the Islands of the Blest. These are my reasons for affirming that Love is the eldest and noblest and mightiest of the gods, and the chiefest author and giver of virtue in life, and of happiness after death.

Aristotle (350 BC)

Aristotle was the first serious agnostic philosopher. To Plato, knowledge and virtue were inseparable; to Aristotle, they were unconnected. Aristotle was not on a search for absolute truth. He was not even certain it existed. Truth, beauty, and goodness were to be observed and quantified from human behavior and the senses, but they were not the legal tender of the land. Goodness in particular was not an absolute, and in Aristotle's opinion it was much abused. Goodness was an average between two absolutes. Aristotle said that mankind should strike a balance between passion and temperance, between extremes of all sorts. He said that good people should seek the "Golden Mean" defined as a course of life that was never extreme. Finally, while Plato argued that reality lay in knowledge of the gods, Aristotle argued that reality lay in empirical, measurable knowledge. To Aristotle, reality was tied to purpose and action. For these reasons, Aristotle became known as the father of modern science.

A passage from Aristotle's *Nicomachean Ethics*:

We may safely assert that the virtue or excellence of a thing causes that thing both to be itself in good condition and to perform its function well. The excellence of the eye, for instance, makes both the eye and its work good; for it is by the excellence of the eye that we see well. So the proper excellence of the horse makes a horse what it should be, and makes it good at running, and carrying his rider, and standing a charge. If, then, this holds good in all cases, the proper excellence or virtue of man will be the habit or trained faculty that makes a man good and makes him perform his function well.

Now, if we have any quantity, whether continuous or discrete, it is possible to take either a larger (or too large), or a smaller (or too small), or an equal (or fair) amount, and that either absolutely or relatively to our own needs. By an equal or fair amount I understand a mean amount, or one that lies between excess and deficiency. By the absolute mean, or mean relative to the thing itself, I understand that which is equidistant from both extremes, and this is one and the same for all. By the mean relative to us I understand that which is neither too much nor too little for us; and this is not one and the same for all. . . . Virtue, then, is a kind of moderation inasmuch as it aims at the mean or moderate amount. . . . Virtue, then, is a habit or trained faculty of choice, the characteristic of which lies in moderation or observance of the mean relative to the persons concerned, as determined by reason, i.e., by the reason by which the prudent man would determine it. And it is a moderation, firstly, inasmuch as it comes in the middle or mean between two vices, one on the side of excess, the other on the side of defect; and, secondly, inasmuch as, while these vices fall short of or exceed the due measure in feeling and in action, it finds and chooses the mean, middling, or moderate amount.

Aristotle's most enduring impact occurred in the area of metaphysics—philosophical speculation about the nature, substance, and structure of reality. It is not physics—concerned with the visible or natural world. Metaphysics is concerned with explaining the nonphysical world. Aristotle, then, advanced the discussion about God, the human soul, and the nature of space and time. What makes this particularly interesting is Aristotle's penchant for delving into the metaphysical by talking about the gods in human terms. Aristotle said, "All men by nature desire to know," and it is by the senses that the gods were known—or not. Faith had nothing to do with it. In other words, Aristotle, for the first time, discussed the gods as if they were quantified entities. He spoke about them as if they were not present. The

Hebrews had done this earlier (Genesis 3), but Aristotle was probably not aware of Moses' text. While some Christian thinkers such as Augustine and Aquinas employed Aristotelian logic in their discussions about God, they never speculated as to God's existence as Aristotle did, but used Aristotle's techniques only to understand more about God.

A passage from Aristotle's *Metaphysics*:

All men by nature desire to know. An indication of this is the delight we take in our senses; for even apart from their usefulness they are loved for themselves; and above all others the sense of sight. For not only with a view to action, but even when we are not going to do anything, we prefer seeing (one might say) to everything else. The reason is that this, most of all the senses, makes us know and brings to light many differences between things. By nature animals are born with the faculty of sensation, and from sensation memory is produced in some of them, though not in others. And therefore the former are more intelligent and apt at learning than those which cannot remember; those which are incapable of hearing sounds are intelligent though they cannot be taught, e.g., the bee, and any other race of animals that may be like it; and those which besides memory have this sense of hearing can be taught. The animals other than man live by appearances and memories, and have but little of connected experience; but the human race lives also by art and reasonings. Now from memory, experience is produced in men; for the several memories of the same thing produce finally the capacity for a single experience.

Aristotle by Francesco Hayez, 1811 (PD-US).

Assignment

A. The most famous concept of Plato's work was the concept of "love." "Love" to Plato was a "form" from which virtue flowed. Compare and contrast this view of love with a view from a man trained in the teachings of Plato: the apostle Paul.

B. Aristotle said that mankind should strike a balance between passion and temperance, between extremes of all sorts, and that good people should seek the "Golden Mean"—a course of life that is never extreme. What problem does this philosophy present to a Christian believer?

C. Aristotle, for the first time, discussed the gods as if they were quantified entities. He spoke about them as if they were not present. What implications did this have for scientific research?

ROMAN HISTORY

First Thoughts . . .

The Romans were the greatest empire builders of the ancient Western world. They created a legacy that is still evident in myriad modern institutions. In many ways, the Roman legacy remains the ideal upon which Western civilization has shaped itself. From a tiny village on the Tiber River to the Euphrates, from the Seine River to Ireland, Roman influence dominated for over 1,000 years. The world has seen nothing like it since and will probably never see anything like it again.

Chapter Learning Objectives . . .

In chapter 11, we will look at three phases of Roman history: the monarchy, the republic, and the empire. We will finish by looking at the mighty Roman military, whose army and navy maintained peace all over the known world.

As a result of this chapter you should be able to:

1. Compare the origin of the city-state Rome to the origin of the city-state Athens.
2. Evaluate a quote from the historian Edward Gibbon concerning religious freedom.
3. Analyze how Christians can prosper in times of persecution.
4. Synthesize data and determine why the Roman army was so effective.
5. Determine why Rome's success in politics was not matched by its moral integrity.

THE MONARCHY

Rome was one of the most important and influential city-states in world history. What Jerusalem was to the religious world, Rome was to the geopolitical world. Romans claimed that in 753 BC, twin boys, **Romulus** and **Remus**, were abandoned next to the Tiber River. A mother wolf purportedly cared for them until they were young adults. Years later, the Roman god of war, Mars, encouraged the boys to build a city where they had been discovered. The two boys built this city; however, they could not get along and ended up at war with each other. Romulus won the battle and the city became known as Rome.

Long before Romulus and Remus there were nomadic people in the Tiber River area who created sedentary villages around 800 BC. The Roman story had begun.

The history of Rome is marked by three epochs. In the first period, from 753 to 509 BC, the city developed from a village to a city ruled by kings. Then the Romans expelled the kings and established the Roman Republic during the period from 509 to 27 BC. It was much like the Greek Republic that existed at about the same time in Athens. The Republic collapsed and Rome was ruled by despotic, if at times benign, emperors from 27 BC–AD 476.

The Italian Peninsula provided the Romans with a secure base from which to expand throughout the Mediterranean and into the European world. Italy was easy to defend and, with its numerous deep-water ports, was an ideal place from which to launch expeditions into the interior Mediterranean world. Italy is a peninsula surrounded on three sides by the sea and protected to the north by part of the Alps mountain range. The climate is generally temperate, although summers are hot in the south.

Altar from Ostia showing the discovery of Romulus and Remus (now at the Palazzo Massimo alle Terme). Photo by Marie-Lan Nguyen, 2006 (PD-US).

Italy is a peninsula jutting out into the Mediterranean Sea west of Greece. Although Italy does not have mountains covering most of its land as does Greece, ancient Italy was poor in mineral resources and surprisingly devoid of useful harbors. However, the most stunning difference between Italy and Greece was Italy's exponentially larger amount of fertile land. While Greece was poor in fertile land, Italy was wealthy in both land and rainfall, so the two nations developed differently. The Romans began and remained largely an agrarian people. Even in its later stages, Roman culture would identify its values and ideals as **agrarian**.

Italy and Greece were different from each other in other significant ways as well. One was that northern Italy was easily accessible from Europe. The Greeks were protected by a formidable mountain range, whereas the Alps to the north of Italy were not quite as invulnerable. Also, Greece had a warlike Greek population to the north—the Macedonians—to serve as a buffer between themselves and other Europeans. The Romans had no such buffer civilization. As a result, conflict was a fairly constant affair in Italy, so the Romans, along with other peoples on the Italian peninsula, developed a military society fairly early in their history. There was very little time to build temples or to write great literary works.

There were already small settlements in Italy around 1500 BC, but somewhere between 900 and 800 BC, the Italian peninsula was settled by an aggressive people group called the Etruscans. The Etruscans, who came from the eastern Mediterranean (possibly Asia Minor), conquered all of Italy from the Arno River in the north to the Tiber River.

The Etruscans lived in independent, fortified city-states that formed small confederacies. In the earliest times, these city-states were ruled by a monarch, but were later ruled by oligarchies, small groups who governed through a council and elected officials. Like the surrounding peoples, the Etruscans were largely agrarian. However, they also had a strong military force that dominated the neighboring communities and forced them to do the agricultural labor on the Etruscan farms. As a result, the Etruscans had time to devote to commerce and industry. In the seventh and sixth centuries BC, the Etruscan military had subjugated much of Italy, including Rome, and regions outside of Italy, such as the island of Corsica.

The Etruscans were a sophisticated people with a Grecian-based alphabet, a powerfully original sculpting and painting tradition, a religion based on human-type gods, which they had learned from the Greeks, and a complicated set of rituals for divining the future, which they handed down to the Romans. Unlike most civilizations of the time, in the Etruscan society, gender inequality seems not to have been very pronounced.

It was on the Tiber River that a small Latin village—the village that would become Rome—was founded. This was the basis of Virgil's classic *The Aeneid*. In *The Aeneid*, a Trojan survivor journeys to the Tiber River to found Rome. Thus, the Romans were in close contact with the Etruscans, whose language, ideals, religion, and civilization comprised the single most important influence on Roman culture.

By a very early period in Rome's history, society was divided into two groups: the **patricians** and the **plebeians**. The patricians, the wealthiest members of society, controlled most of the wealth, trade, power, and the military. Only patricians could serve in the senate or hold appointed or elected offices. The plebeians, the majority of the population, were mainly small farmers and small business owners.

Lucretia by Rembrandt van Rijn, National Gallery of Art, Washington, D.C., 1664 (PD-US).

The plebeians did have a small voice in government, though: The assembly was the governmental body that represented their interests. Early in Roman history a king assumed tertiary control and ruled with the senate in Rome.

During the monarchy, Rome greatly expanded its control over surrounding territories. As Roman territorial power grew, however, its expansion attracted the notice of the powerful Etruscans to the north who, in the middle of the sixth century BC, assumed control of Rome. From the middle of the sixth century, the Roman monarchs came from the Etruscans, and the Latin Romans bitterly resented it. Finally, in 509 BC, when a prince from the ruling Etruscan family, the Tarquins, raped the wife of a patrician, the Romans rose up in revolt and threw the Tarquins out of power. The rape of Lucretia and the overthrow of the Tarquins by Junius Brutus began the decline of Etruscan power and civilization. According to Roman tradition, the king ruled only by consent of the people and in conformity with tradition and the constitution. The Tarquins had broken that tradition, but rather than replace them with a Latin monarch, the Romans dismantled the institution of the monarchy entirely. The age of the Roman Republic, an age that would see the greatest expansion of Roman power and numerous wars, had dawned.

Assignment

Compare the origin of the city-state Rome with the origin of the city-state Athens.

THE REPUBLIC

From its beginning, the Roman Republic was governed by a **senate** and an **assembly**. There was no longer a king, but there were consuls. At the top were two consuls who were patricians elected to the office for one year. These patricians acted as "co-kings" for only a year. In 325 BC, however, the consul system was changed to allow for proconsuls—consuls whose terms in office were extended because of military campaigns.

According to historic Roman tradition, in 494 BC, the plebeians withdrew from Rome and occupied the Sacred Mount. There they declared an alternative government. They formed a tribal assembly, modeled after the Roman assembly, to be led by tribunes who were heads of their tribes. They declared that these tribunes could veto any decision by a Roman magistrate or official, and could veto any decision or legislation by the senate. The assembly itself, like the original Roman assembly, voted by tribe, and the decision of the assembly was binding on all plebeians. In other words, the plebeians had won the right to author their own legislation. Their decisions, however, were not binding on nonplebeians.

The conquest of Italy began soon after the Romans expelled the Tarquins in 509 BC. The Romans' first target was the Etruscans. Allying themselves with other Latins and with the Greeks, the Romans quickly drove the Etruscans from the Italian peninsula. Etruscan civilization came to a brutal end. Rome steadily conquered all the Etruscan territory throughout the fifth and fourth centuries BC.

The Romans, however, were dramatically checked in their conquest of Italy by invasions from another Indo-European people, the Gauls, who lived across the Alps. The Gauls were perennial enemies of the Romans. They burned Rome to the ground, but soon left. It was not until 350 BC that Rome regained enough power to begin asserting dominance over the region again.

From the beginning, Rome was good at occupying cities and successfully administering conquered territories. Some conquered territories were assimilated into Rome with full citizen rights. Others were allowed complete autonomy. Some were allowed to become allies. All, however, paid taxes and provided troops to Rome.

One enemy, **Carthage**, was particularly threatening to Rome's dominance. The third and second centuries BC would see the clash of these two great and powerful cities. At the end of the Punic Wars, Rome would emerge as the most powerful force in the Mediterranean.

The greatest naval power of the Mediterranean in the third century BC was the North African city of Carthage, near present-day Tunis. The Carthaginians were originally Phoenicians, and Carthage was a colony founded by the Phoenician capital city of Tyre (which Alexander the Great conquered). While the Romans were steadily increasing their control over the Italian peninsula, the Carthaginians were extending their empire over most of North Africa. By the time Rome gained control of the entire Italian peninsula, Carthage already controlled the North African coast from western Libya to

Hannibal Barca counting the rings of the Roman knights killed at the Battle of Cannae (216 BC). Marble, 1704 (CC BY-SA 3.0).

the Strait of Gibraltar, and ruled over most of southern Spain, the Gaulish (French) island of Corsica, and the Italian island of Sardinia. When the military forces of the two mighty empires, Rome and Carthage, finally met during the mid-third century BC, a series of wars ensued. They were called the Punic Wars because the Romans called the Carthaginians "Punic," which was short for "Phoenician."

The First Punic War, which broke out in 264 BC, was concentrated on the island of Sicily. Rome utterly destroyed Carthaginian forces, drove them out of Sicily, and occupied Carthaginian Corsica and Sardinia. The Carthaginians were furious.

In 221 BC, a 25-year-old general named **Hannibal** assumed command over Carthaginian Spain. Hannibal marched his army across Europe and, in September of 218 BC, he crossed the Alps and entered Italy. Hannibal's troops soundly defeated the Roman armies they encountered in northern Italy.

The Romans knew that they couldn't beat Hannibal in open warfare. Desperate, they asked **Quintus Fabius Maximus** to become absolute dictator of Rome. Fabius determined to avoid open warfare at any cost and to simply harass the Carthaginian army until it was weak enough to be engaged openly. But when Hannibal marched into Cannae and started decimating the countryside in 216 BC, Fabius sent an army of 80,000 soldiers against him. The Roman army was completely wiped out, suffering its largest defeat ever.

At that point, the situation was nearly hopeless for the Romans. Fabius had been chastened by his defeat and absolutely refused to go against Hannibal, whose army moved around the Italian countryside unopposed. Hannibal, however, didn't have enough soldiers to lay siege to Rome, so all he could do was lay waste to the surrounding countryside.

Then Rome came up with a plan to defeat Hannibal by sending the great Roman general to conquer Hannibal's supply center—Spain. After defeating Spain, Scipio crossed into Africa in 204 BC and took the war to the walls of Carthage itself, forcing the Carthaginians to sue for peace with Rome.

When Hannibal returned home in 202 BC, the Carthaginians took heart and rebelled against Rome in one last gamble. At Zama in northern Africa, Hannibal, fighting against Scipio and his army, met his first defeat. After reducing Carthage to a dependent state, Rome controlled the whole of the western Mediterranean, including northern Africa.

Now Rome turned east toward Macedonia and Greece. By 179 BC they had succeeded in conquering Greece.

Things were different now. As historian Edward Gibbon explains, "Rome had begun as a small city-state. Its constitution, its government, its social structure, and its moral values were those of a small, mainly agrarian state. All of these, the constitution, government, social structure, and values, adapted well to the governing of Italy. The Empire, however, which Rome had stumbled into by accident, provoked a profound crisis in Roman society, government, and morals."

Ultimately a constitutional crisis resulted and a civil war occurred. The war was fought between two great generals, **Julius Caesar** and Pompey. In 48 BC, Caesar defeated Pompey at Pharsalus in Greece. Shortly thereafter, Pompey was assassinated by the Egyptians among whom he had sought refuge. Caesar then turned his forces toward Asia Minor in a conquest so swift that Caesar described it in three Latin words: "Veni, vidi, vici"("I came, I saw, I conquered"). Caesar returned to Rome in 46 BC and had the senate appoint him dictator for ten years. He was given imperium over the Roman Empire and was, basically, above the law and the constitution. Two years later he was appointed dictator for life, and he quickly assumed all the important offices in the government. He reformed the government in many ways, but these reforms were functionally meaningless considering his absolute power. Caesar's absolute power, imperium for life (which made him the imperator, or emperor, of Rome), looked suspiciously like a monarchy, which, for all practical purposes, it was. The Romans, proud of their Republican tradition, deeply resented his power, and in 44 BC, on the Ides (15th) of March, a group of conspirators, led by Gaius Cassius Longinus and Marcus Junius Brutus, assassinated Caesar as he entered the senate in his usual manner, with no bodyguards. This ended the Roman Republican Period.

Assignment

The historian Edward Gibbon also wrote, "The various modes of worship, which prevailed in the Roman World, were all considered by the people as equally true; by the philosopher as equally false; and by the magistrate as equally useful. And thus toleration produced not only mutual indulgence, but even religious accord." Do you agree/disagree with his assessment?

LESSON 3

THE ROMAN EMPIRE

The Republic disappeared when Augustus became Rome's first emperor in 27 BC. This worked fairly well until AD 69, when civil war erupted, after which Vespasian ruled as emperor. When Commodus became emperor in AD 180, it marked the beginning of a sharp decline in the fortunes of the empire that was to continue with hardly a break for 100 years until Constantine became emperor.

The Roman Empire was at its apex. Syria, Egypt, Greece, Gaul (France), Britain, and other countries fell under Roman control. The Roman legions could not be stopped. Augustus, the most famous ruler of this Roman "Golden Age," and many of the emperors who followed him empowered the senate. However, that empowerment was mostly for show, since the emperors, with their strong personal armies, actually ran the Roman Empire.

Nonetheless, Augustus was an able administrator and an inspired leader. To men such as Virgil, the author of *The Aeneid*, Augustus was the "George Washington" of Rome.

Augustus was also aware of the limits of political power. He knew he had to capture the hearts and minds of his subjects. He rewarded Romans who embraced traditional values and punished those who did not. The moral excesses of the late Republic and the early Empire were curtailed. As the result of Augustus' long, skillful reign, he left a legacy of peace and prosperity to the Roman people. Roman patriotism was once more in vogue. Augustus also enlarged the territory of the Empire and improved the defense of the existing frontiers. Like Julius Caesar, he was an inspired administrator whose administration of the provinces was without equal. Historians today view Augustus' reign as the highest point of Roman influence.

The last Roman emperor whose reign we shall examine is **Constantine the Great** (AD 274–337; emperor AD 306–337). Constantine was the first Roman ruler to be converted to Christianity and the last Roman emperor of great import. He founded Constantinople (present-day Istanbul), which remained the capital of the Eastern Roman (Byzantine) Empire (which split from the Western Roman Empire 100 years after Constantine) until AD 1453.

Constantine unified a weakened empire and set the stage for the final victory of Christianity as a world view at the end of the fourth century. By the time of the gathering of the Council at Nicaea, where the Nicene Creed was formulated in AD 325, Christianity was officially the main religion of Rome.

Theodosius I (AD 379–395) was the last ruler of the united Roman Empire. At his death, Theodosius left the eastern portion of the empire to his son Arcadius, and the western portion to his son Honorius. No emperor ever again successfully controlled both east and west.

The Eastern Roman Empire, whose capital was Constantinople, remained strong, while the Western Roman Empire declined steadily due to weak emperors and invading barbarian tribes. The first to go were the outlying frontier territories: Spain, Gaul, and Britain.

Statue of Roman Emperor Augustus

The Eastern Empire continued to prosper. Its emperors were able to defend the Dardanelles, a strategic strait between the Black Sea and the Mediterranean, and, by their strength, to persuade barbarian peoples to invade the Western Empire. In AD 410, the Goths sacked Rome. It was the first time Rome had suffered such an invasion since the Celts had sacked the city in 390 BC, eight centuries earlier.

The Roman Empire was, in the end, overrun by millions of barbarians from Northern and Eastern Europe. Roman armies were designed to defeat other armies, not entire people groups surging toward them. The collapse was completed when Rome itself was conquered by the Visigoth Odoacer and his men in AD 476. The Eastern Roman Empire would last for 1,000 more years, but the Western Empire was finished.

Assignment

Edward Gibbon, in his masterpiece *Decline and Fall of the Roman Empire*, writes, "Public virtue which among the ancients was denominated patriotism, is derived from a strong sense of our own interest in the preservation and prosperity of the free government of which we are members. Such a sentiment, which had rendered the legions of the republic almost invincible, could make but a very feeble impression on the mercenary servants of a despotic prince; and it became necessary to supply that defect by other motives, of a different, but not less forcible nature; honor and religion." When pagan religion was replaced by Christianity in AD 400–500, Rome was doomed. Agree or disagree with Gibbon's conclusions.

Constantine the Great and the vision of a cross in the sky. The book *History of the Church*, c1880.

THE ROMAN MILITARY

The Roman military valued order. Each main section of the army was called a legend. A group of eight soldiers, called a contubernium, shared a tent and ate together. Eight contubernia comprised a century. Centuries—led appropriately by centurions—were grouped into cohorts; and 10 cohorts made a legion composed of 5,000 soldiers.

Copying some of the strategies of the Greek hoplites, Roman soldiers were an unbeatable force. They regularly beat enemies ten or more times their size. The core of the Roman legion consisted of heavily armored infantry. These soldiers fought in closed ranks. They worked as a team. At every level the men of a legion fought together toward ultimate victory. In contrast, most of the armies Rome faced were comprised of courageous but undisciplined warriors whose personal valor might match that of any individual Roman, but who had no chance against a trained army. This combination of superior organization, esprit de corps, and disciplined armored infantry gave the Romans a tremendous advantage in battle.

Roman soldiers practicing military skills

It took some time for this military machine to become effective. In the year 390 BC, Celtic and Gaulish warriors came pouring down the Italian peninsula and crushed a Roman army sent to stop them. Rome was conquered by these barbarians for the last time in 1,000 years.

After this humiliating defeat, the Romans instituted a series of military reforms, and during the subsequent 100 years made their army into a machine of great discipline, efficiency, and strength. The next barbarians to take on the Romans in battle would be slaughtered. In 225 BC, another force of Celts from all over Gaul numbering 50,000 infantry and 20,000 horses and chariots moved down the Italian peninsula. Eighty miles from Rome, two Roman legions comprising 8,000 troops managed to bar the 70,000 barbarians' further advance. The Celts retreated but the Romans attacked anyway. At the end of the battle, some 10,000 Celts had been captured and perhaps as many as 40,000 killed. This story was repeated over and over again all over the known world.

The unbeatable Roman army and navy assured Roman hegemony for a century.

Assignment

Why was the Roman army and navy virtually unbeatable for a thousand years?

ROMAN LIFE

First Thoughts . . .

The Roman Empire was more than ostentatious emperors and gladiator games. It was full of people who had hopes and dreams similar to those that any people would have. The average Roman family consisted of father, mother, children, married sons and their families, and slaves. Women were married at about age 14 and died before they were 30. Men rarely lived to see their 40th birthday. There was no dating or courtship—the father of the family made all important decisions. In the midst of those trying times there were always the gods and the games. Romans loved their religion and their gladiator contests.

Chapter Learning Objectives . . .

In chapter 12, we will look closely at a Roman family and compare it with other ancient families. Next, we will look at Roman religion and speculate upon ways that Christians could evangelize this polytheistic community. Along the way, we will look closely at Roman slavery and the allure of the Coliseum.

As a result of this chapter you should be able to:

1. Compare and contrast Sumerian, Egyptian, Athenian, and Roman families.
2. Pretend that you are an early Christian in Rome and speculate as to ways by which you might encourage these polytheists to become Christians.
3. Analyze why Rome experienced comparatively few slave rebellions.
4. Discuss why Roman Christians objected to slavery.
5. Evaluate why the gladiator games were an accurate metaphor for Roman culture.
6. Compare and contrast the Roman Empire with our "American Empire" of the 21st century.

ROMAN FAMILY LIFE

From the beginning of Roman history, the family was the center of all personal and social relations, and it influenced public and political activities as well. Romans valued stable family life and passed laws to reward families led by two parents. At the same time, religion—which until the middle of the first millennium AD was a form of polytheism—was the other important element that shaped early Roman life. Religion and stable families remained closely connected as the twin pillars of Roman society, especially for the five centuries of the Roman Republic. Later in Roman history, some Romans looked back to these early institutions for the salvation of the Roman Empire.

However, Roman women had very hard lives. The father was the absolute ruler of his family. The state gave him this power. He had the power of life or death over everyone. When a baby was born, it would be laid at its father's feet. If the father picked up the baby, it would live, but if he ignored the baby, it would be taken away to die.

Both boys and girls were educated during their early years (beginning at age seven), a novel practice in ancient cultures. Later, boys were trained in dialectic skills and debate. Formal education ended around age 14. Girls were often married by age 14 or 15. Sons of the wealthy were sent to study in Greece and had formal tutors.

Roman noble families lived in opulent villas with wide-open spaces and private spas. The poor lived in row tenement houses that were perennial fire hazards.

A tunic was the most important part of Roman clothing. Until AD 300, a tunic with long sleeves was perceived as a symbol of effeminacy. A tunic that reached to the ankles was also unsuitable for men. Also, Roman tunics varied in detail determined by the office that was held by their owners. Tunics were worn only at home. When a Roman man went out, he wore a toga.

Ancient Romans ate three meals during the day: breakfast, a second breakfast, and dinner, which was eaten late in the afternoon. The most important and generous meal was dinner. Wealthy Romans ate dinner while lying on a sofa. Dinner consisted of different sorts of meat, fish with vegetables, snacks, fresh or dried fruit, and wine (www.ancient-rome.biz/daily-life.html).

Rich Romans spent their spare time at feasts—an activity that was treated almost as a sport. Public lectures and literary sets were quite popular. Sports and circus games in the Coliseum also provided great amusement for thousands of Romans. A lot of time was spent in the public baths and spas called terms, which were in fact the cultural center of a city.

Assignment

Compare and contrast Sumerian, Egyptian, Athenian, and Roman families.

	Sumerian Families	Egyptian Families	Athenian Families	Roman Families
Gender Roles				
Education				
Religion				
Occupation				

ROMAN RELIGION

Religion was a vital part of Roman life. Roman religion was the basis of explanations for natural phenomena. The Romans, who believed that the gods controlled their lives, spent a great deal of time worshipping them.

The Romans were polytheists. The head god was Jupiter. He ruled with his wife, Juno, the goddess of the sky. Other gods were

Mars, the god of war;
Mercury, the messenger of the gods;
Neptune, the god of the sea;
Janus, the god of the doorway;
Diana, the goddess of hunting;
Vesta, the goddess of the hearth;
Minerva, the goddess of healing and wisdom;
Venus, the goddess of love.

Antique sculpture of Mercury

After the reign of the Emperor Augustus (27 BC–AD 14), the emperor was also considered to be a god and was worshipped on occasion. Each god had a special day that was usually a public holiday. This holiday gave people the opportunity to remember and revere the special god of the day. They often went to a temple dedicated to this god or goddess, where priests sacrificed animals and offered them to the god.

Each family home also had a small altar and shrine. The Romans had personal household gods, who were often more important to Roman families than the public deities.

Assignment

Pretend that you are an early Christian in Rome. You are preparing an evangelism campaign. What are some methods you might use to encourage these polytheists to become Christians?

Statue of the sea god Neptune

ROMAN SLAVERY

Slavery was an important part of Roman life, and was practiced all over the Roman Empire. As the Romans consolidated their position on the Italian peninsula and began the systematic conquest of the Mediterranean region, millions of slaves were incorporated into Roman life and the Roman economy. In fact, there were far more slaves than Roman citizens.

Most slaves were war captives. They were sold soon after they were taken in order to avoid the trouble of feeding and guarding them in a hostile country. Slave families were rarely broken up. Roman masters understood the value of having contented slaves!

A tax was imposed on imported slaves, who were offered for sale with their feet whitened with chalk. Slaves from the East had their ears pierced. A slave was offered for sale with a scroll around his neck describing his character, on which was written the slave's name and nationality and a statement saying that he was free from disease. If the slave had defects not shown in his guarantee, the dealer had to take him back in six months.

The price of slaves varied greatly. Captives sold on a battlefield did not cost much because generals were eager for a quick sale. Like any business, supply and demand determined price.

There were also public slaves, who cared for public buildings and served magistrates and priests, but were owned by the Roman state. Of the slaves kept for profit, the oldest and most important class was that of the farm hands.

A slave might buy his freedom, or he might be freed as a reward for faithful service or some special act of devotion.

There was a noticeable change in the course of slavery as the empire aged. The spread of the Christian church played a role, as many leading Christians were opposed to the institution. Though many in the church, including its priests, owned slaves, the church was at times vocal against

Remains of the Via Appia in Rome, near Quarto Miglio by Kleuske, 2005 (CC BY-SA 3.0).

the institution (www.richeast.org/htwm/greeks/romans/slavery/slavery2.html).

Perhaps the most famous slave was Spartacus, who was actually a free Greek. He may have served as an auxiliary in the Roman army in Macedonia. He deserted the army, was outlawed, captured, and sold into slavery.

In 73 BC, Spartacus led a rebellion during which he defeated two forces of Roman legionary cohorts. For two years Spartacus successfully led a rebellion all over Italy. It is believed that Spartacus died in a final battle that produced so many corpses that his body was never found. The historian Appian reported that 6,000 slaves were crucified along the **Appian Way**.

Assignment

A. While slave rebellions occurred, there really were not very many of them. Why?

B. Why did a number of Roman Christians object to slavery?

THE COLISEUM AND GLADIATORS

The Coliseum, also called the Flavian Amphitheatre, is one of Rome's most enduring monuments to the culture of the ancient Romans. Emperor Vespasian started the Coliseum around AD 72. His son Titus reigned over its completion and the official opening ceremonies about eight years later in AD 80. The Coliseum was the empire's primary stage for gladiatorial combat for nearly four centuries. In a show of Rome's wealth and extravagance, during the opening ceremonies, 100 days of the games were held.

The Coliseum in Rome

The huge theater was originally built encompassing four floors. The first three had arched entrances, while the fourth floor utilized rectangular doorways.

The Coliseum had a total spectator capacity of 45,000–55,000. There were at least 76 numbered entrances and 4 additional entrances reserved for the emperor, other VIPs, and the gladiators (http://www.unrv.com/culture/colosseum.php). The Coliseum was designed for easy crowd dispersal; the entire audience could exit the building in five minutes. Modern stadium builders could learn something from the Romans!

One could purchase "box seats," so to speak, in the Coliseum. Women and the poor sat on the top level. The higher a man's social status, the closer he was to the action.

A sturdy wooden floor covered a basement where the gladiators and animals were kept waiting to perform. Occasionally an emperor held an extravagant affair for which the Coliseum was partially flooded, enabling people to reenact famous Roman naval victories.

What gladiators did was live well and die well. A Roman man at the age of 20 knew he would probably die before he was 30, and he wanted to meet death with honor and dignity. He could observe gladiators do it in the arena, while at the same time living in a highly militaristic culture. Moreover, Roman military tactics invited individual initiative, so the idea of a lone warrior fighting to the death was a powerful motif in Roman life.

The truth is, gladiatorial games proved immediately and immensely popular within the Roman Empire. The per capita income spent on NFL games today pales in comparison to the amount of money that Romans spent on gladiator games! Eventually, the emperors had to regulate how much could be spent on gladiatorial performances to prevent members of the elite from bankrupting themselves. The sheer cost of producing games was stunning. Contests involving animals from distant provinces demonstrated in a material way how far Rome's dominance reached. In a way, then, the gladiator games were a metaphor for what was most "Roman" about the Roman Empire (abacus.bates.edu/~mimber/Rciv/gladiator.htm).

Assignment

Why were the gladiator games an accurate metaphor for Roman culture?

Interior of the Coliseum in Rome, Italy

Chapter 13

ROMAN THOUGHT AND DECLINE

First Thoughts . . .

The British historian Edwin Gibbon begins his epic *The Decline and Fall of the Roman Empire* this way: "In the second century of the Christian era, the Empire of Rome comprehended the fairest part of the earth, and the most civilized portion of mankind. The frontiers of that extensive monarchy were guarded by ancient renown and disciplined valor. The gentle but powerful influence of laws and manners had gradually cemented the union of the provinces. Their peaceful inhabitants enjoyed and abused the advantages of wealth and luxury. The image of a free constitution was preserved with decent reverence: the Roman senate appeared to possess the sovereign authority, and devolved on the emperors all the executive powers of government. During a happy period (AD 98–180) of more than fourscore years, the public administration was conducted by the virtue and abilities of Nerva, Trajan, Hadrian, and the two Antonines." Gibbons argues that the decline and fall of 1,000-year-old Rome occurred within the two generations: "a revolution which will ever be remembered, and is still felt by the nations of the earth." Why?

Chapter Learning Objectives . . .

In chapter 13, we will take a close look at Virgil, the great Roman patriot and orator. Next, we will look at several philosophies that competed for the minds and hearts of Romans. Finally, we will examine the fall of the great Roman Empire.

As a result of this chapter you should be able to:

1. Identify an American author who has extolled America as Virgil in his writings extolled the Roman Empire.

2. Discuss the ultimate outcome of a life focused on pleasure.

3. Evaluate Stoicism.

4. Explain why Neo-Platonism was such a threat to Christianity.

5. Identify the factors that caused the fall of the Roman Empire.

6. Reflect on the state of the "American Empire."

VIRGIL

Publius Vergilius Maro (Virgil) was born on the 15th of October, 70 BC, near Mantua, Italy. He is primarily known as the author of *The Aeneid*, the epic poem that links the birth of Rome to the Trojan War, and thus to the Homeric Cycle. *The Aeneid* is considered the best of classical Latin literature. Its heroic and tragic characters such as Aeneas and the queen of Carthage, Dido, are unforgettable.

Virgil does not show up in any contemporary accounts, and he apparently was reticent to participate in public Roman society. However, he was known as a good man, and although he gained vast public recognition during his lifetime, he is described as being embarrassed by his celebrity. Unlike other poets such as Ovid, who wrote about intimate details of his personal life, Virgil never talked about himself. Virgil died on September 21, 19 BC, and his ashes were entombed near Naples in Posilipo. His tomb, which once was treated like a shrine, has disappeared. Symbolically, Virgil reappears as Dante's escort through the Inferno in *The Divine Comedy*.

The great Latin poet Virgil, holding a volume on which is written *The Aeneid*. On either side stand the two muses: "Clio" (history) and "Melpomene" (tragedy). The mosaic, which dates from the third century AD, was discovered in the Hadrumetum in Sousse, Tunisia, and is now on display in the Bardo Museum in Tunis, Tunisia (CC BY 2.5).

Aeneas Flees Burning Troy by Federico Barocci, Galleria Borghese, Rome, 1598 (PD-US).

Assignment

Virgil's *Aeneid* follows the Trojan warrior Aeneas as he carries his family from his destroyed home, stops in Carthage for a doomed love affair, visits the underworld, and fights difficult battles in Italy. Finally, Aeneas founds Rome. Virgil was the national poet, the champion of Roman expansion. In the 21st century, does America have a "Virgil," an author who encourages patriotism? Who? Why do you choose this person?

EPICUREANISM AND STOICISM

Epicureanism (300 BC)

While the cynic Pyrrhic's writings focused on the value of virtue, Epicurus was advocating an alternative doctrine. Epicurus was the "Jerry Springer" of his age. The aim of human life, he claimed, was to achieve maximum pleasure with the least effort and risk. Sound familiar? This philosophy became the bedrock of postmodernism. Epicurus celebrated the individual's free will and desires. The subjective and personal were paramount. If it felt good, and hurt no one else, it was morally acceptable, even preferred, over any other alternative. Morality was tied to personal fulfillment rather than any external law, deity, or force. This philosophical position invited mankind to a place of selfishness that still is very much with us.

A passage from Epicureanism's *Principal Doctrines*:

If the things that produce the pleasures of profligate men really freed them from fears of the mind concerning celestial and atmospheric phenomena, the fear of death, and the fear of pain; if, further, they taught them to limit their desires, we should never have any fault to find with such persons, for they would then be filled with pleasures from every source and would never have pain of body or mind, which is what is bad. A blessed and indestructible being has no trouble himself and brings no trouble upon any other being; so he is free from anger and partiality, for all such things imply weakness.

Ancient marble head of the greek philosopher Epicurus on display in the British Museum in London.

Death is nothing to us; for that which has been dissolved into its elements experiences no sensations, and that which has no sensation is nothing to us. The magnitude of pleasure reaches its limit in the removal of all pain. When such pleasure is present, so long as it is uninterrupted, there is no pain either of body or of mind or of both together.

Stoicism (300 BC)

Ably represented by Roman emperor Marcus Aurelius, Stoicism became the most influential school of the Roman world. The Stoics taught that one can achieve happiness only by rejecting material comforts and by dedicating oneself to a life of reason and virtue. Human reason was also considered part of the divine character, and therefore immortal. Each person was part of God, and all people form a universal family. Stoicism celebrated the disciplined and controlled human spirit. It became the measuring rod against which all social and religious institutions were measured.

A passage from *Meditations*, by Marcus Aurelius:

Begin the morning by saying to thyself, I shall meet with the busybody, the ungrateful, arrogant, deceitful, envious, unsocial. All these things happen to them by reason of their ignorance of what is good and evil. But I who have seen the nature of the good that it is beautiful and of the bad that it is ugly, and the nature of him who does wrong, that it is akin to me, not [only] of the same blood

Bust of the Roman emperor Marcus Aurelius

The aim of human life, according to Epicurus, was to achieve maximum pleasure with the least effort and risk.

or seed, but that it participates in [the same] intelligence and [the same] portion of the divinity, I can neither be injured by any of them, for no one can fix on me what is ugly, nor can I be angry with my kinsman, nor hate him. For we are made for cooperation, like feet, like hands, like eyelids, like the rows of the upper and lower teeth. To act against one another then is contrary to nature; and it is acting against one another to be vexed and to turn away. Though thou shouldest be going to live three thousand years, and as many times ten thousand years, still remember that no man loses any other life than this which he now lives, nor lives any other than this which he now loses. The longest and shortest are thus brought to the same. For the present is the same to all, though that which perishes is not the same: and so that which is lost appears to be a mere moment. For a man cannot lose either the past or the future: for what a man has not, how can anyone take this from him? These two things then thou must bear in mind: the one, that all things from eternity are of like forms and come round in a circle, and that it makes no difference whether a man shall see the same things during a hundred years or two hundred, or an infinite time; and the second, that the longest liver and he who will die soonest lose just the same. For the present is the only thing of which a man can be deprived, if it is true that this is the only thing which he has, and that a man cannot lose a thing if he has it not.

Assignment

A. What is the ultimate outcome of a life that is focused on pleasure?

B. The Stoics had much truth: Life should be lived simply and completely. However, what is the thing that gives life ultimate and eternal meaning?

NEO-PLATONISM

Neo-Platonism (AD 50)

Neo-Platonism was both a revival of Platonic metaphysics and an effective competitor of Christianity. Central to Neo-Platonism was phenomenology, or the study or description of subjects. Thus, an experience of ecstasy, in which one became one with God, was the source of all reality. For the first time, philosophy dared to cross the threshold from philosophy to experiential religion. Earlier Greek philosophers had crossed the line between metaphysics and ethics, but none had dared to speak of a religious experience as a philosophical phenomenon until the Neo-Platonism defined this religious experience. With unabashed boldness Neo-Platonism argued that science and rationalism were the highest forms of religious experience. This was the "Star Wars" religion of the third century AD. The universe, which emanated from the Force, or Logos, was layered according to stages of purity. The highest goal of life was to rid oneself of dependence on any physical comfort. This bold but strange philosophy/religion invited its followers to experience a rationalistic theophany that came only to those who discarded humanity and embraced divinity. Neo-Platonism evolved into Gnosticism, one of the most powerful heresies of the early church.

Plotinus bust located at the Ostiense Museum, Ostia Antica, Rome, Italy (PD-US).

A passage from *The Six Anneads* by Plotinus:

Pleasure and distress, fear and courage, desire and aversion, where have these affections and experiences their seat? Clearly, either in the Soul alone, or in the Soul as employing the body, or in some third entity deriving from both. And for this third entity, again, there are two possible modes: it might be either a blend or a distinct form due to the blending. And what applies to the affections applies also to whatsoever acts, physical or mental, spring from them. We have, therefore, to examine discursive-reason and the ordinary mental action upon objects of sense, and enquire whether these have the one seat with the affections and experiences, or perhaps sometimes the one seat, sometimes another. And we must consider also our acts of Intellection, their mode and their seat. And this very examining principle, which investigates and decides in these matters, must be brought to light.

Assignment

Neo-Platonism, with its emphasis on the supernatural, was a real threat to early Christianity. What contemporary religions and philosophies compete with Christianity?

THE FALL OF ROME

The decline of the Roman Empire refers to both the gradual disintegration of the economy of Rome and the barbarian invasions that were its final doom. The English historian Edward Gibbon (right, PD-Art), author of *The Decline and Fall of the Roman Empire* (1776), sets AD 476 as the date the Roman Empire fell.

A slow decline occurred over a period of approximately 320 years, culminating on September 4, AD 476, when Romulus Augustus, the last emperor of the Western Roman Empire, was deposed by Germanic chieftain Odoacer. Some say the split into Eastern and Western Empires governed by separate emperors caused Rome to fall. The eastern half became the Byzantine Empire, with its capital in Constantinople (now Istanbul). The western half remained centered in Italy.

Why did Rome fall? Religious abandonment, decadence, economic problems, and military problems caused the fall of Rome. According to Gibbon, the Roman Empire succumbed to barbarian invasions primarily because of the gradual loss of civic virtue among its citizens. Romans had become weak, outsourcing their duties to defend their Empire to barbarian mercenaries, who then became so numerous and ingrained that they were able to take over the Empire. Roman men, he believed, had become effeminate, unwilling to live a tougher, "manly" military lifestyle. He further blamed the degeneracy of the Roman army and the Praetorian guards. In addition, Gibbon argued that Christianity created a belief that a better life existed after death, which fostered indifference toward the present among Roman citizens, thus sapping their desire to sacrifice for the Empire. He also believed its comparative pacifism tended to hamper the traditional Roman martial spirit.

Gibbon sees the primary catalyst of the Empire's initial decay and eventual collapse in the Praetorian Guard, instituted as a special class of soldiers permanently encamped in a commanding position within Rome, a seed planted by Augustus at the establishment of the Empire. He cites repeated examples of this special force abusing its power with calamitous results, including numerous instances of imperial assassination and demands of ever-increasing pay. Other historians, including this author, feel that the collapse was more internal. The collapse occurred because Rome had moved away from its laudable patriotic moorings and had embraced a narcissistic self-centeredness that doomed the Empire.

Walls of Constantinople. Photo by Bigdaddy, 2006 (CC BY-SA 3.0).

Assignment

What caused the fall of the Roman Empire?

Chapter 14

EARLY CHURCH HISTORY

First Thoughts . . .

Christianity began as a small Jewish sect in the eastern Mediterranean region. It quickly grew in size and influence over a few decades, and by the fourth century AD had become the dominant religion within the Roman Empire. Today it is the most populous religion in the world. Why? How could a group of ordinary people such as fishermen and tax collectors, in one generation, turn the world upside down?

Chapter Learning Objectives . . .

In chapter 14, we will examine the explosive growth and expansion of Christianity, as in three generations the Early Church had spread the gospel of Jesus Christ across the known cultural and political world. Next we will look at the everyday lives of early Christians—particularly their inability to build churches. We will look at several persecutions and the resulting martyrdom. Finally, we will apply this new knowledge to the contemporary Church.

As a result of this chapter you should be able to:

1. Discuss God's judgment.
2. Explore the difference between the public and the private lives of Christians.
3. Evaluate the impact of church buildings on Christianity.
4. Gauge the impact of Constantine on church history.
5. Discuss why Christians are such available targets for political leadership of a hosting country.
6. Evaluate the importance of Christians making decisions that may lead to persecution.

THE BIRTH OF THE CHURCH

In the first five years after the death and resurrection of the Lord Jesus Christ, the Church He founded became the major religion of the greatest empire the world has ever known. This cultural revolution—for Christianity was always more than just a "religion"—began with a man who was both wholly human and wholly God. During His three-year earthly ministry, He wrote nothing, created no organization, and owned no property.

The original group of "followers of Jesus Bar Joseph" was a minor sect of Judaism that continued to observe strict Judaic customs, including dietary laws. This was to change quickly.

Nero (below), the cruel, unstable Roman emperor at that time, instituted a major persecution of Christians. Many Jews were mistaken for Christians and were also persecuted. The result was that most Jewish people sought desperately to separate themselves from Christians. In a way, then, the Christian church withdrew from Judaism because of persecution by the Romans.

Another important source of the alienation of Christianity from its Jewish roots was the change in the membership of the Church that took place by the end of the second century when Christians with Gentile backgrounds began to outnumber Jewish Christians. The Early Church decided against requiring that new converts become "Jewish" before they would be accepted as Christians. Clearly, the work of the apostle Paul was influential in this regard (Acts 15).

Paul, a former Pharisee who had studied Plato and the **Talmud**, was the one who formulated, in his many letters to several early Christian congregations, much of the theology of the Early Church.

Within 30 years after Christ's death, His followers were called "Christians," and within four short centuries, without

Christ under cross by Ludovico Pogliaghi, Milan, 1906.

any army, navy, or air force, Christians had "conquered" the known world with the gospel. In the same way, while Rome was conquered by the barbarians, the Christians "conquered"—captured the hearts and the souls of—the barbarians. Today, Christianity is the most populous religion in the world.

One should not suppose that Judaism was the only source from which Christian converts were drawn. During the Early Church's infancy, there were at least five primary religious beliefs competing for the souls of people. First, of

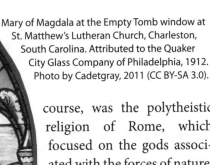

Mary of Magdala at the Empty Tomb window at St. Matthew's Lutheran Church, Charleston, South Carolina. Attributed to the Quaker City Glass Company of Philadelphia, 1912. Photo by Cadetgray, 2011 (CC BY-SA 3.0).

course, was the polytheistic religion of Rome, which focused on the gods associated with the forces of nature. This was mostly a religion of superstition rather than ethical teachings. By the time of Pentecost, the emphasis on these gods had already begun to decline.

A greater threat was the mystery religions, which invited converts not only to be in relationship with deities, but also to use this relationship to gain power. These religions taught that the entire world was inhabited by good spirits and evil spirits, both of which could be persuaded by rituals and formulas to perform certain acts of power.

Perhaps most popular among these mystery religions was Mithraism, whose ancient Persian god, Mithras, was supposedly born from a rock. His worshippers had a complex system of seven grades of initiation, with ritual meals. They met in underground temples, which survive even today.

Other world views/religions also competed for people's hearts and minds. The more educated in the Roman Empire were being influenced by the major philosophical teachings of that era. For instance, according to the teaching of Plato, the physical world was merely an imperfect copy of a spiritual world that consisted of divine thoughts and ideas called "forms." Through knowledge, a person would strive to be more and more like the forms or spiritual types of his physical surroundings. Salvation, then, was nothing more than bringing down to earth the spirit of god.

By far the greatest threat to Christianity was **Gnosticism**, which was popular among the followers of Plato. Salvation, according to the Gnostics, came through the knowledge of the spirit world and denial of the material. As it is today, Gnosticism was practiced among intellectual centers (e.g., universities) of the empire. Gnosticism incorporated elements of Judaism and Christianity, which confused many early converts. Gnosticism invited believers to embrace a spirituality that was both appealing and sustaining. It was "spiritual" but not confessional.

Beginning in Jerusalem, the Christian faith competed against these cultural and religious worldviews, and won. Battle after battle ensued until a sort of orthodoxy emerged with the creation of the Roman Catholic Church.

All natures, all formed things, all creatures exist in and with one another and will again be resolved into their own roots, because the nature of matter is dissolved into the roots of its nature alone.
—The Gospel of Mary Magdalene
(a Gnostic writing)

Mithraic altarpiece found near Fiano Romano, near Rome, and now in the Louvre. Photo by PHGCOM, 2006 (CC BY-SA 3.0).

Assignment

A. Gnosticism, a particularly dangerous and effective first-century heresy, argued for a fundamental dualism between good and evil and salvation through "gnosis" or knowledge. What are contemporary manifestations of that heresy?

B. One early Christian Gnostic, Marcion (AD 165), argued that Jesus was not really a man, but was instead a god in human "garb." What is the danger of advancing such a view?

THE NEXT CENTURY

Jerusalem was the center of Christianity until its destruction by Roman armies in AD 70, but from this center Christianity spread to other cities and towns in Palestine and beyond.

One place in particular was **Antioch**. Perhaps the most successful Christian church, Antioch sent out more missionaries than any other early church. Interracial, full of rich and poor, Antioch was a palatable alternative to the social, racial, and ethnic segregation that had become part of the early Roman Empire. To fellowship one with another, Christians literally climbed over walls that were built by the Romans to keep groups segregated. **Deacons** acted on behalf of neglected ethnic minority widows (Acts 6:1–6). Philip carried the gospel across ethnic/racial lines (Acts 8:4–17). Peter met with a Gentile (the first-century equivalent of a minority!), Cornelius, and defended his actions to the Church (Acts 10:1–11:30). Paul and Barnabas brought together Gentiles and Jews at Antioch in Pisidia (Acts 13:46–52). And, Paul actively pursued the Gentile Timothy and drew him into ministry (Acts 16:1–5). Particularism was recognized—not ignored, not hidden—but it was not an obstacle to fellowship.

Christian teaching was particularly radical. Paul wrote that there was neither Jew nor Greek in Christ Jesus (Gal. 3:28). Paul emphasized that three major first-century social distinctions no longer mattered in Christ: ethnicity, socio-economic status, and gender. Paul stressed, "You are one in Christ Jesus." The 1st- century Church, as I mentioned earlier, struggled with many problems. For instance, Hellenist (Greek) widows, traditionally neglected by the Jews, were now being neglected by Hebrew Christians (Acts 6:1).

Paul not only wrote extensively to the churches about the faith, but he made four missionary journeys. He did perhaps more than any other man to advance the cause of the gospel.

As a Jewish sect, the primitive Christian church had shared the status of Judaism in the Roman Empire, and

The Siege and Destruction of Jerusalem by the Romans Under the Command of Titus, A.D. 70 by David roberts, 1850 (PD-US).

enjoyed the fruits of Roman toleration. However, Emperor Nero, in AD 68, singled out Christians as enemies. The grounds for hostility toward the Christians were not always the same, and often opposition and persecution were localized. The loyalty of Christians to "Jesus as Lord," however, was irreconcilable with the worship of the Roman emperor as lord, and emperors such as Trajan, Claudius, and Marcus Aurelius, who ruled during periods of social stress and conflict, saw the Christians as a great threat. Finally, by the fourth century, Christianity had grown so much that Emperor Diocletian decided it had to be eradicated. He tried, but failed, to accomplish that goal.

What was the Early Church fellowship? First, it met in homes, and although this imposed size limits on its fellowship, it also permitted the Church to enjoy the intimacy and care giving that this arrangement afforded. The Church, for instance, shared a meal every time it met—a practice that eventually evolved into an *agape*, or Eucharist meal. There is much debate about what sort of leadership emerged. I believe that the position of pastor initially emerged from the deacons, who historically were called to serve, not to govern. The Presbyters, or elders, governed. There was no board of trustees. The pastor was identified by, and selected for, his gifts, which were manifestly evident in every pastor.

Sometimes a husband-and-wife team shared the pastoral leadership. (This should not offend the reader—even today some couples informally function as leadership teams with the man designated as the official pastor.) Later an Episcopal form of government arose that was very similar to the present Roman Catholic witness.

An early and strong movement was Monasticism. Renunciation of the world, or **Monasticism**, had in fact nourished the growth of Christianity from the start, and by AD 300, persons who wished to embark on an ascetic life had many exemplars from which to choose. As young people had in the past pursued wisdom by going to the philosopher, so now Christian youth sought out Christian ascetics under whom they might learn the new Christian philosophy. In Egypt, the church leader Origen taught new converts about Christianity and encouraged them with his ascetic lifestyle, including sleeping on the floor, fasting, and abstaining completely from all alcohol.

Roman Triumphal arch panel copy from Beth Hatefutsoth, showing spoils of Jerusalem temple. Photo by Steerpike (CC BY-SA 3.0).

Assignment

A. The Early Church welcomed everyone, male and female, Gentile and Jew. As a result, it was perceived as a radical body. How has the church today lost some of its radicalness?

B. In AD 39–40, Philo of Alexandria (15 BC–AD 50) led a Jewish contingent to ask Emperor Caligula (AD 37–41) to end the persecution of Jews in Egypt. Caligula refused to listen to Philo, who later told his fellow ambassadors that God would punish Caligula. Not long after that, Caligula was assassinated. Does God punish people in this way?

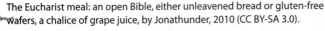
The Eucharist meal: an open Bible, either unleavened bread or gluten-free wafers, a chalice of grape juice, by Jonathunder, 2010 (CC BY-SA 3.0).

CHRISTIANITY AND ROME

From the beginning, Roman authorities perceived Christians as a threat. This was primarily because Christians (like Jews) refused to worship any god but the true God. However, the Christians, unlike those of other religions, also refused to serve in the army. And although they did not openly subvert the civil authorities, Christians did not enthusiastically embrace public office either. These things, among others, conspired to unleash a series of persecutions against Christians that continued off and on until Emperor Constantine gave the Christian faith "most favored status" in the Roman Empire.

Most readers will have heard of the early Christians' secret meetings in the **catacombs** (tombs), which were hollowed out underneath Rome. Roman authorities were naturally reluctant to search for or to persecute Christians who were hiding in the creepy catacombs. Thus, the very thing that represented death to others represented life to the Christians.

As stated previously, this persecution of Christians ended with the reign of **Constantine**. One of the most influential acts of Constantine the Great was his decision in AD 330 to move the capital of the empire from Rome to the city of Byzantium at the eastern end of the Mediterranean Sea. The new capital, named Constantinople, also became the home base of a new Christian church. While western Christianity became increasingly centralized around the Pope (Bishop of Rome), eastern city fellowships—Constantinople, Jerusalem, Antioch, and Alexandria—developed separate from one another; so although worship practices evolved along similar lines, church government and minor doctrines evolved much differently.

In conclusion, things are not all that different today. In the 21st century, Christians must be clever and resourceful: "His intent was that now, through the church, the manifold wisdom of God should be made known to the rulers and authorities in the heavenly realms, according to his eternal purpose which he accomplished in Christ Jesus our Lord"

Byzantine architecture of the Hagia Sophia (the Church of the Holy Wisdom or Ayasofya in Turkish), a famous historic landmark in Istanbul (Constantinople), Turkey.

(Eph. 3:10–11). However, it is not good enough just to be smart; we must also be fighters, because we are in a culture war that can be won only by those who know how to fight well.

To be successful in any campaign, one must know the enemy. The enemy of the people of God is not flesh and blood; it is the spirit of this age—powers and principalities.

It is widespread immorality and incipient mediocrity that threatens the very underpinnings of modern civilization.

This enemy can be overcome by preparedness, not by manipulation; by good, not by evil. The weapons are the whole armor of God—truth, righteousness, peace, faith, salvation, and God's Word (Eph. 6). We who are Christians must understand that in Christ we are more than conquerors (Rom. 8:37), and we need to act like it!

We know absolutely that someday every knee shall bow before Jesus Christ, and every tongue shall confess that He is Lord (Phil. 2:10–11). This is no small comfort to Christian warriors.

Catacombs of Saint Paul in Malta.

Vital, confessional Christians still have much work to do in today's culture. Many Christian apologists warn us that at some point people will become fed up with the excesses and dysfunctional aspects of our culture, and that as modern mainline culture fails to sustain people in their hedonistic pursuit of self-interest, they will want something more. This culture of hopelessness and superfluity is evident in the billboards that line highways, in the songs that play on radios, in the movies that entertain in theaters. Culture is exemplified in university courses and on best-seller lists. It is now questionable whether modern cultural order is capable of nourishing the freedom, responsibility, and civility that people require to sustain vital lives. Modernity (a word to describe modern culture) creates problems far deeper than drugs. It creates a crisis of cultural authority in which beliefs, ideals, and traditions are losing their compelling force in society. There is a numbness spreading across the land that presents great opportunity for Christians.

This author prays that we who follow Christ will make the most of our opportunities to influence our world for Him. Christians should be encouraged that in the near future many people will be looking to sources of stability and strength for direction. By default, those Christians whose lives are lived well and who have a purpose for living, beyond the next paycheck, will have an irresistible appeal.

While living in a hostile culture, Christians must prepare to live and to thrive in the city of God. Christians must with vitality

and readiness live in the world without succumbing to the world's system (John 15:19).

To this hopeless, secular world, history is mundane; it is merely utilitarian. To the Christian, history is sacred, fraught with opportunity. To secular society, history is not didactic; it helps people feel better. To the Christian, history is full of important lessons, and it challenges people to be all they can be in Christ. To secular people, time and space are finite entities full of fearful pitfalls. To the Christian, no matter how bad things are, because God is alive and well, time is holy and the land is holy. Secular people act out of no purpose or design. In contrast, Christians know that God is in absolute control of history. In a way that is not mawkish or condescending, Christians must be tirelessly hopeful. We can do that by speaking the truth of God's Word in places of deception.

Assignment

A. In AD 231, in defiance of Roman law, a private house in the city of Dura-Europas on the Euphrates River was opened for Christian worship. No legal Christian church building was built and occupied for another 100 years. What effect did the inability to build/own church buildings have on the Early Church?

B. Constantine required everyone—Christian and pagan alike—to cease all work on Sunday in order to honor the Lord. Was Constantine correct in doing this?

Head of Constantine's colossal statue at the Capitoline Museums. Photo by Jean-Christophe Benist, 2007 (CC BY-SA 3.0).

MARTYRS

A Christian martyr is one who is killed for following Christ, through stoning, crucifixion, burning at the stake, or other forms of capital punishment. The word *martyr* comes from a Greek word meaning "witness." Martyrs, as described in Scripture, are those who overcome Satan by the shed blood of Jesus Christ, and willingly give their lives rather than renounce their Christian faith (Rev. 12:11).

At first, the term "martyrdom" applied to apostles, and connoted the high office to which only the most esteemed believers were called. Once Christians started to undergo persecution, the term came to be applied to those who suffered hardships for their faith. Finally, the early Christian period before Constantine I became the "classic" age of martyrdom. A martyr's death was considered a "baptism in blood," cleansing one of sin as baptism in water did. Early Christians venerated martyrs as powerful intercessors, and their final words were treasured as inspired by the Holy Spirit.

An early morning fire prompted Emperor Nero's persecution of Christians on July 19, AD 64. It broke out in a small shop by the Circus Maximus and spread rapidly to other regions of Rome, raging for nine days and destroying much of the city. This was the worst in a series of fires that beset the crowded city, home to more than a million people, packed tightly into apartment blocks of wooden construction, among narrow streets and alleyways. Only two areas escaped the fire, one of which housed a large Jewish population.

Nero was at his seaside villa in Anzio when the blaze began, but he delayed returning to the city. Rumors began that he himself had set the fire in order to rebuild the city according to his own plans.

To stop the rumors, Nero decided to blame someone else, and he chose a group of renegade Jews called Christians, who had caused trouble before, and already had a bad reputation in the city.

Instead of executing the Christians immediately at the usual place, Nero executed them publicly in his gardens nearby and in the circus. "Mockery of every sort accompanied their deaths. Covered with the skins of beasts, they were torn by dogs and perished, or were nailed to crosses, or were doomed to the flames and burnt, to serve as a nightly illumination, when daylight had expired."

Most thought Nero went too far. "There arose in the people a sense of pity. For it was felt that they (the Christians) were being sacrificed for one man's brutality rather than to the public interest" (Tacitus).

Assignment

A. Emperor Decius (249–251) required that everyone possess a certificate proving he had sacrificed to the gods. Some Christians either made sacrifices or purchased certificates of sacrifice from commissioners, which caused many believers to criticize them for "selling out" to the Romans. Some other believers argued that it was no big deal; that sacrificing to gods or buying a certificate under false pretenses really didn't matter. Still other believers argued that it was no one else's business what they did. What do you think?

B. In February AD 303, when augurs could no longer find the usual signs on the livers of sacrificed animals, Emperor Diocletian consulted the oracle of Apollo at Miletus, who said that the gods blamed the Christians. At this provocation, Emperor Diocletian started a genocide campaign that nearly wiped out Christians. Why are Christians such available targets for political leadership of a host country?

C. During the Diocletian persecution, a young Christian woman—Pelagia of Tarsus—refused to marry an unbeliever—one of Emperor Diocletian's sons—even though she was fond of him and he was in love with her. Despondent because he couldn't marry Pelagia, Diocletian's son committed suicide. Diocletian then had Pelagia burned at the stake. Was Pelagia right in making her decision? Would marrying Diocletian's son really have been such a big deal? What would you have done?

Chapter 15

CHRISTIANITY SPREADS

First Thoughts . . .

Old Testament Levitical priests had a duty to tend the fire in the tent of meeting, to keep it roaring and bright. The sacred fire was to be safe but huge. The fire on the altar, the eternal flame on which sacrifices were offered to God, was not to go out. Other duties could slide; other tasks could be deferred; but the fire on the altar was never to go out. At all costs and inconvenience, they were to preserve this sacred fire where God's people came to offer their gifts and rededicate themselves to Him.

Throughout the centuries, believers have served well as fire tenders. Brother Lawrence, Martin Luther, and others fanned the flames and kept the fire burning. "The secret things belong to the LORD our God, but the things revealed belong to us and to our children forever, that we may follow all the words of this law" (Deut. 29:29). This is a gathered inheritance kept alive by men and women of faith. We will look at that gathered inheritance together and thank God for the generations of faithful Christians who came before us.

Chapter Learning Objectives . . .

In chapter 15, we will examine more closely pagan attacks on Christianity and the Christians' responses. Next, we will examine the beginning of the monastic movement. Josephus, a Jewish contemporary of Jesus' disciples, recorded an extrabiblical account of the early Christian church. Using Josephus' writings, and other sources, we will look at the Early Church and discuss how the new faith emerged from Judaism.

As a result of this chapter you should be able to:

1. Analyze Celsus' criticism of Christianity and Origen's refutation.

2. Analyze how Christians can remain relevant in the contemporary world without compromising the integrity of their faith.

3. Appraise the importance of Benedict to church history.

4. Evaluate the importance of Josephus' writings.

5. Observe the impact of unforgiveness on world history.

6. Delineate how Christianity emerged from Judaism and maintained its integrity as a movement.

A GATHERED INHERITANCE

Origen (AD 185?–254?)

Origen may well have been the most accomplished biblical scholar of the Early Church. By age 18 he was a respected Old Testament scholar, and by the end of his life he was the leading Christian apologist. He specialized in answering the charges of the highly educated pagan (mostly Greek) community. He targeted the unapproachable Celsus, an influential second-century Platonist of Alexandria and perhaps the first serious critic of Christianity.

A passage from *Contra Celsus* by Origen:

> After this, through the influence of some motive which is unknown to me, Celsus asserts that it is by the names of certain demons, and by the use of incantations, that the Christians appear to be possessed of (miraculous) power; hinting, I suppose, at the practices of those who expel evil spirits by incantations. And here he manifestly appears to malign the gospel. For it is not by incantations that Christians seem to prevail (over evil spirits), but by the name of Jesus, accompanied by the announcement of the narratives which relate to Him; for the repetition of these has frequently been the means of driving demons out of men, especially when those who repeated them did so in a sound and genuinely believing spirit. Such power, indeed, does the name of Jesus possess over evil spirits, that there have been instances where it was effectual, when it was pronounced even by bad men, which Jesus Himself taught (www.newadvent.org/).

Origen, church father. From Greek Wikipedia (PD-US).

Benedict of Nursia (AD 480?–547)

Benedict, the father of Western monasticism, was born into a wealthy Italian family, but was repelled by the excessive lifestyles manifested in his city-state. As a result, he withdrew to Monte Cassino where he built his famous monastery. Benedict established an austere rule of life adopted by most Western monasteries. Monks were not permitted to own property. Benedict also devoted much of his time to the needs of the poor.

Saint Benedict. Detail from a fresco by Fra Angelico, c1437 (PD-US).

Assignment

A. What was Celsus' criticism of Christianity and what was Origen's refutation?

B. Origen was a man fervently committed to the cause of Christ. Yet, as often happens, many of his followers misunderstood Origen and corrupted his message. How can we be faithful to the gospel, yet try to ensure that our followers will not corrupt what we say?

C. What does Benedict mean when he says "The heart becomes broadened"?

A passage from *The Rule of Benedict*:

We are about to found therefore a school for the Lord's service; in the organization of which we trust that we shall ordain nothing severe and nothing burdensome. But even if, the demands of justice dictating it, something a little irksome shall be the result, for the purpose of amending vices or preserving charity; thou shalt not therefore, struck by fear, flee the way of salvation, which cannot be entered upon except through a narrow entrance. But as one's way of life and one's faith progresses, the heart becomes broadened, and, with the unutterable sweetness of love, the way of the mandates of the Lord is traversed. Thus, never departing from His guidance, continuing in the monastery in his teaching until death, through patience we are made partakers in Christ's passion, in order that we may merit to be companions in His kingdom.

Exterior of old mosque in Alexandria

A BOOK REVIEW

E. R. Dodds, in his book *Pagan and Christian in an Age of Anxiety*, discusses a fourth-century way of dealing with hostile environment. Christianity triumphed over paganism because Christianity rejected all gods but accepted all people. Christians promised eternal life in heaven yet they showed love to all persons. Christianity exhibited compassion, conviction, clarity, and community. The Christian belief that they were duty-bound to love their neighbors as themselves, whether part of the household of faith or not, resulted in a disproportionate amount of Christian provision and caring for the sick and the helpless in times of famine, plague, and crisis, of which there were many. Pagan clergy ran for the hills in times of emergency: "Every man for himself!" The greater proportion of Christian sick nursed back to health as well as the number of grateful, rescued non-Christians converting swelled the ranks of Christianity. Dodd places great stress on the tight community structure of the religion, the impression made upon outsiders by the courage of the martyrs, the large-hearted generosity of believers in times of crises, and the monotheistic "intolerance" that made Christian faith an all-or-nothing commitment, not a mere membership in a moose lodge like Mithraism, the Isis cult, etc., all of which were mutually tolerant, interpenetrating, redundant, and thus commanding little loyalty. By implication Dodd warns 21st-century Christians that they must look again to what worked so well in the third century (Book Review).

Assignment

In these early years of the 21st century, the emerging post-Christian world is challenging Christians in unprecedented ways. Yet, there is value in looking again at the Early Church. What can contemporary Christians learn from the Early Church that can help us survive and thrive in our unbelieving, often hostile world?

JOSEPHUS

Josephus (right), also known as Yosef Ben Matityahu (Joseph, son of Matthias), who became known, in his capacity as a Roman citizen, as Titus Flavius Josephus, was a first-century Jewish historian who survived and described in writing the destruction of Jerusalem in AD 70. Josephus spent his life in and around Rome as an advisor and historian to three emperors. For centuries, the works of Josephus were more widely read in Europe than any books other than the Bible. They are invaluable sources of eyewitness testimony to the development of Western civilization, including the foundation and growth of Christianity in the first century.

This is the way Josephus described Jesus: "Now there was about this time Jesus, a wise man, if it be lawful to call him a man; for he was a doer of wonderful works, a teacher of such men as receive the truth with pleasure. He drew over to him both many of the Jews and many of the Gentiles. He was [the] Christ. And when Pilate, at the suggestion of the principal men amongst us, had condemned him to the cross, those that loved him at the first did not forsake him; for he appeared to them alive again the third day; as the divine prophets had foretold these and ten thousand other wonderful things concerning him. And the tribe of Christians, so named from him, are not extinct at this day." Josephus also discussed James, the brother of Jesus: "Festus was now dead, and Albinus was but upon the road; so he assembled the Sanhedrim of judges, and brought before them the brother of Jesus, who was called Christ, whose name was James, and

some others, [or, some of his companions]; and when he had formed an accusation against them as breakers of the law, he delivered them to be stoned: but as for those who seemed the most equitable of the citizens, and such as were the most uneasy at the breach of the laws, they disliked what was done." Next to the Bible, this extrabiblical source had a great impact on Western understanding of church history.

Image of Josephus from *The Complete Works of Flavius Josephus* published by Attic Books (original printed c1850).

Assignment

Josephus wrote, "Now there was about this time Jesus, a wise man, if it be lawful to call him a man; for he was a doer of wonderful works, a teacher of such men as receive the truth with pleasure. He drew over to him both many of the Jews and many of the Gentiles. He was [the] Christ. And when Pilate, at the suggestion of the principal men amongst us, had condemned him to the cross, those that loved him at the first did not forsake him; for he appeared to them alive again the third day; as the divine prophets had foretold these and ten thousand other wonderful things concerning him. And the tribe of Christians, so named from him, are not extinct at this day." Why is Josephus' extrabiblical description so important to the authentication of the origins of Christianity?

AUGUSTINE

"One must believe in order to understand and understand in order to believe," Augustine wrote. It was never clear to Augustine where philosophy ended and theology began. For that reason alone Augustine was one of the most important theologians in world history. This man of God did perhaps more than any other person to claim philosophy as a discipline for God. Augustine argued that Christian faith and philosophical understanding were complementary. Augustine spoke for a generation of believers at the end of the Roman Empire. Through Augustine, Plato's division of the world into the reality of True Being as well as the separation of the soul from the body were given Christian interpretations. Augustine's "beatific vision of God" (*Confessions*, Book IV, Ch. 16) was very similar to Plato's "gazing upon the forms."

A passage from *City of God* by Augustine:

> Though there are very many and great nations all over the earth, whose rites and customs, speech, arms, and dress, are distinguished by marked differences, yet there are no more than two kinds of human society, which we may justly call two cities, according to the language of our Scriptures. The one consists of those who wish to live after the flesh, the other of those who wish to live after the spirit. . . . Thus the things necessary for this mortal life are used by both kinds of men and families alike, but each has its own and widely different aim in using them. The earthly city, which does not live by faith, seeks an earthly peace, and the end it proposes, in the well-ordered concord of civil obedience and rule, is the combination of men's wills to attain the things which are helpful to this life. The heavenly city, or rather the part of it which sojourns on earth and lives by faith, makes use of this peace only because it must, until this mortal condition which necessitates it shall pass away.

Augustine by Sandro Botticelli, c1480 (PD-US).

Assignment

When Augustine was a bishop in the Roman Catholic Church, Christians were facing terrible persecution by the Romans. Many—actually most—of the priests and other leaders of whom Augustine had charge denounced their faith. When the persecution ended, many former leaders repented and were reinstated in the Church. However, the Donatists rejected this decision and founded their own church. Donatists were North African believers who, despite losing loved ones to torture and death, had not given in to persecution and no longer wanted to be associated with a church whose leaders had caved in when faced with persecution. Were the Donatists right or wrong in their decision? Why?

Chapter 16

JAPANESE HISTORY

First Thoughts . . .

The word "Japan" does not appear in history until AD 57 when it is first mentioned in Chinese histories. The Chinese historians tell us of a land divided into 100 or so separate tribal communities without writing or political cohesion. The Japanese are latecomers in Asian history. These warrior people ultimately dominated all of Asia. Where did the Japanese come from? Why did they settle on the islands? What was life like for them?

Chapter Learning Objectives . . .

Most of us have seen movies or read books about the samurai. We will discuss this enigmatic warrior class in the context of early Japanese history. Next, we will look at Japanese religion and literature. In short, we will explore 3,000 years of Japanese history and ruminate on what is distinctly "Japanese" and how and why it arose.

As a result of this chapter you should be able to:

1. Identify historical trends that emerged from the beginning of Japanese history.
2. Understand the role that the Samurai assumed in Japanese society.
3. Discuss several Christian objections to Buddhism.
4. Define Shintoism and discuss why it thrived in Japan.
5. Analyze why Japanese women produced more art than their Western counterparts.
6. Explain why Japanese ballads celebrated only regal subjects.

EARLY JAPANESE HISTORY

Japan is a study in contrasts. On the one hand, it became Asia's first industrialized nation. On the other hand, it is still a very conservative nation.

Japan may be the most cosmopolitan nation in Asia, if not the world. It is so dependent on world markets that it imports virtually all of its iron ore, bauxite, oil, copper, and nickel. Japan relies on foreign supplies for over 90 percent of its coal, natural gas, and lead. Over 85 percent of its total energy is imported from abroad. It is perhaps the greatest importer of agricultural goods. Japan is second only to the United States in terms of the total value of its industrial exports. It is the world's greatest exporter of automobiles, and has the greatest number of merchant ships in the world.

Yet the Japanese people are more intimately tied to their ancient ancestral roots than they are to events happening in the rest of the world. Third- and fourth-generation Japanese, when asked where they are "from," still name the "old home" of their ancestors. Their lives are tied more closely to the ancient rural agricultural rhythms than to the modern industrial cities where they reside (Louis G. Perez, The History of Japan. Westport, CT. Greenwood Press. 1998 (www.questia.com).

How did Japan become a land of so many contrasts?

"Japan" first appeared in AD 57 in Chinese histories, where it was referred to as "Wa." The Chinese historians described Wa as a land divided into numerous tribal communities that shared no written language or political connection. The Japanese did not start writing their histories until around AD 600.

Early middle Jōmon pottery, Tokyo National Museum, 5000-4000 BC. Photo by Chris 73, 2005 (CC BY-SA 3.0).

Where did the Japanese come from? The first settlers of Japan were from the Korean peninsula in the third century BC. The second great push in Japanese history was contact with China from AD 200 forward. From the Chinese, who demanded that Japan be a tribute state to China, the Japanese adopted forms of government, religion, and literature genres.

What permeates every aspect of Japanese culture is its geography. Japan is a series of islands—more than 3,000 islands, of which 600 are inhabited. The four main islands, Honshu, Kyushu, Shikoku, and Hokkaido, dominate Japanese history. The largest island is Honshu, but the overall geographical area of the inhabited islands is less than that of California. All the islands are mountainous and subject to a variety of natural disasters, especially earthquakes and tsunamis. The mountainous terrain leaves its mark on Japanese culture; since the mountains provide natural and difficult barriers, political life in Japan organized as regional rather than national governments (http://www.wsu.edu).

Jōmon is the oldest and the first recorded culture in Japanese history. Jomon culture is also known as "Tree Culture" because trees were an important element in building construction. The invention of pottery was the most significant turning point in the development of Jōmon culture. With increasing food surpluses, small villages gradually became big villages, and there is evidence of trading among villages as well as the holding of ceremonies.

The Jōmon lived in small, relatively self-sufficient village communities. Eventually, clusters of villages united in small territorial or tribal units under local chieftains. By the second and third centuries, small-fortified villages appeared.

Assignment

What historical trends emerge from the beginning of Japanese history?

THE EMPEROR

The Yamato State

The earliest Japanese state was ruled by **Yamato kings**. The Yamato state, in AD 500, was really a loose hegemony. Yamato is the richest agricultural region in Japan. The Yamato kings located their capital at Naniwa (modern-day Osaka) and enjoyed a hegemony over the surrounding aristocracies that made them powerful and wealthy.

During this period, Japan had a presence on the Korean peninsula itself. Korea was in its most dynamic cultural and political period. Korean rulers understood the strategic importance of Japan and so entered into alliance with the Yamato state and worked hard to form an alliance that affected Japanese culture for centuries.

Yamato emperors expanded their rule over all of the main islands of Japan except Hokkaido. This ultimately brought great upheaval in Japanese society. Likewise, a widespread smallpox epidemic in 735–737 indelibly changed early Japan. Perhaps one-third of the population perished during those two years.

Despite such signs of imperial power, the political role of the emperor shrank in importance during the ninth century. Often the emperor was a child or a youth without the personal character, skills, and experience needed to play a strong political role. Emperors thus became figureheads whose main function was to preside over official ceremonies and religious rituals. Political power in the imperial court shifted into the hands of influential aristocratic families, most of which descended from the clan chieftains who had been allied with the Yamato rulers in the sixth and seventh centuries.

Armored samurai with sword and dagger by Felice Beato, c1860 (PD-US).

Samurai of the Chosyu clan, during the Boshin War period by Felice Beato, c1860 (PD-US).

The aristocrats supplanted royal authority. Aristocrats held the highest offices, inherited their positions, and paid no taxes. Aristocratic families dominated the political and cultural activities of the imperial court until the 12th century.

The Confucian and Buddhist civilian control of the country seriously undermined aristocratic civilian control.

The Samurai

As the effective influence of the imperial court gradually waned during the 9th century through the 12th century, power moved away from the emperor to local warriors ("bushi" or "samurai"). The warriors were typically landholders, many, minor landholders—yeoman farmers, really. They were not necessarily rich noblemen. They lived in small, fortified compounds, and they offered the surrounding peasant communities succor and protection. Often warriors served as local district officials, judges, even priests, but they remained quintessential warriors. Much of their time was devoted to the cultivation of warfare. As a result, they were extremely effective administrators and warriors. With their land holdings, military skills, and administrative skills, the warriors were a powerful presence in Japanese society.

In time, samurai families joined together for protection into larger groups based on kinship ties. The emperor, with no standing army, relied on samurai families to maintain local law and order.

By the middle of the 13th century, samurai had become so valuable to the emperor that he appointed a "head samurai" called a "shogun." A shogun was a military governor, so to speak, who answered directly to the emperor. He was responsible for maintaining peace in the provinces. He arbitrated differences between rival samurai and other divergent groups.

In 1232 the shogun promulgated the Joei Code, which clarified the duties of samurai and other officials. The code also restrained unruly samurai by requiring them to respect the rights of the religious temples and shrines.

Samurai on horseback. Artist unknown, c1878 (PD-Japan_oldphoto).

Assignment

Who were the samurai and what role did they assume in Japanese society?

Illustrated Story of Night Attack on Yoshitsune's Residence at Horikawa, 16th Century (PD-US).

JAPANESE RELIGIONS

Buddhism arrived in Japan from China. This highly existential religion was especially popular among middle-class merchants. Buddhism, which was essentially atheism, allowed its participants to separate their moral behavior from their religious activity. This was definitely a convenient religion for aggressive entrepreneurs.

Siddhartha Gautama, known as Buddha, the "Awakened," was the son of the ruler of a kingdom in northern India. Determined to renounce the world, at the age of 29, he abandoned his wife and son and society in general and practiced severe asceticism. After seven years, he concluded that this had brought him no nearer to the wisdom he sought. He claimed that, in the midst of his travail, as he sat under the sacred fig-tree at Bodhi Gay, he suddenly saw the Great Truths, and was "born again" as Buddha.

He resolved to bestow on others the Four Great Truths and the eightfold path. Beginning his ministry at Benares, he first converted five monks who had previously been his fellows in asceticism, then many of the noble youth of the city, then 1,000 Brahman Hindu priests. The rest of his life was spent in wandering about and preaching his new creed, which spread with extraordinary rapidity.

Shinto is the indigenous "spirituality" of the Japanese people. It is not really a religion; it is more a set of practices to establish a connection between present day Japan and its ancient past. It is a form of ancestor worship.

Shinto practices were first recorded and codified in the written historical records of the Kojiki and Nihon Shoki in the seventh and eighth centuries. Shinto today is a term that applies to public shrines suited to various purposes such as war memorials, harvest festivals, romance, and historical monuments, as well as various sectarian organizations. Practitioners express their diverse beliefs through a standard language and practice, adopting a similar style in dress and ritual, dating from around the time of the Nara and Heian Periods (Wikipedia Free Encyclopedia).

The word Shinto ("way of the gods") was adopted from the written Chinese combining two kanji: "shin," meaning kami; and "tō," or "do," meaning a philosophical path or study (originally from the Chinese word *tao*). Kami are defined in English as "spirits," "essences," or "deities" that are associated with many understood formats; in some cases being humanlike, some animistic, others associated with more abstract "natural" forces in the world (mountains, rivers, lightning, wind, waves, trees, rocks). It may be best thought of as "sacred" elements and energies. Kami and people are not separate; they exist within the same world and share its interrelated complexity.

Writings by Buddha:

Then overjoyed with joy was I,
Delighted with a keen delight;
And thus with pleasure saturate
I sat me down with legs across.
And while cross-legged there I sat,
I thus reflected to myself:
"Behold! in trance am I adept,
And all the Powers High are mine.
Nowhere throughout a thousand worlds
Are any seers to equal me;
Unequalled in the magic gifts
Have I this height of bliss attained.

The Great Buddha statue, Kōtoku Temple, Kamakura, Japan

Assignment

A. What are several Christian objections to Buddhism?

B. What is Shintoism and why did it thrive in Japan?

JAPANESE LITERATURE

Five hundred years before Europeans were writing novels, Japanese writers created the genre. European novelists of course were unaware of most of these works. Early novels include the 11th-century *The Tale of Genji* by Murasaki Shikibu and the 14th-century *Romance of the Three Kingdoms* by Luo Guanzhong.

The Tale of Genji was written chapter by chapter in installments, as Murasaki delivered the tale to women of the aristocracy (the yokibito). It has many elements found in a modern novel: a central character, a very large number of major and minor characters, and a well-developed plot. All characters age in step and all the family and feudal relationships are consistent among all chapters. Japanese literature is one of the oldest and richest national literatures. It may seem strange to Western literary tastes, but that in no way denigrates the literature. Japanese is new, refreshing, and offers Western readers many important insights into this Far Eastern culture. Indigenous Japanese literature, such as the haiku verse, has had a substantial impact on literature in many parts of the world.

The *Pillow Book* is a book of observations and musings recorded by **Sei Shōnagon** during her time as court lady to **Empress Consort Teishi** during the 990s and early 1000s in Heian Japan. The book was completed in the year 1002.

The literature of the Japanese people mirrors the political history of the nation. Like the history of Japan, the literature has been affected by alternating periods of isolation from the outside world and engagement with it. In fact, Japanese called their historical periods by the names of the places, that were the seats of government.

Japanese literature in particular is indebted to Chinese influences. Chinese literature was introduced to Japan sometime during the 3rd century AD. Nevertheless, during

Murasaki Shikibu shown writing at her desk at Ishiyama-dera inspired by the Moon by Suzuki Harunobu, c1767 (PD-US).

the ancient period at least, literature evolved with a particularly unique flavor.

A consistent theme in Japanese literature over the centuries has been the tension within a truly severe caste system. Japanese literature is also quite sensitive to the place of nature in life. In that sense, Japanese literature would fall into the Romantic worldview category. Finally, Japanese literature manifests an uncharacteristically large number of female writers compared with other cultures.

Scholars customarily divide the general history of Japan into periods based on changes in governmental institutions, such as the Heian period (794–1185), the Muromachi period (1333–1603), and the Tokugawa period (1603–1868). The literary history of Japan can be broken down according to these same periods. The major dividing line between the traditional and modern periods of the country is the Meiji Restoration of 1868, which also signaled a new era of modernization and contact with the West.

Very early in its existence, Japanese literature exhibited several nuances. The development of the **waka** in Japanese literature was as radical an event as the development of the sonnet or iambic pentameter rhyme in Western literature.

Originally waka were composed to celebrate victories in battle or for religious reasons. This tradition of poetry for public occasions carried through to the first great age of written waka in the seventh and eighth centuries, with highly wrought *nagauta* (long poems), consisting of alternating "lines" of five and seven syllables, being composed for performance on public occasions at the imperial court. At the same time, *tanka* (short poems) consisting of five "lines" in the pattern of 5-7-5-7-7 syllables, became a useful shorthand for private communication between friends and lovers, and the ability to compose a *tanka* on a given topic became an essential skill for any gentleman or lady at court. While a young man today would send flowers as a token of affection for a young lady, in 11th-century Japan, a young man would send a tanka. Over time, the *tanka* became a preferred manifestation of the Japanese poetry genre.

Finally, the initial 5-7-5 of a *tanka* became a poetic form on its own, the haiku, and great poets were discovered among the samurai warriors as well as the townsfolk of early modern Japan.

Looking Three Times at the Thatched Hut, hanging scroll, ink on silk. Located at the Palace Museum. This painting is from the *Romance of the Three Kingdoms* where Liu Bei entreats Zhuge Liang to join him, visiting his thatched hut three times, by Dai Jin during the early Ming Dynasty (PD-Art).

Assignment

Japanese women produced more art than their Western counterparts. Why?

Minamoto no Yoritomo, the first shogun (1192–1199) of the Kamakura shogunate by Fujiwara No Takanobu, 1179 (PD-US).

Chapter 17

INDIAN (SOUTH ASIAN) HISTORY

First Thoughts . . .

Mark Twain quipped, "India is the cradle of human race, the birthplace of human speech, the mother of history, the grandmother of legend, and the great-grandmother of tradition. Our most valuable and most astrictive materials in the history of man are treasured up in India only!" The Indus River Valley civilization began in India around 2500 BC. From this auspicious beginning, Indian people groups spread over, and conquered, the South Asian subcontinent.

Chapter Learning Objectives . . .

We will examine India's history from the Indus River Valley civilization to the present. We will examine Indian religions and, in the process, look at history-maker Thomas, the apostle who founded Christianity on the South Asian subcontinent.

As a result of this chapter you should be able to:

1. Discuss historical trends that emerged in Indian history.

2. Identify at what point India gained a national identity.

3. Contrast the British invasion of India with other invasions.

4. Describe the challenges Thomas encountered in taking the gospel to India.

5. Discuss why a Christian would want to study Hinduism.

6. Analyze how Indian culture was connected to Hinduism.

HISTORY OF INDIA

Scholar Will Durant explained, "India was the mother of our race and Sanskrit the mother of Europe's languages. She was the mother of our philosophy, mother through the Arabs of much of our mathematics, mother through Buddha of the ideals embodied in Christianity, mother through village communities of self-government and democracy. Mother India is in many ways the mother of us all."

India is a success story. India's population recently exceeded 1 billion people. Yet a noted Indian historian said, "Although it is difficult to accept, the Indians totally lacked the historical sense." The ancient Indians made great inroads into astronomy, physics, mathematics, and all kinds of literature and arts, but never seriously documented their history. In Hindi culture, history was not important.

India's history began in the northwest around 3000 BC, with the Indus Valley, or Harappan, civilization, when an agricultural economy gave rise to extensive urbanization and trade. The second stage occurred around 1000 BC when the Ganga-Yamuna river basin and several southern river deltas experienced extensive agricultural expansion and population growth.

By AD 700, India began to connect with surrounding countries. India's connection with Europe began with visits from Portuguese explorers, traders, and missionaries, beginning in 1498. The Europeans, primarily the English, arrived in force during the early 17th century, and by the 18th century had made a profound impact on India. India was forced, for the first time, into a subordinate role within a world system based on industrial production rather than agriculture. Today, India is the most populous democracy in the world.

Throughout India's history, religion has been the carrier and preserver of culture. Closely allied with religious belief, and deeply rooted in history of India, caste remains an important feature of Indian society. Caste is a system of classifying and separating people from birth within thousands

Hindu children of high caste, Bombay, India by the Keystone View Company, c1922 (PD-US).

of different groups labeled by occupation, ritual status, social etiquette, and language (www. indianchild.com/history_of_india2.htm).

Indus River Valley

The earliest known civilization in India, the starting point in its history, dates back to about 3000 BC. Discovered in the 1920s, it was thought to have been confined to the valley of the River Indus, hence the name Indus River Valley civilization. This civilization was a highly developed urban one, and two of its towns, Mohenjodaro and Harappa, represent the high-water mark of the settlements. Thus, this civilization is now better known as the Harappan civilization. Mohenjodaro and Harappa are now in Pakistan, and the principal sites in India include Ropar in Punjab, Lothal in Gujarat, and Kalibangan.

A city-settlement of the the Indus Valley Civilization, c2600–1500 BC. Photo by Comrogues, 2010 (CC BY 2.0).

This ancient civilization was well developed for its time. It had an organized government. Craftsmen worked with several metals. Farmers domesticated animals, including camels, goats, water buffaloes, fowls, and chickens.

The cities of the Indus Valley were well planned and even had manholes! The Indus people had public buildings that included the Great Bath at Mohenjodaro. Indus cities were paved and laid at right angles. Streets faced north, south, east, or west. Indus houses had protection against noise, odors, and thieves. Houses faced streets and were at least two stories high. Life was centered in an enclosed courtyard, and there was a balcony over the courtyard. Each house had its own well, and one even had a large bathtub. Indus houses had a brick staircase to lead to upper levels and roof (www.eapen.com/jacob/report/indus.html).

Aryans and Vedic Age

A group called the Aryans entered India through Khyber Pass (connecting India and Persia) in 1500 BC. They established small farming communities across the state of Punjab. The Aryans introduced the domesticated horse and developed the Sanskrit language. Both were to play fundamental roles in the shaping of Indian culture.

Sanskrit, the forerunner of Hinduism, was the basis and the unifying factor of the majority of Indian languages. The Aryans composed the hymns of the four Vedas, the great philosophic poems that are at the heart of Hindu thought.

Religion ultimately formed the nation that emerged. Religion defined and encouraged the caste system. With society being divided on the basis of castes, conflicts and disorders were bound to arise. A need arose, therefore, for a strong external force to enforce these divisions and to arbitrate these conflicts. This gradually led to full-fledged state systems, including vast empires.

By 3000 BC, most of North India was knit together in the first great Indian empire by Chandragupta Maurya. His son Bindusara extended the Mauryan Empire over virtually the entire subcontinent. The greatest Mauryan emperor was Ashoka the Great (286–231 BC), whose successful campaigns culminated in the annexation of Kalinga (modern-day Orissa).

Assignment

What historical trends emerged in Indian history?

ALEXANDER THE GREAT

In 327 BC, Alexander the Great conquered northwest India. Alexander left behind Greek governors to rule over Indian territories won by him. But with time, these regions lost out to Indian states through conflict and slow absorption.

By AD 400, the **Gupta Empire** had lasted for more than two centuries. It covered a large part of the Indian subcontinent. The Gupta rulers patronized the Hindu religious tradition, so orthodox Hinduism reasserted itself in this era. Great strides were made in literature and the arts.

Invasions by the White Huns signaled the end of this era. After the decline of the Gupta Empire, northern India split up into a number of separate Hindu kingdoms and was not unified again until the arrival of the Muslims.

While kingdoms rose and fell in the north of India, the south remained generally stable. Buddhism gradually became popular in northern India, but Hinduism continued to flourish in the south. The prosperity in the southern parts of the country was based upon the long-established trade links of India with other civilizations. The Egyptians and Romans had trade relations with southern India through sea routes, and later, links were also established with Southeast Asia. Other outside influences in the south included the arrival of Jesus' disciple Thomas in Kerala (AD 52), who brought Christianity to India.

Islamic Invasions

An event of immense and lasting impact in Indian history was the invasion of the Muslims. Lured by tales of the fertile plains of the Punjab and the fabulous wealth of Hindu temples, Mahmud of Ghazni first attacked India in AD 1000. Other raiders from Central Asia followed him, but they

Akbar on an elephant by Miniatur der Moghulschule, c1609 (PD-Art).

were no more than small bands of scouts. It was only in 1192 that Mohammed of Ghori, who had been expanding his power all across the Punjab took Ajmer. The following year his general, Qutb-ud-din Aibak, took Varanasi and Delhi and, after Mohammed Ghori's death in 1206, became the first of the Sultans of Delhi.

The most important Islamic empire was that of the **Mughals**, a Central Asian dynasty founded by Babur early in the 16th century. Babur was succeeded by his son Humayun. During the reign of Humayun's son, Akbar the Great (1562–1605), Indo-Islamic culture reached its peak in the areas of tolerance, harmony, and a spirit of enquiry. Mughal culture reached its zenith during the reign of Akbar's grandson Shahjehan, a great builder and patron of the arts. Shahjehan moved his capital to Delhi and built the incomparable Taj Mahal at Agra.

A major competitor of the Mughals and their Brahmin allies was Shivaji and his Marathas.

When Nadir Shah of Persia attacked Delhi in 1739, he defeated both the Mughals and the Marathas. Soon, though, everyone fell to the British.

The British established political supremacy over eastern India after the Battle of Plassey in 1757. They gradually extended their rule over the entire subcontinent, either by direct annexation or by exercising leadership over the entire nation.

Unlike all former rulers, the British did not settle in India to form a new local empire. The British sought to absorb the entire subcontinent into their commonwealth. India offered unlimited material wealth to their expanding empire.

A century of accumulated grievances erupted in the mutiny by Indian soldiers in the British army in 1857. This was the signal for a spontaneous uprising among the Mughals, which doomed Mughal rule and assured British hegemony.

There was not a serious attempt at Indian independence until Mahatma Gandhi led a nonviolent revolt after World War II. Gandhi, a British-trained lawyer of Indian origin from South Africa, adopted a radical traditional Indian style of living, which won him wide popularity and transformed him into the undisputed leader of India's independence movement.

India achieved independence on August 15, 1947.

Assignment

A. At what point did India have a national identity?

B. In what ways was the British invasion of India different from other invasions?

The Taj Mahal is located in Agra, India, and is the finest example of Mughal architecture.

THOMAS THE DISCIPLE

Thomas (also called Didymus—the Greek word for "twin"), one of the twelve disciples, is believed to have been the twin brother of Matthew. He was first called Jude, the son of James and a grandson of Alpheus. Some texts have stated that Thomas was the twin of James, not of Matthew, so it's obvious that little is actually known about Thomas.

Thomas is most often remembered for his doubting and for having been missing from the Upper Room when Jesus appeared to the disciples after His resurrection. When told by the other disciples that they had seen Jesus alive, Thomas had difficulty believing that Jesus had actually risen from the dead. Thomas said, "Unless I see the nail marks in his hands and put my finger where the nails were, and put my hand into his side, I will not believe it" (John 21:20). But after he saw the Lord for himself, he believed fervently.

Thomas preached in Persia, in Parthia, and also in India. Thomas was the one who helped build a palace in India, and is credited with the founding of Christianity in that country.

San Thome Basilica in Chennai is built over the site where St. Thomas is believed to be originally interred. Photo by PlaneMad, 2007 (CC BY-SA 2.5).

Hymns of St. Ephraem, edited by Lamy:

It was to a land of dark people he was sent, to clothe them by Baptism in white robes. His grateful dawn dispelled India's painful darkness. It was his mission to espouse India to the One-Begotten. The merchant is blessed for having so great a treasure. Edessa thus became the blessed city by possessing the greatest pearl India could yield. Thomas works miracles in India, and at Edessa Thomas is destined to baptize peoples perverse and steeped in darkness, and that in the land of India.

Assignment

What challenges did Thomas encounter when he brought the gospel to India?

The Incredulity of Saint Thomas by Caravaggio, (PD-US, PD-Art).

INDIAN RELIGIONS

Hinduism

Hinduism is a way of life based on the teachings of ancient scriptures like the Vedas and the Upanishads. The word *dharma* connotes "that which supports the universe" and effectively means any path of spiritual discipline that leads to God. In that sense, Hinduism is another form of Universalism. Hinduism can be compared to a fruit tree with (1) its roots representing the Vedas and the Upanishads, (2) the thick trunk symbolizing the spiritual experiences of numerous wise teachers, (3) its branches representing various theological traditions, and (4) the fruit itself, in different shapes and sizes, symbolizing various sects and subjects (www.hinduism.about.com/library/).

The **Vedas** are the most sacred books of India. They are the original scriptures of Hindu teachings. Vedic literature with its philosophical maxims has stood the test of time and is the highest religious authority for all sections of Hindus in particular and for mankind in general.

The main ancient sources of information with regard to these Hindu beliefs and practices are the Ramayana and the Mahabhrata. The former is a highly artificial production based on legend and ascribed to one man, Valmiki. The latter, a "huge conglomeration of stirring adventure, legend, myth, history, and superstition," is a composite production, begun probably as early as the fourth or fifth century before Christ, and completed by the end of the sixth century of our era. It represents many strata of religious belief.

Hindu Proverbs

"A man in this world without learning is as a beast of the field. "

"Anger has no eyes."

"Can the monkey know the taste of ginger?"

"Dig a well every day to drink water every day. "

"Eating while seated makes one of large size; eating while standing makes one strong."

"It is better to walk than to run; it is better to stand than to walk; it is better to sit than to stand; it is better to lie than to sit."

Assignment

Why would a Christian want to study Hinduism?

Lakshmi, Hindu goddess of wealth, prosperity, light, wisdom, fortune, and fertility.

Sadhu at the ghats in Varanasi, India.

Chapter 18

PERSIAN HISTORY

First Thoughts . . .

The Persian Empire was the largest known empire. It gave southwestern Asia and adjoining regions an unprecedented degree of organization. The Persians built roads and established the first important postal system in history to maintain communication between the emperor and his commonwealth. Known for their religious tolerance, the Persians respected the traditions of the people they conquered, as in allowing the Israelites to rebuild their holy city of Jerusalem. Through Judaism and, later, Christianity, Persia's Zoroastrian faith would have a powerful if indirect effect on the spiritual life of the West. All of this was to change with the advent of Islam, which was neither tolerant nor enlightened. The Persians, now called the Iranians, entered a sort of Dark Age.

Chapter Learning Objectives . . .

In chapter 18, we will examine Persian history from its advent in the mountain valleys of Euro-Asia and its expansion into the West. We will see how Islam transformed the culture and ethos of the Persian/Iranian people. Finally, we will look at an important religion, Manichaeism, which became the prototype of later Western polytheistic faiths (e.g., Transcendentalism).

As a result of this chapter you should be able to:

1. Explain what historical trends emerge in Persian history.
2. Discuss why the Islamic invasion threatened Persian society and culture.
3. Tell what two European powers had designs on Iran/Persia and why.
4. Speculate upon why Manichaean religion is so popular today.
5. Explore legends about the wise men from the East.
6. Describe what historical trends emerge in Persian history.

ANCIENT PERSIA

Background

The country has always been known to its own people as Iran (land of the Aryans), although for centuries it was referred to as Persia by the Europeans, mainly due to the writings of Greek historians. Most people today know Iran for its carpets, its caviar, its militant Islam, and its importance as one of the world's major oil producers. Yet, Persia/Iran has always been one of the oldest and richest cultures in the world.

For more than 3,000 years Persia was a battleground between Asia and Europe. Under **Cyrus the Great**, it became the greatest empire in the world. Successive interactions with Greeks, Arabs, Mongols, and Turks brought great diversity into Persian culture. The Aryan (Iranian) people came into Iran during the second millennium BC. This vigorous civilization was destroyed in one night by Alexander, who conquered Persia and began the Hellenistic period.

Iranians

Iran (Persia) emerged as a civilization in the Susian plain, under the influence of nearby Mesopotamia in the Tigris-Euphrates valley.

Around 3500 BC, Mesopotamian farmers—Sumerians (see chapter 1)—lived in Iran. The Sumerians, who lived in Babylon and constituted the most advanced and complex civilization in the world at that time, settled in Iran in 3200 BC.

In 3000 BC, the Akkadians drifted into the northern Sumerian territory, where they adopted some aspects of Sumerian culture. Around 2340 BC, Sargon, the ruler of the Akkad region, conquered all the inhabitants of the land from the Mediterranean Sea to the Caspian Sea in the north to the Persian Gulf in the south.

The Guti, primitive Iranians, among other tribes living in the mountainous areas, controlled many of the routes that crossed western Iran. They were able to capture Susa, its capital. The Guti occupied Persia for several centuries. At the height of its glory, the Guti succeeded in defeating Assyria and Babylon.

By 900 BC Assyria was busy restoring its control over Babylonia, and by 700 BC their empire included the entire Tigris-Euphrates region, and all the eastern shore of the Mediterranean. It was the most powerful empire the world had yet seen. The Assyrians were ruthless, violent people, and many see this period as the Dark Ages of Persian history (www.art-arena.com/iran1.html).

The Medes and the Persians

Around 2000 BC, invaders broke through to the Iranian plateau, either from the Caucasus or through Central Asia. The most famous of these tribes, the Persians (Parsa) and the Medes (Mada), settled in what became Persia.

Under the rule of Cyaxares (633–584 BC), the Medes put an end to centuries of war against the Assyrians. Their capture of Nineveh in 612 BC finally brought down the Assyrian Empire. For more than half a century, the Medes ruled a vast empire with borders stretching from Afghanistan to Turkey.

Cyrus the Great monument at Sydney Olympic Park Photo by Siamax, 2007 (CC BY-SA 3.0)

The Persian army emerged as a serious player under the leadership of Achimenes, whose descendant, Cyrus, brought the Achaemenian Empire onto the stage of world history. Cyrus was the descendant of a long line of Persian kings and should be referred to as Cyrus II, having been named after his grandfather. The last leader of the Medes, Astyages (585–550 BC), was defeated and captured by Cyrus in 549 BC.

In 546 BC, Cyrus II attacked the powerful kingdom of Lydia. From that point on, Cyrus was master of all Asia Minor. In 539 BC, Cyrus II conquered Babylon.

Cyrus was succeeded by his son Cambyses II (530–522 BC).

Cyrus cylinder in the British Museum. Photo by Mike Peel (www.mikepeel.net) 2010 (CC BY-SA 2.5).

Parthians

In 171 BC, the Parthians, a nomadic mountain tribe from the North, conquered Persia. In addition to the nomads who were a constant menace to its eastern frontier, Parthia had to face another powerful adversary, Rome. For almost three centuries, Rome and Parthia battled over Syria, Mesopotamia, and Armenia without ever achieving any lasting results.

Assignment

For more than 3,000 years Persia was a melting pot of civilizations and demographic movements between Asia and Europe. Under Cyrus the Great, it became the center of the world's first empire. Successive invasions by the Greeks, Arabs, Mongols, and Turks developed the nation's culture through rich and diverse philosophical, artistic, scientific, and religious influences, but Persia was still able to maintain its national identity. What historical trends emerge in Persian history?

Carving of Persian (rounded hats) and Median Soldiers in traditional costume with Farvahar on Persepolis by Arad (CC BY-SA 3.0).

ISLAMIC KINGDOMS

Abu Bekr, the first successor of the Prophet Mohammed, was head of the Moslem (Muslim) community from AD 632 to 634. He seized Syria, then Jerusalem, and finally Damascus in 638. In 635, other Arab troops crossed the Euphrates River. Arab horsemen overran Persia. In the course of the seventh century, victorious Muslim armies overran Persia, and the Sassanian Empire (AD 226–652), fabled for the splendor of its court, crumbled. The conquest proved to be far more than military, for it introduced a new religion into Persia and opened an entirely new chapter in Iranian history. The country whose soldiers had subdued faraway Yemen, captured Jerusalem, and marched to the gates of Constantinople only a few decades earlier, now was ruled by Arab governors for some 200 years before it could assert its identity again. During that time, the majority of the Persians converted to Islam. With conversion came a new spirit and a new social order. As the unity of the overwhelming and transcendent Allah was impressed upon the converts, the characteristic belief in the dualism of the Iranian religion disappeared. Gone, too, were the class distinctions, which had been the backbone of Sassanian social and political organization. The powerful Zoroastrian church was reduced to a marginal institution catering to the spiritual needs of a declining community (www.art-arena.com/hlit.htm).

The Mongols, whose regime lasted less than 100 years, eventually conquered the Islamic regime. The Mongol conquest of the Persian world brought terrible destruction and large-scale massacres. In 1258, Genghis Khan's grandson, Kublai Khan, conquered Persia.

The Timurids

A Tamerlane of the Timurid dynasty dominated all of Persia from 1387 until the 18th century. Then the Afghans came.

Afghan rule in eastern Iran lasted only a short time (1722–1729). In 1795, victorious, Qajar leader Agha Muhammed Khan established the new Qajar dynasty. He brought the whole country under his authority and was crowned "Shah" (king) in Tehran in 1796.

The 19th and early 20th centuries were dominated by conflict between Russia and Great Britain. Russia hoped to reach the Persian Gulf and the Indian Ocean through Iran, and Great Britain wanted to protect its sea and land routes to India and to slow down Russian expansion. The Qajar monarchs were incapable of establishing a sound fiscal policy, and to compensate for this, they progressively disposed of Iran's economic resources to foreign powers in return for small sums of money that satisfied their immediate financial needs.

Increasing dissatisfaction with governmental incompetence and corruption, together with resentment of foreign political and economic control, led to a revolt. There was a demand for a constitution, which was signed by Muzzaffer od-Din Shah (above) on December 30, 1906. This led to the formation of the first "Majlis" (parliament). In 1908, everything changed with the discovery of oil.

During World War I (1914–1918), Britain and Russia launched allied attacks from Iran against the Ottoman (Turkish) Empire. In 1919, Britain induced the Iranian prime minister to sign an agreement making Iran a virtual protectorate of Britain (similar to India). There was so much opposition among Iranian nationalists that the treaty quietly died in 1921.

Nationalism

Reza Shah Pahlavi, a leader of Iranian nationalists, removed all enemies and in 1925 became leader for life.

Reza Shah had ambitious plans for what he called the modernization of Iran.

Reza Shah's son, Mohammad Reza Shah Pahlavi, became Shah of Iran in 1942.

Meanwhile, Iran's political system became increasingly open. Ordinary citizens were invited to become involved.

Then the Iranians nationalized the oil industry. This angered Great Britain. Americans, too, became involved, and sponsored a revolution that put **Mohammad Reza Pahlavi** into power. He ruled Iran as shah (king) from 1941 until the powerful Muslim religious leader Ayatollah Khomeini overthrew him in January 1979.

The Iranian Revolution transformed Iran from a monarchy under Shah Mohammad Reza Pahlavi to an Islamic republic. Now populist and Islamic economic and cultural policies replaced Iran's rapidly modernizing, capitalist economy. Much industry was nationalized, and Western influences banned.

Khomeini served as leader of the revolution or as Supreme Leader of Iran from 1979 to his death on June 3, 1989. This era was dominated by the consolidation of the revolution into a theocratic republic under Khomeini, and by the costly and bloody war with Iraq. On September 22, 1980, the Iraqi army invaded Iran and precipitated the Iran–Iraq War. The attack took revolutionary Iran completely by surprise.

Although **Saddam Hussein** and his Iraqi forces made several early advances, by 1982, Iranian forces had pushed the Iraqi army back into Iraq. Khomeini sought to export his Islamic revolution westward into Iraq, especially on the majority Shi'a Arabs living in the country. The war then continued for six more years until 1988, when Khomeini, in his words, "drank the cup of poison" and accepted a truce mediated by the United Nations.

Succeeding Khomeini as president was pragmatic conservative Ali-Akbar Hashemi Rafsanjani, who served two four-year terms and focused his efforts on rebuilding Iran's economy and war-damaged infrastructure, though low oil prices hampered this endeavor. During the Persian Gulf War in 1991 the country remained neutral, restricting its action to the condemnation of the U.S. and allowing fleeing Iraqi aircraft and refugees into the country.

Rafsanjani was succeeded in 1997 by the reformist Mohammad Khatami. His presidency was soon marked by tensions between the reform-minded government and an increasingly conservative and vocal clergy. This rift reached a climax in July 1999 when massive anti-government protests erupted in the streets of Tehran. The disturbances

Mohammed Reza Pahlavi, Shah of Iran, and his wife, Queen Farah, prepare to depart after a visit to the United States. Photo by MSgt. Denham (USAF), 1977 (PD-US).

lasted over a week before police and pro-government vigilantes dispersed the crowds.

Khatami was reelected in June 2001, but the religious Guardian Council repeatedly blocked his efforts. Conservative elements undermined the reformist movement, banning liberal newspapers and disqualifying candidates for parliament. Mohammad Khatami was reformist president of Iran from 1997 to 2005. In June 2003, anti-government protests by several thousand students took place in Tehran. Several human rights protests also occurred in 2006. In the Iranian presidential election in 2005, Mahmoud Ahmadinejad, the mayor of Tehran, became the sixth president of Iran, after winning 62 percent of the vote in the run-off poll, against former president Ali-Akbar Hashemi Rafsanjani. During the authorization ceremony he kissed Khomeini's hand in demonstration of his loyalty to him. Mahmoud Ahmadinejad is the current president of Iran. He is an outspoken opponent of Israel and the US, and his regime is generally perceived as a rogue regime.

Assignment

A. Why did the Islamic invasion threaten Persian society and culture?

B. What two European powers had particular interest in Iran? Why?

MANICHAEAN RELIGION

Mani, born in western Persia (approximately 210–275 AD), was a religious preacher and the founder of Manichaeism, an ancient religion that was once widely embraced but is now considered nonexistent. Augustine of Hippo, the famous church father, embraced this religion before he was converted to Christianity.

As a young man, Mani claimed to have had a revelation that salvation was possible through education and self-denial. He later claimed to be the Holy Spirit promised by Jesus (John 14). Mani called himself "the Last Prophet," joining a succession of men he believed were guided by God, including Noah, Abraham, Zoroaster, Hermes, Plato, Buddha, and Jesus Christ.

Bema Psalms

Psalm 223

Let us worship the Spirit of the Paraclete.

Let us bless our Lord Jesus who has sent us the Spirit of Truth. He came and separated us from the Error of the world, he brought us a mirror, we looked, we saw the Universe in it.

When the Holy Spirit came he revealed to us the way of Truth and taught us that there are two Natures, that of Light and that of Darkness, separate one from the other from the beginning.

The Kingdom of Light, on the one hand, consisted in five Greatnesses, and they are the Father and his twelve Aeons and the Aeons of the Aeons, the Living Air, the Land of Light; the great Spirit breathing in them, nourishing them with his Light.

But the Kingdom of Darkness consists of five storehouses, which

Painter Mani presenting king Bukhram-Gur with his drawing by Alishir Navoi, c1521, (PD-US).

are Smoke and Fire and Wind and Water and Darkness; their Counsel creeping in them, moving them and inciting them to make war with one another.

Now as they were making war with one another they dared to make an attempt upon the Land of Light, thinking that they would be able to conquer it. But they know not that which they have thought to do they will bring down upon their own heads.

But there was a multitude of angels in the Land of Light, having powers to go forth to subdue the enemy of the Father, whom it pleased that by his Word that he would send, he should subdue the revels who desired to exalt themselves above that which was more exalted than they.

This too is the way of the Father, who sent his strong son; and he produced from himself his Maiden equipped with five powers, that she might fight against the five abysses of the Dark.

When the Watcher stood in the boundaries of light, he showed to them his Maiden who is his soul; they bestirred themselves in their abyss, desiring to exalt themselves over her, they opened their mouth desiring to swallow her.

He held her power fast, he spread her over them, like nets over fishes, he made her rain down upon them like purified clouds of water, she thrust herself within them like piercing lightning. She crept in their inward parts, she bound them all, they not knowing it.

When the First Man had finished his war the Father sent his second son. He came and helped his brother out of the abyss; he established this whole world out of the mixture that took the place of the Light and the Darkness.

He spread out all the powers of the abyss to ten heavens and eight earths, he shut them up into this world once, he made it a prison too for all the powers of Darkness, it is also a place of purification for the Soul that was swallowed in them.

The sun and moon he founded, he set them on high, to purify the Soul. Daily they take up the refined part to the height, but the dregs however they erase. Mixed, they convey it above and below.

This whole world stands firm for a season, there being a great building which is being built outside this world. So soon as the builder shall finish, the whole world will dissolve and set on fire that the fire may smelt it away.

All life, the relic of Light wheresoever it be, he will gather to himself and of it depict and image. And the counsel of death too, all the Darkness, he will gather together and make a likeness of its very self, it and the Ruler.

Tiffany stained-glass window of St. Augustine, in the Lightner Museum, St. Augustine, Florida, by Louis Comfort Tiffany, date unknown (CC BY-SA 3.0).

In a moment the living Spirit will come. He will succor the Light. But the counsel of death and the darkness he will shut up in the dwelling that was established for it, that it might be bound in it for ever.

There is no other means to bind the Enemy save this means; for he will not be received to the Light because he is a stranger to it : nor again can he be left in his land of Darkness, that he may not wage a war greater than the first.

A new Aeon shall be built in the place of the world that shall dissolve, that in it the powers of the Light may reign, because they have performed and fulfilled the will of the Father entire, they have subdued the hated one, they have over him for ever.

This is the Knowledge of Mani, let us worship him and bless him. Blessed is every man that shall have trust in him, for he it is shall live with all the Righteous. Glory and victory to our Lord Mani, the Spirit of Truth, that cometh from the Father, who has revealed to us the Beginning, the Middle, and the End. Victory to the soul of the blessed Mary, Theona, Pshaijmnoute.

Assignment

The Manichaean cult has experienced a comeback in the last few years. Why do you think Manichaeism would be so popular among contemporary people?

Islamic Mosque

THE WISE MEN

The wise men of the Christmas story came from the East (Matthew 2:1) Legend states that they were from Persia (Iran). If that is true, they were probably Magi—priests from the Zoroastrian religion. Following an astronomical phenomenon—a star—they no doubt had traveled for weeks. While we do not know their names and can't even confirm there were three, we know that their entrance into the nativity story forever affected the course of history.

The Gospel of Matthew, the only one of the four Gospels to mention the Magi, states that they came "from the East" to worship the Christ, "born King of the Jews." Although the account does not tell how many Magi there were, the three kinds of gifts they presented led to a widespread assumption that there were three. Their identification as kings in later Christian writings is linked to Old Testament prophecies such as that in Isaiah 60:3, which describe the Messiah being worshipped by kings.

Traditions identify a variety of different names for the Magi. In the Western Christian church they have been commonly known as Melchior, Caspar, and Balthassar.

They probably were Babylonian or Persian. The majority belief was they were from Babylon, which was the center of Zurvanism, and hence astrology, at the time; and they may have retained knowledge from the time of their Jewish leadership by Daniel.

According to the Gospel of Matthew, the Magi found Jesus by following His star, which thus traditionally became known as the Star of Bethlehem.

On finding him, they gave him three symbolic gifts: gold, frankincense, and myrrh. Warned in a dream that Judean king Herod intended to kill the child, they decided to return home by a different route. This prompted Herod to resort to killing all the young children in Bethlehem, an act called the Massacre of the Innocents, in an attempt to eliminate a rival heir to his throne. Jesus and His family had, however, escaped to Egypt beforehand. Nonetheless, Herod murdered all male citizens younger than age two in one of the most infamous crimes in world history.

Today, the celebration of the visit of the Wisemen is one of the most revered aspects of the Christmas season.

Assignment

Why is the biblical account of the wise men an important part of the Christmas story?

Chapter 19

CHINESE HISTORY

First Thoughts . . .

Chinese civilization began around 2500—2000 BC, about 1,000 years earlier than Western European civilization (1000 BC) and more than 3,000 years before European-American civilization (AD 1600). A rich culture thrived in the lower Huang He (Yellow River) Valley of northern China. What makes the civilization unique in world history is its continuity through more than 4,000 years. No other civilization can make that claim! The Chinese kept voluminous records from the beginning. The strange thing is that throughout China's history, its scholars alluded to its cultural separateness from its contiguous neighbors. Thus, Chinese people, it seems, have always had a sense of their unique cultural identity.

Chapter Learning Objectives . . .

In chapter 19, we will begin by examining Chinese history. We will see dynasties emerge that alternately struggled with domestic conflict and foreign invasions. Next, we will see how the dynasties collapsed, were replaced with a republican government, and, shortly thereafter, fell to a Communist regime. Finally, we will look at Chinese religions and reflect upon how they connected with and transformed Chinese people.

As a result of this chapter you should be able to:

1. Compare Chinese civilization with European civilization, c. AD 500–1000.

2. Delineate historical trends that emerge in Chinese history.

3. Evaluate Communism's appeal to the Chinese people.

4. Predict the future of the People's Republic of China.

5. Explain why Daoism would work better in a totalitarian regime than in a democracy.

6. Explore why Confucius, who never claimed to be a deity and never set out to found a religion, became, after his death, both a deity and the focus of a religion.

7. Discuss why European technology quickly surpassed Chinese technology.

ANCIENT CHINA

Chinese history, until recently, was written mostly by royal patrons and scholars. The aristocracy wrote the history and made every effort to paint a thorough and flattering picture of its influences. Since little social history emerged, historians know little about common people in early Chinese history. Generally speaking, historians described a Chinese political pattern of dynasties, or political kingdoms, one following another in a cycle of birth and death.

Certain themes emerged in Chinese history. Unlike Japan, which was relatively isolated on an island, mainland China was a crossroad between warring groups. Inevitably, each new conqueror put his mark on China, and as a result, China became an amalgamation of several different cultures. Chinese culture readily absorbed the culture and politics of surrounding cultures.

At the same time, Chinese dynasties were acutely aware of their vulnerability and constantly sought to protect themselves from unfriendly neighbors. They were always advanced technologically and used this advance whenever possible. Thus, they fought with gunpowder before anyone else and built the longest wall in world history. As a result, China was threatened but not conquered until the 13th century when the Mongols from the North conquered all of China.

The Mongols were illiterate, and perhaps no more than 700,000 in number. They were herdsmen on the grassy plains north of the Gobi Desert in what is now Mongolia. Before AD 1200, the Mongols were fragmented, moving about in small bands headed by a chief, or khan, and living in portable felt dwellings, called, by the Mongols *ger*. From his late teens to age 38 in 1200, a Mongol named Temujin (Temüjin) rose as khan over various families. He was a good manager, collecting people of talent. After some success, Temujin took the title Universal Ruler, which translates to Genghis Khan. Genghis Khan conquered China and most of Asia, but his father, Kublai Kahn, actually ruled China.

Genghis Khan, artist unknown, c 14th century (PD-US, PD-Art).

China came under foreign rule for the second time in the 17th century when the Manchus conquered them. As one can see, the tension of embracing and warring against nearby countries empowered much of Chinese history.

Inevitably, though, Chinese culture and politics eventually triumphed. The superiority of their technology, their political institutions, and the sheer weight of their numbers assured Chinese success over all their opponents. Nonetheless, assimilation and rapprochement continued over the centuries through conquest and colonization until what is now known as China emerged under a unified rule.

At the same time, the Chinese also left an indelible mark on Japan, Korea, Tibet, and Mongolia—important rival and neighboring civilizations.

From 2000 BC to the early 20th century, a succession of dynasties or kingdoms ruled increasingly large parts of China. Leadership emerged in these dynasties among educated men who were recruited to serve as government officials based on their skills rather than their lineage. This was a propitious event for Chinese political leadership throughout its emergence as a world power. When European intrusions began in the 16th century, the complexion of Chinese leadership was changed. The old dynastic rule was sorely tested by foreign and dangerous technology and ideology. By the early 20th century, China had had enough and instigated a revolution against the ruling monarchy and foreign entrepreneurs alike. In 1949, the Chinese Communist Party took over as China's current government.

It is time now to return to a general overview of Chinese history.

Xia (c. 2200–c. 1750 BC)

The first dynasty to emerge in Chinese history was the Xia Dynasty. The Xia were famous for their decorated teapots. No one really knows for sure, but the Xia probably had writing similar to today's written Chinese. Most of the Xia people were farmers who used bronze (vs. iron) weapons to defend themselves. For the first time, a ruling class emerged. The ruling families used elaborate and symbolic rituals to exhibit their governing power. Most Xia practiced polytheism that emphasized communication with spirits for help and guidance. (A similar religion emerged among Native Americans at approximately the same time.)

The Xia Dynasty lasted more than 400 years and was ruled by 17 kings over 14 generations. Ultimately the lack of experience among the ruling class caused the downfall of the most famous of the early Chinese dynasties.

Shang (c. 1750–c. 1040 BC)

The Shang Dynasty had more advanced bronze weaponry and produced the most complete record of Chinese writing. They were also one of the earliest civilizations to practice human sacrifice. They liked human sacrifice—a lot. When a king died, more than 100 slaves would join him in the grave.

Bronze yuè axe from the Shang Dynasty. Photo by Vassil, 2007 (PD-US)

A king was endowed with supreme authority. In order to secure his power, he insisted that his subjects practice ancestral and nature worship. He then proclaimed himself the agent or the worldly descendent of all supreme beings. To make sure that a Chinese king had adequate help in the afterlife, personal slaves were often buried alive as human sacrifices, together with animal offerings. Given the price of slaves, later Shang dynasties replaced human beings with life-size clay figures, some of which were discovered several years ago.

The Shang monarchy practiced a truly strange sort of succession that caused much confusion and ultimately led to its downfall. After a king died, no one knew who exactly should be king. This finally led to civil war!

Zhou (c. 1100–256 BC)

The Zhou Dynasty's dominance is traditionally divided into two periods: Western Zhou (11th century BC to 711 BC), and Eastern Zhou (770 BC to 221 BC). The Zhou reigned for 800-plus years. This was a time of "high culture" in China.

The Zhou practiced father-son succession, which greatly stabilized the kingdom. The Zhou dynasty set up a feudal type regime, presaging European feudalism, which arose 1000 years later. This form of government created a ruling class and a resulting bureaucracy that extended far beyond the royal family. This economical form of government produced the longest and most stable regime in Chinese history. Zhou city-states became progressively centralized and established efficient political and economic institutions.

The Zhou still didn't rule all of what is present-day China, but they ruled more of it than any previous dynasty. They were located in the middle of the principalities, giving rise to what the Chinese call the Middle Kingdom. The Zhou were able to maintain peace and stability for a few hundred years; then in 771 BC, the capital was sacked by barbarians from the West. The Zhou recovered and ruled for 500 more years.

Pit of oracle bones. The oracle bones are pieces of bone or turtle plastron bearing the answers to divination during the late Shang Dynasty (1766-1050 BC). Photo by Chez Cǎsver, 2006 (CC BY 2.0).

During this time, three major religions emerged: Daoism (or Taoism), Confucianism, and Legalism.

Daoism is based on study of the Dao, literally translated "The Way." The book of Daoism, the *Dao de Jing, The Way and Virtue*, was written by Lao-zi. Daoists set the tone for Chinese religions for centuries through pithy sayings, aphorisms, and salient metaphors. In fact, Daoism, in form and function, profoundly influenced the later development of Cha'an (also known as Zen) Buddhism.

The philosopher Confucius, who lived during the Zhou period approximately 500 years before Christ, said: "A gentleman has three things to guard against. In the days of thy youth, ere thy strength is steady, beware of lust. When manhood is reached, in the fullness of strength, beware of strife. In old age, when thy strength is broken, beware of greed." Confucius believed that only virtuous, morally upright men should be rulers. He developed a sort of works righteousness theology. Many people consider Confucian thought to be, like Daoism (Taoism), a form of atheism.

Legalism derived its views from a philosopher named Xun-zi, who believed that man is essentially selfish and, therefore, evil. Because mankind is basically, irretrievably bad, legalism advocated an active secret police and other forms of totalitarianism.

Toward the end of the Zhou period, huge battles occurred. These were the first massive battles in world history. An army of almost a million men was not an uncommon size. Nonetheless, in 771 BC, the Zhou court was sacked, and its king was killed by invading barbarians allied with rebel lords. The Zhou dynasty ended.

Assignment

The Shang king's rule was based equally on religious and political power. He played a priestly role in the worship of his ancestors, and he was the political leader of China too. Compare this leadership paradigm with what emerged in Europe, c. AD 500–1000.

MIDDLE HISTORY

Qin (221–206 BC)

In 221 BC, the first emperor of China, Qin Shihuangdi, conquered the rest of China after a few hundred years of disunity. Qin Shihuangdi was ruthless. He murdered hundreds of his enemies. Also, Qin utilized iron weapons that were vastly superior to bronze implements. Qin began what later became the Great Wall of China. The Great Wall was not finished until 2,000 years later, during the Ming dynasty. When Emperor Qin Shihuangdi died in 210 BC, the Qin Empire fell.

Han (206 BC–AD 220)

This short period of Chinese history reflects a prosperous time in her history. During this era, Buddhism was introduced to the culture, as the Han family ruled from the city of Changian. The boundaries of China established during this era have changed only slightly.

The Great Wall of China between Jiankou and Mutianyu.

Three Kingdoms (220–265)

The end of the Han Dynasty was followed by a long period of disunity and civil war. It began with the Three Kingdoms. These three kingdoms were the Wei in northern China, the Shu to the west, and the Wu in the east. During this period of history, Buddhism spread throughout China. Tea was discovered in the south during this period and became an important export product. Porcelain and other fine pottery were also developed during this time. Ts'ao Ts'ao ruled the kingdom of Wei. This was the strongest of the kingdoms, and Ts'ao Ts'ao nearly unified all of China under his rule. He was defeated by Sun Ch'üüan and Liu Pei in the battle of the Red Cliff. This defeat was the beginning of the division into three kingdoms. The Wei and Shu kingdoms were both centralized, while the Wu kingdom was ruled by a confederation. The Wei kingdom eventually captured the Shu kingdom in AD 263.

Ts'ao Ts'ao's army consisted of both Chinese and barbarians, the Hsiung-nu, the Hsien-pei, the Wu-huan, and the Ch'iang. This resulted in assimilation among the people, which had not occurred in the past. In the future, these assimilated nomads would form independent kingdoms in northern China. The Ssu-ma was a militant family that rose to power very quickly. One of its members, Su-ma Yen, founded the new Chin Dynasty in AD 265.

Chin Dynasty (AD 265–420)

Su-ma Yen, later named Wu Ti, began the Chin Dynasty and ruled from AD 265 to 289. Emperor Wu Ti reunified China, ending the period of the Three Kingdoms. Now there was no longer a serious danger of being invaded. Therefore, the emperor ordered his army to disband. However, not all complied, which proved to be Wu Ti's undoing, as he was killed during one of the revolts led by rogue princes. The Chin Dynasty was never strong again.

A sidebar to this story is the Dynasties of the North and the South, which lasted from AD 317 to 589. During this time period, the North and the South were split and two separate streams of dynasties formed.

Sui (AD 589–618)

The Sui Dynasty reunified China. It also accomplished many public works. The Grand Canal was extended northward. The Grand Canal of China is the world's oldest and longest canal, longer than the Suez and Panama Canals. The Grand Canal is 1,114 miles long with 24 locks and some 60 bridges.

The Sui also continued to build the Great Wall along the northern borders, and Confucianism began to regain popularity as the nobles gained importance.

Tang (AD 618–907)

The Tang Dynasty extended the boundaries of China into Siberia, Korea, and Vietnam. They also opened the so-called Silk Road into Afghanistan.

The Silk Road had been around for hundreds of years. It was a trade route to the West. However, the most significant "trade good" carried along this route was not silk, but Buddhism, which came to China from India via the northern branch of the Silk Road.

During the Tang Dynasty, China had its first empress—Empress Wu, who was a ruthless dictator. The Empress Wu was not a nice person. She made Lady Macbeth look like Mother Theresa! She murdered her own son! Empress Wu and her successors ineffectively ruled China. For that, and other reasons, the Tang Dynasty ultimately collapsed.

Northern Song (960–1125)
Southern Song (1127–1279)

The Song (pronounced Soong) Dynasty was another great dynasty. The Song Dynasty brought all sorts of advances in agriculture and technology. For the first time, rice was grown in abundance for all Chinese.

The stable Song system set in place a social order that still exists today. And the system worked. In fact, it worked almost too well. This is important because one of the factors behind the Industrial Revolution in Europe was that Europeans didn't have enough laborers to work the fields. This created an incentive to produce labor-saving devices for the mass production of products. There was no such incentive in China, which had a surplus of human labor and plenty of food to feed its multitudes. The "if it isn't broken, don't fix it" attitude in China lasted into the 20th century.

In spite of the Song Dynasty's accomplishments, it was ultimately a failure. Its reign marked the end of indigenous Chinese rule and the beginning of barbarian invasions. The northern half of China was conquered by barbarians. Then 150 years later, the Mongols, fresh from conquering everything between Manchuria and Hungary, invaded and occupied China proper.

Assignment

What historical trends emerge in Chinese history?

MONGOLS TO THE REPUBLIC

Yuan (Mongol) (1279–1368)

While the period of Mongol rule was called a dynasty, and it was extensive in effect and duration, it was in fact a government of occupation. And although the Mongols used existing civil governmental structures, they introduced a new language. They also replaced many senior administrators.

The Mongols came from central Asia, approximately where Mongolia is today. They were fierce warriors. By the middle of the 13th century, the Mongols had created a pretty serious empire. They had conquered northern China, Korea, and most of Central Asia, and had twice penetrated Europe to the Danube River. With the resources of his vast empire, Kublai Khan (1215–94), grandson of Genghis Khan (1167?–1227) and leader of the Mongols, established the first alien dynasty to rule all China—the Yuan (1279–1368). The Mongols' extensive western European contacts produced a fair amount of cultural exchange. The first records of travel by Westerners date from this time. The most famous traveler of the period was the Venetian Marco Polo, whose account of his trip astounded the people of Europe and captured the imagination of men like Christopher Columbus.

Ming (1368–1644)

The Ming Dynasty (1368–1644) eventually conquered the Mongols. The Ming Dynasty was known for its cruelty and excesses. At one point 40,000 opponents were beheaded! Nonetheless, the Ming Dynasty reestablished the Chinese empire.

Long wars with the Mongols, incursions by the Japanese into Korea, and harassment of Chinese coastal cities by the Japanese in the 16th century weakened Ming rule, which was conquered by the Manchus in 1644.

Portrait of Kublai Khan during the Yuan era by Anige (also known as Araniko) of Nepal (PD-US, PD-Art).

Qing (Manchu) (1644–1911)

The Manchu/Qing Dynasty copied Chinese institutions and philosophy to a much greater extent than did the Mongols of the Yuan. In fact, the Manchus were extremely suspicious of Western contact and resisted all outside influence as long as possible. However, European governments eventually succeeded in setting up trading posts all along the Chinese coast., where Western trade goods were accompanied by Western culture.

On the one hand, the West did its best to undermine

what it considered to be restrictive trading and governmental regulations. On the other hand, they did their best to prop up the ailing Qing, the most notable example being the crushing of the Boxer Rebellion in 1900 by foreign troops (primarily U.S. forces). What the Western powers were interested in was the carving up of China for their own purposes, and that, paradoxically, required keeping China together.

Republican China (1911–1949)

On May 4, 1919, about 3,000 students from various Beijing universities gathered in Tiananmen Square and held a mass protest. The May 4th Movement, born at that rally, was the first true nationalist movement in China. (Student activists at the "Beijing Spring" in 1989 intentionally drew parallels with the May 4th Movement.)

In the early 1920s, Dr. Sun Yat-sen, the leader of the (up-to-then unsuccessful) Nationalist Party, accepted Soviet aid and began a movement to unify China. When Sun died of cancer in 1925, the new leader, Chiang Kai-shek, launched his famous "Northern Expedition"—all the way from Guangzhou to Shanghai. Chiang Kai-shek slaughtered many of the Chinese Communists. Among those Communists who managed to escape the carnage was a young librarian named Mao Zedong.

The Nationalists almost managed to destroy the Communists. In 1934, the Nationalists were closing in on the remaining Communist positions, when, under the cover of night, the Communists began the Long March. The number of Communists declined from 100,000 to about 8,000 during that terrible year.

While all this was occurring, the Japanese occupied Manchuria. To a large degree, ironically, the Japanese invasion saved the Communist party.

In 1937, the Japanese invaded China proper from their bases in Manchuria. At this point the Nationalist Government ignored the Communists and warred against the Japanese. In the interlude, the Communists consolidated their control over northern China in preparation for the resumption of the civil war that would occur after the Japanese had been defeated.

Statue of Mao in Lijang. Photo by Roy Niekerk, 2007 (CC BY-SA 1.0).

At the end of World War II, the war between the Nationalists and the Communists began again. The Nationalists were defeated and fled to Taiwan. The People's Republic of China was founded in 1949 with Mao Zedong as its first premier.

The People's Republic of China (1949–)

In 1950, China intervened in the Korean War, and, while there was no clear victor, China experienced grievous losses. Communist Russia and China were strong allies.

In 1958, Mao, who was growing increasingly distant from Moscow, launched the Great Leap Forward. The idea was to mobilize the peasant masses to increase crop production by collectivizing the farms and using the excess labor to produce steel. Mao created the greatest man-made famine in human history. From 1958–1960, poor planning and bad management combined to starve 30 million people to death.

By 1962, its break with the Soviets complete, China started to position itself as the "other" superpower while it recovered from the Great Leap. In 1966, Mao launched the Great Proletarian Cultural Revolution. In terms of the chaos, bloodshed, and destruction, it was comparable to the French Revolution.

One reason Mao was able to pull off the Cultural Revolution was his self-appointment as emperor! Among the notable achievements of the early 1970s was Mao's decision to seek rapprochement with the United States, as dramatized by President Richard M. Nixon's visit to China in February 1972.

When Mao died in 1976, Deng Xiaoping emerged as the new leader. Since then, China has slowly emerged from isolation and joined the world as a major economic and military power.

Assignment

A. Why did Communism appeal so strongly to the Chinese people?

B. Based on the past, what do you think the future holds for the People's Republic of China?

C. Technology played a key role in military and political victories that emerged in early Chinese history. Compare that to the geopolitical situation that exists today.

CHINESE RELIGIONS

Laozi (570 BC–490 BC)

The doctrines of Daoism (or Taoism) are set forth in *The Way and Its Power* by Laozi. Daoism teaches against the unnatural and artificial. Whereas plants and animals act spontaneously in the ways appropriate to them, humans have separated themselves from the Way (Dao) by analysis and evaluation. Daoism is an ancient type of "tree hugging" religion. It is a form of stoicism that argues for a sort of fatalistic surrender to the Cosmos. Daoism argues that agriculture is the most superior lifestyle, in which life can follow the most natural course. The British romantics (e.g., Byron, Coleridge, Shelley) and American romantics (e.g., Emerson, Thoreau) experimented with forms of Daoism.

Huge stone statue of the ancestor of Taoism named Laozi in Fujian, China.

Dai Temple in Mount Tai, Tai'an, Shandong, China. Photo by Jiang, 2007 (PD-US).

Taoist Writings

The ancients who were skillful at the Tao
Did not illuminate the people
But rather kept them simple.
When the people are difficult to rule
It is because of their cleverness.
Therefore
If you use cleverness to rule the state
You are a robber of the state.
If you don't use cleverness to rule the state
You are a blessing to the state.

If you understand these two points, you know the proper norm for governing
To be continuously understanding the proper norm is called
Mysterious Virtue.
How deep and far-reaching Mysterious Virtue is!
It makes all return
Until they reach the Great Norm.

Confucius (551 BC–?)

Confucius was born in a distinguished family in China, 551 BC. The name Confucius is the Latin form of the Chinese characters Kung Foo-tsze, meaning "the master, Kung." His father was governor of a province, but not a man of great wealth. Confucius himself entered government service but enjoyed teaching more. He became a public teacher and soon attracted numerous disciples. At that time in China, as in Greece, wise persons attracted disciples who literally made it a vocation to listen and to record their sayings. When Confucius was nearly 50, in the year 500 BC, he again took public office. In spite of some success, he lost the support of his emperor in 496 BC. Until Confucius' death in

Confucius Temple, Taiwan

478 BC, he wandered from state to state, sometimes well-treated, sometimes enduring severe hardships. After his death, his wisdom was universally recognized and, in Chinese religion that worshiped wisdom more than a deity, he was venerated. Sacrifices were offered to him, temples built in his honor, and a cult established that has lasted almost 2,000 years. Confucius, like the Greek Socrates, did not regard himself as an innovator, but as the preserver of ancient truth and ceremonial propriety. He created no theology nor cosmology but only moral epigrams and political aphorisms. Nonetheless, Confucius had a great impact on world history (Stobaugh: *World Literature*).

each of them will serve as my teacher. I will pick out the good points of the one and imitate them, and the bad points of the other and correct them in myself.

Assignment

A. Why would Daoism work better in a totalitarianism regime than in a democracy?

B. Why would a person like Confucius, who never claimed to be a deity and never wanted to found a religion, become, after his death, both a deity and the focus of a religion?

Confucius' quotes:

He who learns but does not think is lost. He who thinks but does not learn is in great danger.

In vain have I spent in thought whole days without food, whole nights without sleep! Study is better.

I am not one who was born in the possession of knowledge. I am one who is fond of antiquity, and earnest in seeking it there.

If I am walking with two other men,

Statue of Confucius in the temple of Confucius in Beijing.

Chapter 20

THE MIDDLE AGES

First Thoughts . . .

While the Sui Dynasty ruled in China, in Europe, in AD 410, Alaric, king of the German Visigoths, led his army into northern Italy. The Visigoths had come to ask the Roman authorities to grant their people land. The Romans ignored Alaric's request and he destroyed Rome. As the Roman Empire collapsed, Europe entered a vast and varied period of history commonly referred to as the Dark Ages. The Early Middle Ages saw the continuation of trends set in Late Antiquity—depopulation, a slowing of urbanization, and increased barbarian invasion. North Africa and the Middle East, once part of the Eastern Roman Empire, were conquered by Islam. Later in the period, the establishment of the feudal system allowed a return to systemic agriculture. There was sustained urbanization in Northern and Western Europe. During the High Middle Ages (c. 1000–1300), Christian-oriented art and architecture flourished and Crusades were mounted to recapture the Holy Land. The influence of the emerging nation-state was tempered by the ideal of an international Christendom. The codes of chivalry and courtly love set rules for proper behavior, while the Scholastic philosophers attempted to reconcile faith and reason.

Chapter Learning Objectives . . .

In chapter 20, we will begin with an overview of the Middle Ages. Then we will examine the importance of the Church and of St. Francis of Assisi. Finally, we will look at some of the major philosophies that emerged during those centuries.

As a result of this chapter you should be able to:

1. Evaluate Marco Polo's impact on medieval history.
2. Contrast the life of a typical noblewoman with that of an average peasant woman.
3. Discuss the Saracens and their threat to Europe.
4. Explain how religion and superstitions mixed during the Middle Ages.
5. Reflect upon the impact of St. Francis on world history.
6. Evaluate the pros and cons of Scholasticism.
7. Understand the impact of the Middle Ages on world history.

END OF AN EMPIRE TO THE REFORMATION

The term "Middle Ages" applies to the time span from the collapse of the Roman Empire to the Renaissance and the Reformation. When we think of the Middle Ages, we picture knights in shining armor, Robin Hood, dragons, lavish banquets, kings, queens, wandering minstrels, and magnificent sword fights. The fact is, though, life in the Middle Ages was anything but glamorous. Life generally was harsh, tentative, and downright dangerous. People did not live very long; those who made it to "old age" usually died before age 40.

The Middle Ages, or the Dark Ages, stretched roughly from the end of the Roman Empire (AD 476) to the 15th century (AD 1500). The Middle Ages began with the collapse of the Roman Empire, and although Roman culture continued to predominate for a while, it was soon replaced by feudalism.

Feudalism was a system of life characterized by strict adherence to status, station, and position. In this feudal system, the king—who was at the top of the status pyramid—awarded land grants to his most important nobles, barons, and bishops in return for their loyalty. At the bottom of the status pyramid were the very poor people— the peasants, also called serfs. In exchange for the privilege of living and working on land owned by a nobleman, his peasants were offered protection. And they were "his" peasants. Everything they had—their food, homes, and animals—belonged to the lord of the manor. These peasants were not free people. They could choose neither where they wanted to live nor the jobs they wanted to perform. Yet because they were protected by the owner of the fief, most were glad to stay close to his manor and do his bidding

Normally the peasants farmed part-time and worked at a trade the rest of the time. They gave a portion of their earnings to the lord of the manor as a form of rent. These manors were isolated, with occasional visits from peddlers, pilgrims on their way to the Crusades, or soldiers from other fiefdoms.

Joan of Arc's Death at the Stake (Right-Hand Part of The Life of Joan of Arc Triptych). Artist unknown, 1843 (PD-US, PD-Art).

Nobles, however, were not such docile subjects. They divided their land among the lesser nobility, who became their vassals. Many of these vassals became so powerful that the kings had difficulty controlling them. In 1215, the English barons formed an alliance that forced King John to sign the Magna Carta. While it gave no rights to ordinary people, the Magna Carta limited the king's powers of taxation and required trials before punishment was meted out. It was the first time an English monarch came under the control of the law, setting a precedent for later constitutions.

On the feudal manors, however, the lord was master. A lord, working with the local priest, acted as a judge in carrying out the laws of the manor.

It was particularly tough to be a woman in this world. Women mostly performed household tasks such as cooking and sewing. However, the serf women could also be called on to hunt for food and fight beside their husbands if their home was attacked. There were also some rare instances where medieval women were blacksmiths, merchants, and apothecaries (pharmacists). Some women were capable of sorcery and healing. Others became nuns and devoted their lives to God and spiritual matters. Famous women of the Middle Ages included Joan of Arc, who led French troops against an English invasion. She was, however, an exception.

Homes—even beautiful castles—were not very comfortable in the Middle Ages. Most medieval homes were cold, damp, and dark. Sometimes it was warmer and lighter outside the home than inside. For security purposes, windows, when they were present, were very small openings with wooden shutters that were closed at night or in bad weather. Besides, most medieval persons thought it was unhealthy to breathe too much fresh air. Peasant families ate, slept, and spent time together in very small quarters, rarely more than one or two rooms. The houses had thatched roofs and were easily destroyed.

Castles were more elaborate than the peasants' homes, but were still dark and dreary inside. Tapestries were hung on the stone walls, providing not only decoration but also an extra layer of warmth. The stones in castles stayed cold most of the winter, and once they were hot in the summer, they stayed oppressively hot for most of the season. Because only the extremely wealthy could afford panes of glass, sometimes only churches and royal residences had glass windows. Most used cheesecloth as window coverings to keep out the bugs.

Nonetheless, populations of medieval towns and cities increased significantly. Great plagues broke out several times during the Middle Ages with devastating results. An outbreak of bubonic plague, called **the Plague or Black Death**, struck Europe and the Mediterranean area from 1347 through 1351. These plagues had been preceded by a cycle of ancient plagues between the sixth and eighth centuries AD. These diseases killed one in three—25 million—of all Europeans.

In 1260, Marco Polo traveled east from Europe. In 1265, he arrived at Kaifeng, the capital of the Mongol Empire ruled by Kublai Khan (also known as the Great Khan). In 1269, he returned to Europe with a request from Khan for the Pope to send 100 missionaries to the Mongol Empire, supposedly to help convert the Mongols to Christianity. The

Leeds castle in Kent, England

missionaries were not sent, but Marco Polo returned and set up a trade route to China!

Europeans, thanks to Marco Polo, knew a great deal about China, but they couldn't do much about it until they were able technologically, by means of their advanced sailing ships, to reach the Far East. This is discussed in greater detail in the history unit entitled "Conquistadors, Cartier, and Colonization."

Wars were common. The Crusades (a subject of another chapter) against the Muslim Turks were fought for three centuries, and the Hundred Years' War in which England fought against France lasted from 1337 to 1453. In the early Middle Ages, fully armored knights ruled much of the battlefield. They scorned the foot soldiers, who were usually just peasants forced to fight by their lords. But by the 15th century, knights were fast becoming obsolete and ordinary soldiers were becoming more important. Technological advances such as the crossbow made orthodox warfare obsolete. Lords started employing mercenary soldiers who hired themselves out to the lord who offered the most money.

Yet when we imagine life in the Middle Ages, most of us still picture knights and jousting tournaments. Tournaments started in France in the 11th century. Held to entertain royalty, they were also public contests of courage and skill.

A type of medieval sport, the joust consisted of two knights on horseback, spears drawn, charging at each other from opposite directions. They were separated by only a low wooden fence. The winner remained on his horse. If both fell off, they would resume their battle on the ground, using swords. Normally it was not a fight to death, but knights were often badly hurt. Their armor, which weighed almost 75 pounds, quickly heated up inside. Their horses were also outfitted with armor. Knights followed a system of behavior called chivalry—a code of honor by which the spirit of medieval knighthood was preserved and advanced. There were tacit rules: Normally a knight would not attack an unarmed enemy; under no circumstances would he harm an innocent spectator; and he was expected to treat ladies with great respect. Often a lady would give her scarf to her favorite knight to spur him on to new feats of courage. Jousting tournaments were the highlight of dull castle life.

During the Middle Ages, possibly the greatest threat to Christian Europe was the Saracens. The term Saracens was used by the ancient Romans to refer to people who inhabited the deserts near the Roman province of Syria and who were distinct from Arabs. The term was later applied to Arab peoples in general. By the time Europeans began to chronicle the Crusades, Saracens became synonymous with Muslims. The Saracens, who conquered most of the Mediterranean world, almost completely overran Europe. The Spanish hero El Cid and the French hero Roland played important roles in military campaigns that ultimately stopped the Saracen incursion into Europe.

Assignment

A. Marco Polo described the attempt to invade Japan by Kublai Kahn, whose efforts were thwarted when his ships were destroyed by a typhoon. This "Divine Wind" or "Kamikaze" was a term resurrected by the Japanese during World War II to describe their pilots who flew suicide missions against American naval ships. Does God intervene, as Marco Polo supposed, on the side of one army or another in a conflict? Give reasons for your opinion.

B. Contrast the lives of a noblewoman and a peasant woman in the Middle Ages.

C. Why were the Saracens such a great threat to Medieval Europe? What do you think would have happened if they had succeeded in conquering all of Europe?

THE ROMAN CATHOLIC CHURCH

The Catholic Church was the only church in Europe during the Middle Ages. Therefore, church leaders played leading roles in government and in everyday life. The bishop was an advisor to kings. The village priest, who was a central part of peasant life, served as doctor, teacher, counselor, and pastor.

As the population of Europe expanded, the little Roman-style church buildings were replaced by huge cathedrals. Monasticism expanded and increased. Churches became places of safety where people could fervently seek the Lord. Monasteries in the Middle Ages were based initially on the rules set down by St. Benedict in the sixth century. Later, the Order of St. Francis, the Society of Jesus, and the Cistercian Society emerged. The monks took vows of poverty, chastity, and obedience to their leaders. They were required to perform manual labor and were forbidden to own property or to leave the monastery. Monasteries and nunneries were safe havens for pilgrims and other travelers.

Monks typically worshiped in the monastery chapel eight times a day. In a ritual including chants, hymns, and prayers from the divine offices and the Mass, the first office, "Matins," began at 2 a.m. The next seven followed at regular intervals, culminating in "Vespers" in the evening and "Compline" before the monks retired at night. Between prayer times, the monks read or copied religious texts and music. This was an important practice that enabled the Scriptures to be preserved accurately over a century. Monks were often well educated, and they devoted their lives to writing and learning. For example, the seventh-century Venerable Bede, an English Benedictine monk, wrote a history of England entitled *An Ecclesiastical History of the English People.*

Pilgrimages were an important part of religious life in the Middle Ages. Many people made journeys to visit holy shrines such as the Church of St. James in Spain, the Canterbury Cathedral in England, and of course sites in Jerusalem and Rome. Chaucer's *Canterbury Tales* is a series of stories told by 30 pilgrims en route to Canterbury.

Assignment

A. Civilizations as early as the Chaldeans in southwestern Asia were among the first to claim spiritual belief in plants that never existed—a practice that continued during the Middle Ages. One of the most amazing beliefs was that a tree existed that had barnacles that opened to reveal geese. Why were such explanations presented and why did people believe them?

B. Important in the celebration of Christmas was the banquet, which varied in generosity according to the resources of the celebrants. Churches and houses were decorated with ivy, mistletoe, holly, or, for the first time, with a Christmas tree. The gift-giving of the season was represented by the New Year Gift, which continued a tradition of Roman origin. The later Christmas present was not part of a Medieval Christmas. In fact, the Medieval Christmas was an eclectic event. What part of Christmas was Christian and what part was pagan?

Left tower of Cathedral of Santiago de Compostela.

FRANCIS OF ASSISI

Francis of Assisi, an Italian preacher, founded the Franciscan Order. Born into the family of a wealthy cloth merchant, as a young man, Francis led a worldly, carefree life. Yet Francis demonstrated a tender heart by once giving all that he had to a beggar, for which he was rewarded with a beating from his father. In 1201, after a military campaign, Francis suffered in prison for a year. He then endured a long illness. Francis committed his life to Christ and lost the desire for the things of this world. He identified with the poor.

Clad in a rough garment, barefoot, and, after the evangelical precept, without staff or scrip, he began to preach repentance. He was soon joined by his first follower, a prominent fellow townsman who contributed all he possessed to the work. Within a year Francis had 11 followers, although he chose not to be ordained as a priest.

When Francis began to work among the most desperate of the poor and infirmed, his father legally disinherited him. Francis then wore the simplest of garments and devoted himself to working with lepers. For the rest of his life, having only the most basic of material possessions, Francis devoted himself to living and working among the poor. He was also purported to have a special ministry among animals. Francis' love and concern for all living beings, based entirely on his love for God, is a great inspiration to us all.

Statue of St. Francis of Assisi holding a cross.

Assignment

Describe a humble Christian who, perhaps unknown to other people, has had a positive impact on the world.

SCHOLASTICISM AND ERASMUS

Scholasticism (1100–1300)

During the 11th century a revival of philosophical thought began as the result of a group of mostly Christian thinkers, notably Thomas Aquinas. Adherents of this movement, which became known as Scholasticism, attempted with varying degrees of success to use natural human reason—in particular, the philosophy and science of Aristotle—to understand the metaphysical content of Christian revelation. Scholasticism attempted a dangerous task that many judged to be a failure based on this premise: Christianity can never be a philosophy before it is a religion. Nonetheless, as Aquinas argued, the fact that God's knowledge is absolute does not mean that philosophical speculation, particularly Aristotelian speculation, is an automatic threat to Christian faith.

A passage by Thomas Aquinas:

Just as God is not an existence according to this existence, but rather the nature of an entity is eminently in Him, and so He is not in all ways devoid of entity; so even He is not in all ways devoid of knowledge that He may not be known. But He is not known by the mode of other existing things, which can be comprehended by the created intellect. Although God stands more distantly from every intelligible thing, according to the propriety of nature than the intelligible from the sensible, nevertheless, the notion of knowablity is more befitting to God.

Portrait of Desiderius Erasmus of Rotterdam with Renaissance Pilaster by Hans Holbein the Younger, 1523 (PD-US, PD-Art).

Erasmus (1466–1536)

Everyone is familiar with the Renaissance, a time of artistic awakening in the 16th century. Erasmus was part of the Northern European Renaissance. He led Europe, philosophically, from the Scholasticism of the Middle Ages to the Rationalism of the Enlightenment. Europe was a willing traveler.

A priest, a scientist, a genius, Erasmus made an indelible mark on his era. Perhaps the most enduring philosophical thought he advanced was his discussion about the self. Erasmus, for the first time, discussed things like happiness being centered in the self or personhood of a man or a woman. Happiness was based on some narcissistic notions of self-love. While Erasmus did not create a system of psychology, he nonetheless started a discussion that would be revived in the works of Descartes and Freud.

A passage from *In Praise of Folly* by Erasmus:

Fourteenth-century image of a school by Laurentius de Voltolina, c14th century, (PD-US).

Lastly, what is that in the whole business of a man's life he can do with any grace to himself or others—for it is not so much a thing of art, as the very life of every action, that it be done with a good mien—unless this my friend and companion, Self-love, be present with it? Nor does she without cause supply me the place of a sister, since her whole endeavors are to act my part everywhere. For what is more foolish than for a man to study nothing else than how to please himself? To make himself the object of his own admiration? And yet, what is there that is either delightful or taking, nay rather what not the contrary, that a man does against the hair? Take away this salt of life, and the orator may even sit still with his action, the musician with all his division will be able to please no man, the player be hissed off the stage, the poet and all his Muses ridiculous, the painter with his art contemptible, and the physician with all his slip-slops go a-begging. Lastly, you will be taken for an ugly fellow instead of youthful, and a beast instead of a wise man, a child instead of eloquent, and instead of a well-bred man, a clown. So necessary a thing it is that everyone flatter himself and commend himself to himself before he can be commended by others. Lastly, since it is the chief point of happiness "that a man is willing to be what he is," you have further abridged in this my Self-love, that no man is ashamed of his own face, no man of his own wit, no man of his own parentage, no man of his own house, no man of his own manner of living, not any man of his own country; so that a Highlander has no desire to change with an Italian, a Thracian with an Athenian, not a Scythian for the Fortunate Islands. O the singular care of Nature, that in so great a variety of things have made all equal! Where she has been sometimes sparing of her gifts she has recompensed it with the mote of self-love; though here, I must confess, I speak foolishly, it being the greatest of all other her gifts: to say nothing that no great action was ever attempted without my motion, or art brought to perfection without my help.

Assignment

A. The Scholastics tried to argue from rationalism that God exists and that He is omnipotent. Why is this so difficult?

B. Erasmus suggested something that was innocuous enough: that people should primarily be concerned with their happiness. Why is this a dangerous notion?

Chapter 21

THE CRUSADES

First Thoughts . . .

Regarding the Crusades of the 11th through the 13th centuries, G. K. Chesterton wrote, "High ideas were besmirched by cruelty and greed, enterprise and endurance by a blind and narrow self-righteousness, and the Holy War itself was nothing more than a long act of intolerance in the name of God, which is a sin against the Holy Ghost." Some people, however, do not share his negativity. The late Dr. Bruce Shelley, a staff member of *Christianity Today* magazine, wrote, "Many Muslims, for instance, still reckon that the crusades initiated centuries of European aggression and exploitation. Some Catholics want the Pope to apologize to the world for them. Liberals of all stripes see the crusades as examples of bigotry and fanaticism. Almost all these opinions are, however, based on fallacies. The denigrators of the crusades stress their brutality and savagery, which cannot be denied; but they offer no explanation other than the stupidity, barbarism and intolerance of the crusaders, on whom it has become conventional to lay most blame. Yet the original justification for crusading was Muslim aggression; and in terms of atrocities, the two sides' scores were about even." What really happened in the Crusades? Why did they occur?

Chapter Learning Objectives . . .

In chapter 21, we will begin by looking at the causes and results of the Crusades. Next, we will analyze opposing views of those wars. Along the way we will discuss the excesses of both Christian and Islamic warriors. We will examine the role of women in the Crusades. Finally, we will analyze the worldview of Francis Bacon, who was an extremely influential philosopher during the Crusades period.

As a result of this chapter you should be able to:

1. Understand the causes and results of the Crusades.
2. Discuss the views of Christians and Islamic people concerning the Crusades.
3. Discuss the lives of Christian European women in the Crusades.
4. Evaluate the views of the philosopher Francis Bacon.
5. Examine when or if ever the Christian should force his faith on others.

CAUSES AND RESULTS

Recently some evangelical Christian organizations have ceased calling their outreach efforts "crusades," calling them "encounters" instead. Why? Widespread negative feelings about the Medieval Crusade movement created a present-day concern that non-Christian groups would think negatively about any Christian activity called a "crusade." We will examine the Crusades and make some judgments about whether or not they were appropriate.

The Crusades were a religious movement. They were also military campaigns. Specifically, the Crusades were a series of wars by European Christians to recapture the Holy Land from Islamic peoples. The Crusades began in 1095 and ended in the late 13th century. Originally, the Crusades were a united effort to reclaim the site of the crucifixion of Jesus Christ, and other biblically sacred places, for Christian believers. Later, the Crusades assumed economic and social goals. The Crusades became a form of colonization (although the word "colony" was not used until the 15th century).

In a broad sense, then, the Crusades were a combination of militant Christianity and European expansion. The Crusades combined religious interests with secular and military enterprises. In many ways this was an unhappy marriage.

Crusaders influenced and were influenced by international communities. Europe—indeed, the world—would never be the same after the Crusades.

How and why did the Crusades occur? In AD 814, after the death of Charlemagne, king of the Holy Roman Empire, and the subsequent collapse of his empire, Christian Europe was under attack and on the defensive. Magyars, cousins of the Moguls, nomadic people from Asia, conquered and pillaged central Europe until the 10th century. Likewise, beginning in about 800, several centuries of Viking raids disrupted life in northern Europe and even threatened Mediterranean and Russian cities. But the greatest threat by far came from Islamic invaders.

By the eighth century, Islamic forces had conquered North Africa, the eastern shores of the Mediterranean, and most of Spain. They were, in fact, threatening most of Europe. Islamic armies established bases in Italy, greatly reduced the size and power of the Byzantine Empire, and nearly captured its capital, Constantinople. The Byzantine Empire, which had preserved much of the classical civilization of the Greeks and Romans and had defended the eastern Mediterranean, was barely holding its own against the enemy. Islam was also more than a military threat; it was a cultural threat. It offered an alternative civilization to what was supposed to be the vastly superior Western European culture. This was shocking and disconcerting to Western Europe, to say the least. The threat of a rival culture and religion was a threat no other force posed. This was true especially of the Vikings and the Magyars, who killed the body but rarely converted the soul.

European civilization rose to the challenge. By the 11th century the balance of power had veered toward the West. They had stemmed the tide of Islam. As a result, the Church grew much stronger. The pope was now the most powerful religious and political figure in Europe. His influence brought unity across national and cultural barriers. His authority superseded all other authority and encouraged a supranational identity. Thus, for the first time in many years, the popes were able to effectively unite European popular support behind them, a factor that contributed greatly to the popular appeal of the first Crusades.

Furthermore, Europe's population was booming. Superior agriculture, a cessation of the worst plagues, and improved hygiene conspired to rapidly expand European populations. As the middle class expanded, there was a need for new adventures and enterprises for bored second sons and nouveau riche entrepreneurs looking for an outlet for their growing surplus of time and resources. A Crusade was just what the doctor ordered!

Another impetus was the growth of a sophisticated and generally healthier urban population. These populations were aware of the Middle East and saw its potential market and territorial opportunities.

This is not to imply, however, that the Crusades were first and foremost anything other than a religious quest. Nonetheless, human and economic resources could now support new enterprises on the scale of the Crusades. A growing population and more surplus wealth also meant greater demand for goods from elsewhere. European middle class people had always looked to the Mediterranean; now they sought greater control of the goods, routes, and profits. They wanted to cut out the middle man. Thus secular interests merged with religious interests in discussions about the Holy Land. Those things, combined with the Pope's newfound ability to mobilize and focus all of Europe, made the Crusades a real possibility.

It was against this background that Pope Urban II, in a speech at Clermont, France, in November 1095, called for a great Christian expedition to free Jerusalem from the **Seljuk Turks**, a new Muslim power that had recently begun actively harassing peaceful Christian pilgrims traveling to Jerusalem. The Pope was spurred by his position as the spiritual head of Western Europe, by the temporary absence of strong rulers in Germany (the Holy Roman Empire) or France who could either oppose or take over the effort, and by a call for help from the Byzantine emperor, Alexius I. These various factors were genuine causes and useful justifications for the Pope's call for a Crusade. In any case, the Pope's speech—well reported in several chronicles—appealed to thousands of people of all classes. It was the right message at the right time.

The First Crusade commenced with the explicit and singular purpose of freeing Jerusalem from Islamic rule. It became much more.

The Crusaders faced many obstacles. They had no tertiary leader and no agreement with the Byzantine emperor whose territory they would have to traverse. In fact, different leaders followed different routes to Constantinople, where they agreed to meet. Robert of Flanders and Bohemond of Taranto went by sea, while Godfrey of Bouillon and Raymond of Toulouse traveled by land. On their way, an amazing thing happened. As the Crusaders marched eastward, a vast host of people with all sorts of motives joined them. Few knew what to expect. They knew little about the Byzantine Empire or its religion, Eastern Orthodox Christianity. Few Crusaders had sympathy for the Eastern Orthodox religion, which did not recognize the pope, used the Greek language rather than Latin, and had very different forms of art and architecture. It did not look a thing like their "down home" religion, and they naturally were suspicious. They knew even less about Islam or Muslim life, and were more or less persuaded that the only good Muslim was a dead Muslim.

Orthodox Christians looked like the Islamic infidels to the Crusaders. Thus, many innocent Byzantines, along with other innocent bystanders—especially Jewish people—were killed by the Crusaders. Also, from the beginning, the Crusaders often massacred Muslims without giving them an opportunity to convert to Christianity.

Nonetheless, the Crusades proceeded. Ultimately the First Crusade at least achieved its goal. A siege of Jerusalem culminated in a bloody Christian victory in July 1099, in which many of the inhabitants were massacred.

Now what were they to do? Having achieved their goal, many Crusaders were ready to go home. Others felt that the next step should be the creation of a permanent Christian presence in the Holy Land. The result was the establishment of the Latin Kingdom of Jerusalem, governed first by Godfrey of Bouillon, who took the title of Defender of the Holy Sepulcher, and then by his brother Baldwin, who ruled as king. Three other Christian states were formed as well.

Islamic rulers were not passive in the face of Christian invasion. They dealt a major blow to Christian power in 1144, when they soundly defeated the Crusaders in a major battle.

In particular, news of the fall of most of Palestine reverberated throughout Europe, and the Second Crusade was called by Pope Eugenius III. The Second Crusade resulted in many Western casualties. The only military gains during this action were made in what is now Portugal, where English troops helped free the city of Lisbon from the Moors.

The Second Crusade through the end of the Third Crusade in 1192 illustrated the problems inherent in every Crusade. The same tensions and disunity that existed in Europe began to assert themselves again in the Holy Land. Christian knights fought each other. This disunity undermined the whole effort and was a poor witness to indigenous people. As Indian leader Ghandi observed 800 years later: "I would have become a Christian if it was not for the Christians."

After the failure of the Second Crusade, it was not easy to see how there might be a Third Crusade. However, there was a great spiritual upheaval that offered a way. In the 1120s and 1130s Crusaders took vows of chastity and obedience patterned after those of monasticism. At the same time they were professional soldiers, willing to spend long periods in the East to achieve their goal.

In the years between the failure of the Second Crusade and 1170, when the Muslim prince Saladin came to power in Egypt, the Palestinian Latin States were on the defensive but were able to exist. But in 1187 Saladin took Jerusalem. The situation had become desperate. In response to the Church's call, three Western rulers undertook to lead their forces in person. These were Richard the Lion-Hearted of England, Philip II of France, and Frederick I, called Frederick Barbarossa, the Holy Roman Emperor.

The Crusaders were unable to recapture Jerusalem or much of the former territory of the Latin Kingdom. They did succeed, however, in wresting from Saladin control of a chain of cities along the Mediterranean coast. By October 1192, much smaller Latin Kingdoms were established. There were smaller and less successful Crusades, but the major Crusade effort had ended.

The Crusades were military and religious failures. On the other hand, the Crusades made Western Europe more cosmopolitan. Perhaps the Crusades also brought Europe out of the end of the Dark Ages.

Saladin and Guy de Lusignan after battle of Hattin in 1187 by Said Tahsine, 1954 (PD-US).

The most important effect of the Crusades was economic. The Italian cities prospered from the transport of Crusaders and replaced Byzantines and Muslims as the primary merchant-traders in the Mediterranean. The Crusades also provoked such Atlantic powers as Spain and Portugal to seek trade routes to India and China. Their efforts, through such explorers as Christopher Columbus, opened most of the world to European trade dominance and colonization. They also shifted the center of commercial activity from the Mediterranean to Central Europe.

Assignment

In AD 637 Islamic general Caliph Omar conquered the city of Jerusalem, the center of the Christian world and a magnet for Christian pilgrims. The city's Muslim masters exhibited religious tolerance. No new churches were to be built, and crosses could not be publicly displayed outside church buildings, but the pilgrims were allowed to continue their treks to the holiest shrines of Christendom (although they were charged a toll). Things stayed the same for more than 400 years. Then, in the latter part of the 11th century (1076), Turkish Muslims conquered Jerusalem. Now, vicious attacks were waged on the Christian pilgrims and their sacred shrines in the Holy City. The Holy Land was now in the smothering grip of infidels, and the Europeans determined that something had to be done. In response, Pope Urban II called a conference at the city of Clermont, France, in 1095, and exhorted the assembled multitude to wrest the Holy Land from the hands of the Muslims, assuring them that God would absolve them from any sin associated with the venture. The First Crusade was the most successful in that it actually accomplished what it set out to do—conquer Jerusalem. But it had its problems. Led by Peter the Hermit and Walter the Penniless, one poor group marched across Europe to Constantinople, only to be slaughtered by the Turks soon after crossing into Asia Minor. What was the allure of a "Crusade" to otherwise poor pilgrims?

OPPOSING VIEWS OF THE CRUSADES

Christian View

This selection is by Pope Urban II. This speech started the First Crusade (1095–1099).

A speech by Pope Urban II:

Although, O sons of God, you have promised more firmly than ever to keep the peace among yourselves and to preserve the rights of the church, there remains still an important work for you to do. Freshly quickened by the divine correction, you must apply the strength of your righteousness to another matter which concerns you as well as God. For your brethren who live in the east are in urgent need of your help, and you must hasten to give them the aid which has often been promised them. For, as the most of you have heard, the Turks and Arabs have attacked them and have conquered the territory of Romania [the Greek empire] as far west as the shore of the Mediterranean and the Hellespont, which is called the Arm of St. George. They have occupied more and more of the lands of those Christians, and have overcome them in seven battles. They have killed and captured many, and have destroyed the churches and devastated the empire. If you permit them to continue thus for awhile with impunity the faithful of God will be much more widely attacked by them. On this account I, or rather the Lord, beseech you as Christ's heralds to publish this everywhere and to persuade all people of whatever rank, foot-soldiers and knights, poor and rich, to carry aid promptly to those Christians and to destroy that vile race from the lands of our friends. I say this to those who are present, it meant also for those who are absent. Moreover, Christ commands it.

All who die by the way, whether by land or by sea, or in battle against the pagans, shall have immediate remission of sins. This I grant them through the power of God with which I am invested. O what a disgrace if such a despised and base race, which worships demons, should conquer a people which has the faith of omnipotent God and is made glorious with the name of Christ! With what reproaches will the Lord overwhelm us if you do not aid those who, with us, profess the Christian religion! Let those who have been accustomed unjustly to wage private warfare against the faithful now go against the infidels and end with victory this war which should have been begun long ago. Let those who for a long time have been robbers now become knights. Let those who have been fighting against their brothers and relatives now fight in a proper way against the barbarians. Let those who have been serving as mercenaries for small pay now obtain the eternal reward. Let those who have been wearing themselves out in both body and soul now work for a double honor. Behold! on this side will be the sorrowful and poor, on that, the rich; on this side, the enemies of the Lord, on that, his friends. Let those who go not put off the journey, but rent their lands and collect money for their expenses; and as soon as winter is over and spring comes, let them eagerly set out on the way with God as their guide.

Statue of Urban II in Clermont-Ferrand. Sculpted by Henri Gourgouillon. Photo by Mussklprozz, 2005 (CC BY-SA 3.0).

Islamic View

This is a sermon presented by the Islamic Mullah Mohammed Ben Zeky on the first Friday after Saladin's capture of Jerusalem.

Taken from Joseph F. Michaud's *The History of the Crusades, Vol. III* translated by W. Robson :

Praise to God, who has raised Islamism into glory by his aid; who has abased polytheism by his power; who rules worldly things by his will; who prolongs his blessings according to the measure of our gratitude; who defeats infidels by his stratagems; who gives power to dynasties, according to his justice; who has reserved future life for those who fear him, by an effort of his goodness; who extends his shadow over his servants; who has caused his religion to triumph over all others; who gains the victory over his servants without anyone being able to oppose him; who triumphs in his caliph, without anyone being able to resist him; who orders what he wills, without any being able to make objections to it; who judges according to his will, without anyone being able to avert the execution of his decrees. I praise this God for having by his assistance rendered his elect victorious; for the glory he has given them; for the aid he has granted to his defenders; I praise him for having purified the house filled with pollution from the impieties of polytheism. I praise him inwardly and outwardly. I give testimony that there is no other God but this God; that he is the only one, and has no associate; the only one, the eternal one, who begets not, neither is he begotten, and has no equal. O men! Publish the extraordinary blessing by which God has made easy to you the recapture and deliverance of this city which we had lost, and has made it again the centre of Islamism, after having been during nearly a hundred years in the hands of the infidels. This house was built and

Baldwin of Boulogne entering Edessa in February 1098 by J.Robert-Fleury, 1840 (PD-US, PD-Art).

its foundations laid for the glory of God and in the fear of Heaven. For this house is the dwelling of Abraham; the ladder of your prophet (peace be with him!). . . . For God said, the Messiah will not deny that he is the servant of God; God has no son, and has no other God with him. They have been in impiety, they who have said that the Messiah, the son of Mary, was God.

Assignment

A. Would Pope Urban's arguments persuade you to join the Crusade? Why? Why not?

B. Why was Mullah Mohammed Ben Zeky so pleased that the Christian "infidels" had been defeated?

C. In the spring of 1097, a host of more than 100,000 crusaders joined forces on the eastern side of the Bosporus.

The combined army then fought its way along the coast of the Mediterranean, reaching the gates of Jerusalem in June of 1099. The following is a contemporary account of the capture of Jerusalem:

"Exulting with joy we reached the city of Jerusalem on Tuesday, June 6, and we besieged it in a wonderful manner. . . . During the siege we were unable to find any bread to buy for about the space of ten days, until a messenger came from our ships; also we were afflicted by great thirst, so much so that in fear and terror we had to water our horses and other animals six miles away. The fountain of Siloam, at the foot of Mount Zion, sustained us, but the water was sold among us at a high price. . . . We sewed up skins of oxen and buffaloes in which we brought the water six miles. The water we drank from such receptacles was fetid, and what with foul water and barley bread we daily suffered great affliction and distress. Moreover the Saracens hid near all the springs and wells and ambushed our men, killing and mutilating them and driving off the animals into their dens and caverns. Then our leaders planned to attack the city with machines, in order to enter it and adore the sepulcher of our Savior. They made two wooden towers and many other machines. . . . Day and night on the fourth and fifth days of the week we vigorously attacked the city on all sides; but before we made our assault the bishops and priests persuaded all by their preaching and exhortation that a procession should be made round Jerusalem to God's honor, faithfully accompanied by prayers, alms, and fasting. Early on the sixth day we attacked the city on all sides and could do nothing against it. We were all surprised and alarmed. Then, at the approach of the hour at which our Lord Jesus Christ deigned to undergo the passion of the cross for us, our knights in one of the towers fought bravely, amongst them Duke Godfrey and his brother, Count Eustace. One of our knights climbed on to the wall of the city. When he reached the top, all the defenders of the city quickly fled along the walls and through the city. Our men followed and pursued them, killing and hacking, as far as the temple of Solomon, and there was such a slaughter that our men were up to their ankles in the enemy's blood. . . . The emir who commanded the tower of David surrendered to the Count [of St. Giles] and opened the gate where pilgrims used to pay tribute. Entering the city, our pilgrims pursued and killed the Saracens up to the temple of Solomon. There the Saracens assembled and resisted fiercely all day, so that the whole temple flowed with their blood."

In what ways is this account encouraging and, at the same time, shocking?

D. In the year 1187, the Muslim leader Saladin conquered the city of Jerusalem as well as most of the Crusader strongholds throughout the Holy Land. In response, the kings of Europe including Frederick Babarossa of Germany (who died en route), Philip II of France, and Richard I (the Lion-Hearted) of England mounted a campaign to rescue the city. The Third Crusade was underway. The key to the campaign's success was the capture of the port city of Acre. King Richard arrived on the scene in June 1191 to find the city under siege by a Christian army. Intensifying the bombardment of the city, Richard and the French King, Philip, slowly broke the city's walls, weakening its defenses while simultaneously starving the occupiers into submission. Finally, on July 12, the Muslim defenders and Crusaders agreed to surrender terms. In exchange for sparing the lives of the defenders, Saladin would pay a ransom of 200,000 gold pieces, release some 1,500 Christian prisoners, and return the Holy Cross. These actions were to be accomplished within one month after the fall of the city. Richard would hold 2,700 Muslim prisoners hostage until the terms were met. Saladin immediately ran into problems completing his part of the bargain. The deadline came without payment of the terms. Saladin offered a compromise. Richard refused to compromise and declared the lives of the Muslim defenders of Acre forfeit.

The following is an eyewitness account of the slaughter of 2,500 captives:

"Then the King of England, seeing all the delays interposed by the Sultan to the execution of the treaty, acted perfidiously as regards his Islamic prisoners. On their yielding the town he had engaged to grant their life, adding that if the Sultan carried out the bargain he would give them freedom and suffer them to carry off their children and wives; if the Sultan did not fulfill his engagements they were to be made slaves. Now the king broke his promises to them and made open display of what he had till now kept hidden in his heart, by carrying out what he had intended to do after he had received the money and the Frank prisoners. It is thus that people of his nation ultimately admitted. The King ordered all the Islamic prisoners, whose martyrdom God had decreed for this day, to be brought before him. They numbered more than three thousand and were all bound with ropes. The Franks then flung themselves upon them all at once and massacred them with sword and lance in cold blood."

Was this slaughter justified? What damage resulted from this decision at that time and in later years?

QUEEN ELEANOR OF AQUITAINE

When thinking about the Crusades, few people consider the dramatic effect on women in those unsettling times. At first women, as ill-prepared as men, set off for the Holy Lands, eager to wash away their sins and receive special glory for their effort to free Jerusalem from Muslim control. However, in the fall of 1096, Pope Urban II decreed that no women, no elderly people, nor children of any age could participate in the Crusades. Despite the pope's ban, some women accompanied their husbands anyway. The best-known participant was Queen Eleanor of Aquitaine, who accompanied her husband on the Second Crusade. Later, Queen Eleanor acted as a regent for her son, Richard the Lion-hearted, while he was away on the Third Crusade. Eleanor survived her son Richard and lived well into the reign of her youngest son, King John.

By and large, though, women did not accompany their husbands, and those who were left behind had to fend for themselves. The absence of a husband, a son, or a guardian sometimes lasted for ten years. Many men never returned. It is reported that in the Second and Third Crusades perhaps 500,000 were lost.

Assignment

If you were a mother or a wife of a Crusader, why would you want to accompany your son or husband?

Palace of Poitiers, seat of the Counts of Poitou and Dukes of Aquitaine in the 10th through 12th centuries, where Eleanor's highly literate and artistic court inspired tales of Courts of Love. Photo by Christophe Finot, 2007 (CC BY-SA 2.5).

ROGER BACON

Roger Bacon (1214–1294)

Roger Bacon was a Franciscan monk who used scientific experiments to uncover data regarding natural laws. He was perceived as a great threat to the Medieval Roman Catholic Church, which asked all theologians to refrain from scientific speculation. While this author would have no problem with theologians who speculate on scientific matters, I would be greatly bothered by scientists who pontificate on theology without first submitting to the authority of Scripture. Bacon was very close to moving in that direction. The problem was, Bacon was a better scientist than a theologian, and he probably should have abandoned the latter and embraced more fervently the former.

The following is a passage Bacon wrote:

> And God wishes all men to be saved and no man to perish, and His goodness is infinite; He always leaves some way possible for man through which he

Statue of Roger Bacon in the Oxford University Museum of Natural History. Photograph taken by Michael Reeve, 2004 (CC BY-SA 3.0).

> may be urged to seek his own salvation. . . . For this reason the goodness of God ordained that revelation would be given to the world that the human race might be saved. . . . And it is not surprising that the wisdom of philosophy is of this kind since this wisdom is only a general revelation made to all mankind because all wisdom is from God.

Study of a Franciscan friar, Roger Bacon. By the late 18th century this study, on Folly Bridge, had become a place of pilgrimage for scientists. Artist unknown, 1775 (PD-US, PD-Art).

Assignment

What does Bacon mean when he implies that scientific knowledge may lead to salvation, but the prerequisite for this revealed wisdom of science is Christian morality? Why is that a dangerous thought?

Romanesque Gothic church ruin in Zsambek , Hungary.

Chapter 22

AGE OF DISCOVERY

First Thoughts . . .

The mid-to-late 15th century has quite rightly been called the Age of Discovery. It was an age in which European ships left the safe coastal waters of the Old World and embarked on their adventures to the New World. First, Portuguese ships, then Spanish, and, in the late 15th and early 16th centuries, British, French, and Dutch ships set out to discover a world that they originally called the Other World—the Indies—but eventually called the New World. The truth is, the costs were minimal but the risks were high. Whole continents were discovered and explored. Why did Europeans take to the oceans beyond their nearby seas? What made the civilizations of the Renaissance turn to discovery? The main motive was economic. Europeans recognized that the Far East was rich in luxuries. One shipload of trade goods from the "Indies" (which we call China) could make a man wealthy for the rest of his life.

Chapter Learning Objectives . . .

In chapter 22, we will begin by looking at an overview of the Age of Discovery. We will then look at a couple of primary source passages and judge whether they are credible sources. Next, we will discuss why Prince Henry the Navigator was so important to Europe.

As a result of this chapter you should be able to:

1. Discuss the factors that prompted two centuries of exploration.

2. Explore the Huguenot persecution.

3. Analyze the cause of religious persecution.

4. Evaluate what makes a primary source reliable.

5. Understand why Portugal led Europe in the initial stages of exploration.

6. Compare different world views that emerged in the 16th century.

7. Explain how the Crusades were connected to the Age of Discovery.

DISCOVERY AND EXPLORATION

Explorers are people who travel to discover or investigate unknown places. Prehistoric men and women who ventured out across the continents were among the first explorers who purposely visited and studied unknown geographic areas. Indeed, Native Americans discovered the West Indies 2,000 years before Columbus. Newfoundland was discovered 1,000 years before the Vikings.

The history of the European voyages of exploration is divided into two areas: the drive to the East, which was pioneered by Portuguese explorers, and the expansion westward across the Atlantic to the New World, initially led by the Portuguese but eventually dominated by the Spanish. The two differ in that Europe knew of India and China for centuries, but couldn't get there easily. The existence of America was easily obtained, but totally unsuspected. When Columbus landed in the Bahamas in 1492, America was still viewed as little more than a barrier between Europe and the true prize of the Indies in the East. It was not recognized as anything valuable.

The golden age of exploration began in the 15th century as sailors from Europe ventured out to explore the world. They located routes across its oceans and continents and defined the earth's physical shape and size.

The Age of Exploration grew out of largely economic impulses. For one thing, Marco Polo had introduced Europeans to exotic spices and teas from China and the East Indies. But Polo's access was a land route access from Venice, Italy, to Peking, China. However, toward the end of the 14th century, the vast empire of Kublai Kahn was breaking up; thus, merchants could no longer be ensured of a safe conduct along the land routes. Second, the growing power of Islamic Turkey blocked European attempts at trade. Still, enormous profits could be made by traders who were able to bring back even one caravan from the Orient. At the same time, technological advances made exploration even more possible. One of these advances was Portugal's development of a new type of ship called the **caravel** (right). The caravel was a particularly seaworthy ship that was both fast and

Portuguese caravel, photographed at the Musee de la Marine, Paris by PHGCOM, 2007 (CC BY-SA 3.0).

dependable. The invention of the caravel would be similar to the transformation of air flight from propeller-driven craft to jet airplanes. At the same time, with the further improvement of the mariner's compass, European traders were ready to leave the land behind and explore the unknown.

In 1260, Marco Polo traveled east from Europe. In 1265,

Marco Polo travelling, from the book *The Travels of Marco Polo* ("Il milione"), originally published during Polo's lifetime. Artist unknown, 1324 (PD-US, PD-Art).

he arrived at Kaifeng, the capital of Kublai Khan's (also known as the Great Khan) Mongol Empire. In 1269, Polo returned to Europe with a request from Khan for the Pope to send 100 missionaries to the Mongol Empire, supposedly to help convert the Mongols to Christianity. The missionaries were not sent, but Marco Polo returned and set up a trade route to China!

Vikings were the first Europeans to cross the Atlantic Ocean. By AD 930, 10,000 Vikings settled in Iceland. Eric the Red sailed from Iceland in 982 and discovered and settled Greenland. In 1002, Eric's son, Leif Ericson, discovered a new land that he called Vinland, which included Newfoundland, Canada, to northern Maine, USA.

Nonetheless, the Portuguese, not the Vikings, led the European world in sea exploration during the 15th century. Portugal went first, around West Africa, and then around the Cape of Good Hope. Finally Portugal reached India and China.

The man chiefly responsible for Portugal's age of exploration was Prince Henry. From 1419 until his death in 1460, Prince Henry sent expedition after expedition southward along the west coast of Africa. Twenty-seven years after Henry's death, Bartolomeu Dias rounded the Cape of Good Hope in 1487. Vasco da Gama (1469–1524) continued sailing into unknown waters along the eastern coast of the African continent. He eventually located a route to India and the East Indies. The first sea route, competing with land routes, was opened to the Far East.

Portugal's dominance of East Indian trade lasted almost a century until the Dutch eventually seized trade routes from them. The Portuguese were entrepreneurs. Christopher Columbus was an explorer. Born in Genoa, Italy, in 1451, Columbus first went to sea at the age of 14. As a young man, he settled in Portugal and married a woman of noble background. After his wife's death in 1485, Columbus and his young son, Diego, moved to Spain. Like all learned men of his time, Columbus knew that the world was round. The problem was he thought the world was much smaller than it actually was. Thus, his decision to sail westward to reach the East made a lot of sense. King Ferdinand and Queen Isabella brought Spain to the exploration table by financing Columbus' westward journey.

By 1550 most Europeans thought that the New World was pretty useless, especially compared with the East Indies. Nonetheless, the Age of Discovery was well underway.

What if an even shorter sea route could be found? Europeans were eager to try new and faster routes to the spice markets of the Indies. Spices were highly valued because they made bland food taste better and helped prevent food from spoiling. Spices such as pepper, cinnamon, nutmeg, ginger, and cloves were like treasures to Europeans. Investors could make a fortune with one boatload of spices from India.

The first accidental circumnavigation of the globe was accomplished by **Ferdinand Magellan**. Like Columbus before him, Magellan believed he could get to the Spice Islands by sailing west. Based on discoveries made by earlier explorers, he knew that he would have to sail around or through the New World to do so. However, because he greatly underestimated the world's size, the journey that he thought would take six to eight months actually took three years!

Magellan easily convinced the teenaged Spanish king, Charles I (also known as the Holy Roman emperor Charles V) that at least some of the Spice Islands lay in the Spanish half of the undiscovered world. He meant to find them if Charles would finance him. Magellan did discover the Philippines, only to be killed there by natives; however, surviving crew members managed to escape to their ships and reach their destination. Now everyone knew: The world was much larger than anyone had imagined.

England entered the exploration game with **John Cabot**. Like Columbus and Magellan, Cabot thought there was a better route to the riches of the Orient by heading west instead of east. He knew that the world was much larger than previously supposed; however, what if a northwestern route could be found? Magellan had not found a southern route, but there might be a route north of the New World. It was worth a try.

King Henry VII of England thought so too, but he was less than generous in his contributions. Cabot was given one small ship less than 70 feet long, called the *Matthew*, and a crew of 18 men. The expedition set sail from Bristol, England, on May 2, 1497, and landed several weeks later on an island that Cabot mistakenly thought was near the coast of Asia. He named the island "new found land," which, of course, is present-day Newfoundland. During a subsequent voyage, Cabot disappeared.

John Cabot's son, Sebastian, picked up the mantle. In 1508, with King Henry VII's support, he set sail to discover western lands. He headed north looking for a strait to take him to the Orient. He was unsuccessful but was anxious to try again. By that time, Henry VIII was in power and he was not interested in subsidizing exploration. Cabot moved to Spain and secured the Spanish ruler's support. He was convinced he could do better than Magellan. In 1526, he set sail with four ships and spent four years sailing off the east coast of South America. He did not find a better passage around the continent and returned to Spain in 1530 in disgrace.

The second circumnavigation of the globe was accomplished by the privateer Francis Drake. Although France and England were not at war, Queen Elizabeth I was concerned about Spanish expansion in the New World. She sent Drake on a mission to explore the New World and to harass England's rivals in Spanish-held territory. The mission was a great success. Drake plundered Spanish shipping in the Caribbean and in Central America and loaded his ship with treasure to take back to Queen Elizabeth. Drake later sailed around the world.

While the English were concentrating on finding a northwest passage to Asia, the French king, Francois I, commissioned Jacques Cartier to find a way west to the Pacific and claim new lands for France. In 1535 Cartier discovered the mouth of the St. Lawrence River. On his second voyage in 1535, Cartier explored the St. Lawrence River and passed the future sites of Quebec and Montreal. Cartier was followed by countrymen Samuel de Champlain and Robert de La Salle. Champlain established the first permanent settlement at Quebec. He discovered Lake Champlain in New York and traveled as far north as Lake Huron. La Salle wanted to establish French rule from the Great Lakes to the Mississippi Valley. He explored the Mississippi River and claimed the surrounding territory of Louisiana for France.

Henry Hudson, an accomplished navigator and sailor, set sail in 1607 from England and sailed closer to the North Pole than any other explorers had. He was looking for a northwest passage to the Orient. In 1608, he set sail once again and discovered that as he rounded the northern tip of Norway, the sun shone 24 hours a day during the Arctic summer. He still failed to find a northwest passage.

In 1609, Hudson sailed for the Dutch East India Company, which provided him with a ship called the *Half Moon* and a crew. The *Half Moon* set sail from Amsterdam and ended up off the coast of present-day Maine, from which they could see the area known today as Cape Cod. The *Half Moon* headed south and sailed to the Chesapeake Bay. Hudson then turned north from the coast of present-day New Jersey. In 1609, he dropped anchor in New York Harbor at the mouth of the Hudson River. Hudson made one more trip north to what is today called Hudson Bay. In spite of being one of the most famous men alive, Henry Hudson was set adrift in a small boat by his mutinous crew and never heard from again.

The final explorer we will mention was British captain James Cook. The contributions of Captain Cook (above, PD-US, PD-Art) were extensive. He charted much of the Pacific Ocean and discovered several island groups. He proved once and for all that there was no northwest passage. The Age of Discovery had ended.

Assignment

What prompted two centuries of European exploration?

RELIGIOUS PERSECUTION

The Huguenots

By the 1560s, Huguenots, unwelcome in France, tried to establish a Protestant state in which they could practice their religion near what is now the city of St. Augustine. Phillip II of Spain would have none of that and dispatched one of his most brutal commanders, Pedro Menendez, at the head of a fleet of 11 ships and 1,000 troops to uproot the French interlopers (who after all were settling on French territory). The Roman Catholic Spanish massacred the French Protestants, but it could just as easily have been the other way around, as Protestants were also murdering Roman Catholics.

An eyewitness account of the Saint Bartholomew's Day Massacre by François Dubois, c1572 (PD-US, PD-Art).

The following is a contemporary account:

On Friday, the 28th September, and while the captain-general was asleep, resting after all the fatigues he had passed through, some Indians came to camp, and made us understand by signs, that on the coast toward the south there was a French vessel which had been wrecked. Immediately our general directed the admiral to arm a boat, take fifty men, and go down the river to the sea, to find out what was the matter. . . . He said there should be in all twelve men to go in a boat, and two of them Indians, who would serve as guides. We set off immediately to descend the river to the sea, in search of the enemy; and, to get there, we had to march more than two leagues through plains covered with brush, often up to our knees in water, our brave general always leading the march. When we had reached the sea, we went about three leagues along the coast in search of our comrades. It was about ten o'clock at night when we met them, and there was a mutual rejoicing at having found each other.

Not far off we saw the campfires of our enemies, and our general ordered two of our soldiers to go and reconnoiter them, concealing themselves in the bushes, and to observe well the ground where they were encamped, so as to know what could be done. About two o'clock the men returned, saying that the enemy was on the other side of the river, and that we could not get at them. Immediately the general ordered two soldiers and four sailors to return to where we had left our boats, and bring them down the river, so that we might pass over to where the enemy was. Then he marched his troops forward to the river, and we arrived before daylight. We concealed ourselves in a hollow between the sand-hills, with the Indians who were with us; and, when it came light, we saw a great many of the enemy go down the river to get shell-fish for food. Soon after we saw a flag hoisted, as a war-signal. Our general, who was observing all that, enlightened by the Holy Spirit, said to us, "I intend to change these [clothes] for those of a sailor, and take a Frenchman with me (one of those whom we had brought with us from

Spain), and we will go and talk with these French-men. Perhaps they are without supplies, and would be glad to surrender without fighting." He had scarcely finished speaking before he put his plan into execution. As soon as he had called to them, one of them swam towards and spoke to him; told him of their having been shipwrecked, and the distress they were in; that they had not eaten bread for eight or ten days; and, what is more, stated that all, or at least the greater part of them, were Lutherans. Immediately the general sent him back to his countrymen, to say they must surrender, and give up their arms, or he would put them all to death. A French gentleman, who was a sergeant, brought back the reply that they would surrender on condition their lives should be spared. After having parleyed a long time, our brave captain-general answered "that he would make no promises, that they must surrender unconditionally, and lay down their arms, because, if he spared their lives, he wanted them to be grateful for it, and, if they were put to death, that that there should be no cause for complaint." Seeing that there was nothing else left for them to do, the sergeant returned to the camp; and soon after he brought all their arms and flags, and gave them up to the general, and surrendered unconditionally. Finding they were all Lutherans, the captain-general ordered them all put to death; but, as I was a priest, and had bowels of mercy, I begged him to grant me the favor of sparing those whom we might find to be Christians. He granted it; and I made investigations, and found ten or twelve of the men Roman Catholics, whom we brought back. All the others were executed, because they were Lutherans and enemies of our Holy Catholic faith. All this took place on Saturday (St. Michael's Day), September 29, 1565.

Magellan's Voyage

On September 20, 1520, Magellan led a flotilla of five ships with a crew of 250 from Spain to find a water passage around the Americas and continue on to the East Indies. This was a true journey into the unknown—equivalent to a present-day manned flight to Mars. The journey was arduous. Magellan didn't live to reach his goal—he lost his life while battling natives on an island in the Philippines. Reduced to two ships, the remainder of his crew pressed on with their mission, successfully reaching the Moluccas—the Spice Islands. Loaded with cloves, the two ships continued

Persecution of the Waldensians in the Massacre of Mérindol in 1545 by Gustave Dore, c1885 (PD-US, PD-Art).

homeward. Finally, on September 6, 1522, almost exactly three years after its departure, a single ship with only 19 crew members aboard returned to Spain. But Magellan's crew had finally reached the East by sailing west.

Our only contemporary account of Magellan's journey comes from the diary of an Italian, Antonio Pigafetta, who was not a member of the crew but a passenger on vacation! The scene is set this way: Magellan persuades one of the Philippine chiefs to convert to Christianity. Magellan hopes to make this chieftain supreme over the remaining local tribes and loyal to the king of Spain. To bolster this chief's local supremacy, Magellan decides that a show of force, particularly the power of his muskets and cannons, will impress the natives into submission. Magellan does not take into account that the reefs along the island's beach will not allow his ships to get into effective range for their cannon. As the battle is joined along the beach, the crew abandons Magellan in panic and the Captain is soon overwhelmed: "When morning came, forty-nine of us leaped into the water up to our thighs, and walked through water for more than two cross-bow flights before we could reach the shore. The boats could not approach nearer because of certain rocks in the water. The other eleven men remained behind to guard the boats. When we reached land, those men had formed in three divisions to the number of more than one thousand five hundred persons. When they saw us, they charged down upon us with exceeding loud cries, two divisions on our flanks and the other on our front. When the captain saw that, he formed us into two divisions, and thus did we begin to fight. The musketeers and crossbow-men shot from a distance for about a half-hour, but uselessly; for the shots only passed through the shields which were made of thin wood and the arms [of the bearers]. The captain cried to them, 'Cease firing cease firing!' but his order was not at all heeded. When the natives saw that we were shooting our muskets to no purpose, crying out they determined to stand firm, but they redoubled their shouts. When our muskets were discharged, the natives would never stand still, but leaped hither and thither, covering themselves with their shields. They shot so many arrows at us and hurled so many bamboo spears (some of them tipped with iron) at the captain-general, besides pointed stakes hardened with fire, stones, and mud, that we could scarcely defend ourselves. Seeing that, the captain-general sent some men to burn their houses in order to terrify them. So many of them charged down upon us that they shot the captain through the right leg with a poisoned arrow. On that account, he ordered us to retire slowly, but the men took to fight, except six or eight of us who remained with the captain. The natives shot only at our legs, for the latter were bare; and so many were the spears and stones that they hurled at us, that we could offer no resistance. The mortars in the boats could not aid us as they were too far away. So we continued to retire for more than a good crossbow flight from the shore always fighting up to our knees in the water. The natives continued to pursue us, and picking up the same spear four or six times, hurled it at us again and again. Recognizing the captain, so many turned upon him that they knocked his helmet off his head twice, but he always stood firmly like a good knight, together with some others. Thus did we fight for more than one hour, refusing to retire farther. An Indian hurled a bamboo spear into the captain's face, but the latter immediately killed him with his lance, which he left in the Indian's body. Then, trying to lay hand on a sword, he could draw it out but halfway, because he had been wounded in the arm with a bamboo spear. When the natives saw that, they all hurled themselves upon him. One of them wounded him on the left leg with a large cutlass, which resembles a scimitar, only being larger. That caused the captain to fall face downward, when immediately they rushed upon him with iron and bamboo spears and with their cutlasses, until they killed our mirror, our light, our comfort, and our true guide. When they wounded him, he turned back many

Ferdinand Magellan, 1581. Engraver unknown, 1810 (PD-US).

times to see whether we were all in the boats. Thereupon, beholding him dead, we, wounded, retreated, as best we could, to the boats, which were already pulling off."

Assignment

A. In the Huguenot passage, who is the speaker? Why would he refer only to Roman Catholics as Christians?

B. How do you react to the speaker's statement that the Holy Spirit led his group to trick and then massacre the Protestants?

C. If you had been a Huguenot in the situation described, would you have quickly converted to save your life?

D. Why do some Christians kill one another "in the name of Christ"?

E. Is the Magellan passage a dependable account of this event? Why or why not?

PRINCE HENRY THE NAVIGATOR

Prince Henry the Navigator (Dom Henrique), more than any European including Columbus, deserves credit for the exploration of the New World. He single-handedly made Portugal a premier power in the Age of Discovery. He is most famous for the voyages of discovery that he organized and financed, which eventually led to the rounding of the southern tip of Africa and the establishment of financially lucrative sea routes to the Indies. Henry was also a very devout Christian. Even though he did not live to see the New World discovered by Columbus, his advances in navigation and seagoing technology made the discoveries possible. Prince Henry the Navigator never left his home in Portugal, but he helped make it possible for the first Europeans to explore Africa. He was truly a history maker.

We imagine that we know a matter when we are acquainted with the doer of it and the end for which he did it. And since in former chapters we have set forth the Lord Infant [Prince Henry] as the chief actor in these things, giving as clear an understanding of him as we could, it is meet that in this present chapter we should know his purpose in doing them. And you should note well that the noble spirit of this Prince, by a sort of natural constraint, was ever urging him both to begin and to carry out very great deeds. For which reason, after the taking of Ceuta he always kept ships well armed against the infidel, both for war, and because he had also a wish to know the land that lay beyond the isles of Canary and that Cape called Bojador, for that up to his time, neither by writings, nor by the memory of man, was known with any certainty the nature of the land beyond that Cape. Some said indeed that Saint Brandan had passed that way; and there was another tale of two galleys rounding the Cape, which never returned. But this doth not appear at all likely to be true, for it is not to be presumed that if the said galleys went there, some other ships would not have endeavored to learn what voyage they had made. And because the said Lord Infant wished to know the truth of this, — since it seemed to him that if he or some other lord did not Endeavour to gain that knowledge, no mariners or merchants would ever dare to attempt it — (for it is clear that none of them ever trouble themselves to sail to a place where there is not a sure and certain hope of profit)—and seeing also that no other prince took any pains in this matter, he sent out his own ships against those parts, to have manifest certainty of them all. And to this he was stirred up by his zeal for the service of God and of the King Edward his Lord and brother, who then reigned. And this was the second reason of his action.

The third reason was that, as it was said that the power of the Moors in that land of Africa was very much greater than was commonly supposed, and that there were no Christians among them, nor any other race of men; and because every wise man is obliged by natural prudence to wish for a knowledge of the power of his enemy; therefore the said Lord Infant exerted himself to cause this to be fully discovered, and to make it known determinately how far the power of those infidels extended.

The fourth reason was because during the one and thirty years that he had warred against the Moors, he had never found a Christian king, nor a lord outside this land, who for the love of our Lord Jesus Christ would aid him in the said war. Therefore he sought to know if there were in those parts any Christian princes, in whom the charity and the love of Christ was so ingrained that they would aid him against those enemies of the faith.

The fifth reason was his great desire to make increase in the faith of our Lord Jesus Christ and to bring to him all the souls that should be saved— understanding that all the mystery of the Incarnation, Death, and Passion of our Lord Jesus Christ was for this sole end—namely the salvation of lost souls — whom the said Lord Infant by his travail and spending would fain bring into the true path. For he perceived that no better offering could be made unto the Lord than this; for if God promised to return one hundred goods for one, we may justly believe that for such great benefits, that is to say for so many souls as were saved by the efforts of this Lord, he will have so many hundreds of guerdons in the kingdom of God, by which his spirit may be glorified after this life in the celestial realm. For I that wrote this history saw so many men and women of those parts turned to the holy faith, that even if the Infant had been a heathen, their prayers would have been enough to have obtained his salvation. And not only did I see the first captives, but their children and grandchildren as true Christians as if the Divine grace breathed in them and imparted to them a clear knowledge of itself.

But over and above these five reasons I have a sixth that would seem to be the root from which all the others proceeded: and this is the inclination of the heavenly wheels. For, as I wrote not many days ago in a letter I sent to the Lord king, that although it be written that the wise man shall be Lord of the stars, and that the courses of the planets (according to the true estimate of the holy doctors) cannot cause the good man to stumble; yet it is manifest that they are bodies ordained in the secret counsels of our Lord God and run by a fixed measure, appointed to different ends, which are revealed to men by his grace, through whose influence bodies of the lower order are inclined to certain passions. And if it be a fact, speaking as a Catholic, that the contrary predestinations of the wheels of heaven can be avoided by natural judgment with the aid of a certain divine grace, much more does it stand to reason that those who are predestined to good fortune, by the help of this same grace, will not only follow their course but even add a far greater increase to themselves. But here I wish to tell you how by the constraint of the influence of nature this glorious Prince was inclined to those actions of his. And that was because his ascendent was Aries, which is the house of Mars and exaltation of the sun, and his lord in the XIth house, in company of the sun. And because the said Mars was in Aquarius, which is the house of Saturn, and in the mansion of hope, it signified that this Lord should toil at high and mighty conquests, especially in seeking out things that were hidden from other men and secret, according to the nature of Saturn, in whose house he is. And the fact of his being accompanied by the sun, as I said, and the sun being in the house of Jupiter, signified that all his traffic and his conquests would be loyally carried out, according to the good pleasure of his king and lord.

Assignment

In what way was Prince Henry the Navigator a history maker?

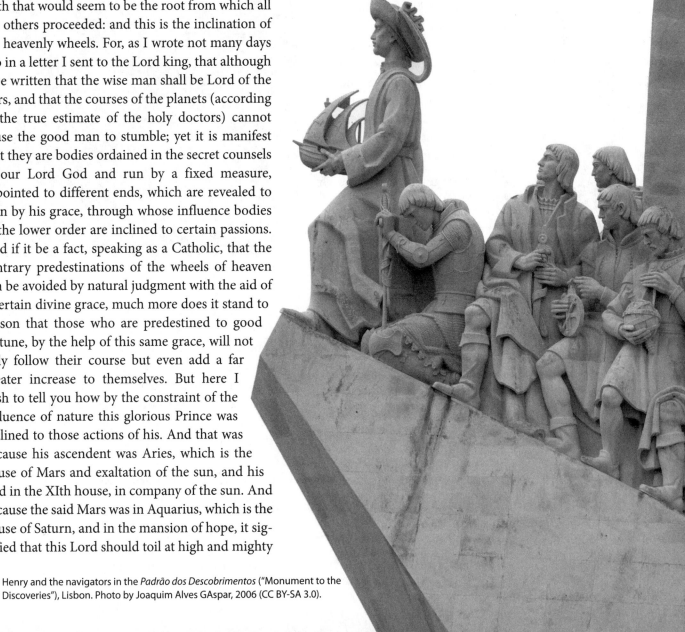

Henry and the navigators in the *Padrão dos Descobrimentos* ("Monument to the Discoveries"), Lisbon. Photo by Joaquim Alves GAspar, 2006 (CC BY-SA 3.0).

MONTAIGNE AND HOBBES

Michel de Montaigne (1533–1592)

Montaigne (below, PD-US), a French nobleman, reintroduced Greek skepticism to Western culture. His skepticism, however, assumed a much more strident tone. "All that is certain is that nothing is certain" could easily have been written by present-day Existentialists. Modern in substance and tone, Montaigne's writings redefined some parameters of 16th-century philosophy. Montaigne's phrase "suspend judgment" became the watchword for European intellectuals. He invited modern Europe to "suspend judgment" in its assessment of newly discovered civilizations in North America and Africa. Montaigne became the champion of later ideologues who embraced cultural neutrality and diversity. He was far ahead of his time.

Passage from *Essays* by Michel de Montaigne:

The laws of conscience, which we pretend to be derived from nature, proceed from custom; every one, having an inward veneration for the opinions and manners approved and received among his own people, cannot, without very great reluctance, depart from them, nor apply himself to them without applause. In times past, when those of Crete would curse any one, they prayed the gods to engage him in some ill custom. But the principal effect of its power is, so to seize and ensnare us, that it is hardly in us to disengage ourselves from its grip, or so to come to ourselves, as to consider of and to weigh the things it enjoins. To say the truth, by reason that we suck it in with our milk, and that the face of the world presents itself in this posture to our first sight, it seems as if

Thomas Hobbes by John Michael Wright, 17th century (PD-US, PD-Art).

we were born upon condition to follow on this track; and the common fancies that we find in repute everywhere about us, and infused into our minds with the seed of our fathers, appear to be the most universal and genuine: from whence it comes to pass, that whatever is off the hinges of custom, is believed to be also off the hinges of reason; how unreasonably, for the most part, God knows.

Thomas Hobbes (1588–1679)

Hobbes was one of the first modern Western thinkers to provide a secular justification for political power. Only Frederick Nietzsche was more pessimistic and prophetic in his message than was Hobbes. Hobbes accurately predicted the nihilism that would be so endemic to the modern era. The philosophy of Hobbes marked a departure in Western philosophy from the religious emphasis of Scholasticism. Hobbes argued that people can either live under the violent, evil power of human nature or accept a state that has absolute power—in other words, a totalitarian state. There was no alternative.

Passage from _Leviathan_ by Thomas Hobbes:

Nature, the art whereby God hath made and governs the world, is by the art of man, as in many other things, so in this also imitated, that it can make an artificial animal. For seeing life is but a motion of limbs, the beginning whereof is in some principal part within; why may we not say, that all automata (engines that move themselves by springs and wheels as doth a watch) have an artificial life? For what is the heart but a spring and the nerves but so many strings and the joints but so many wheels, giving motion to the whole body, such as was intended by the artificer? Art goes yet further, imitating that rational and most excellent work of nature, man. For by art is created that great Leviathan called a Commonwealth or State, in Latin civitas, which is but an artificial man, though of greater stature and strength than the natural, for whose protection and defense it was intended; and in which the sovereignty is an artificial soul, as giving life and motion to the whole body; the magistrates and other officers of judicature and execution, artificial joints reward and punishment, by which fastened to the seat of the sovereignty every joint and member is moved to perform his duty, are the nerves, that do the same in the body natural; the wealth and riches of all the particular members are the strength; salus populi, the peoples safety, its business; counselors, by whom all things needful for it to know are suggested unto it, are the memory; equity and laws, an artificial reason and will; concord, health; sedition, sickness; and civil war, death. Lastly, the pacts and covenants, by which the parts of this body politic were at first made, set together, and united, resemble that fiat, or the let us make man, pronounced by God in the creation.

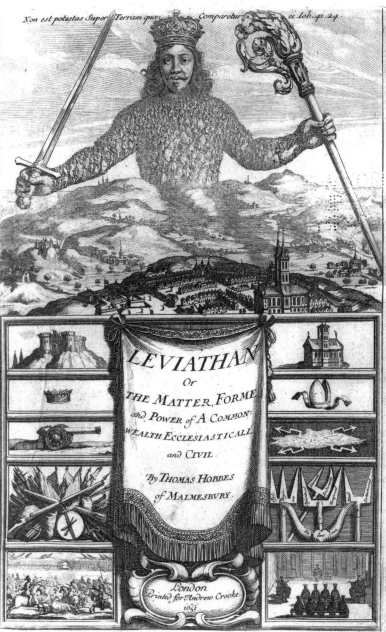

The frontispiece of the book _Leviathan_ by Thomas Hobbes. Artist unknown, 1651 (PD-US).

Assignment

A. Is it possible to "suspend judgment"?

B. Why is Hobbes so popular among Marxist historians?

Portuguese Nanbanjin arriving at Japan much to the surprise of locals, detail from Nanban panel from Kanō Domain, c1593 (PD-US, PD-Art).

Chapter 23

THE RENAISSANCE

First Thoughts . . .

The mention of the Renaissance evokes images of nude human sculptures and realistic, brightly colored paintings. The modest, godly, unpretentious, halo graced paintings of the Middle Ages were in the past. "Renaissance" is the French term for "rebirth." Historians first used it in about 1840 to describe the period from the 14th to the 16th centuries, implying a rediscovery of rational civilization (exemplified by Greece and Rome) after the medieval centuries. The term "Middle Ages," also coined by historians, had a much more negative meaning. The truth is, it is impossible to establish clear dividing lines between medieval and Renaissance periods. In art (particularly sculpture), stylistic hints of the coming Renaissance appeared well before 1300, and the study of classical literature was well underway before the Renaissance began. Nonetheless, for our purposes, the Renaissance is the first modern era to dawn in the European pantheon.

Chapter Learning Objectives . . .

Chapter 23 begins by looking at an overview of the Age of Discovery. We will then consider a couple of primary source passages and judge whether they are credible sources. Next, we will discuss why Prince Henry the Navigator was so important to Europe.

As a result of this chapter you should be able to:

1. Discuss the origin of the Renaissance and its implications for future generations.
2. Explore the link between the Renaissance and nationalism.
3. Analyze Renaissance art.
4. Explore the emergence of modern science during the Renaissance.
5. Evaluate the works of Petrarch and Machiavelli.

THE RENAISSANCE: PART ONE

The word Renaissance means "rebirth." In many ways this is a misnomer because many things did not change from 1500 to 1700. Nonetheless, for the first time, the period from AD 500 to 1500 was known as the "Middle Ages," and what now was called the "modern age" or "Renaissance" occurred afterwards. People did not have as strong a sense of time as we have today. We talk about this or that period, but people living in 1500 thought little about the past and even less about the future, since most would live only 35 or 40 years.

Much like Americans who lived through the Great Depression, Renaissance people had a ubiquitous feeling of gratefulness that they had survived bad times and were now living in good times. They had crossed the chasm called the Middle Ages and they were in the promised land. Everything "medieval" was old-fashioned. Everything new was better. Europeans thought they had rediscovered the superiority of Greek and Roman culture after many centuries of intellectual and cultural decline. Now the sky was the limit. They could go farther than even the Greeks and Romans went. There was, in other words, incredible hope that mankind could solve most any problem, overcome almost any challenge.

The Renaissance included a series of cultural and scientific events that occurred during the 15th and 16th centuries. But it was much more than that. The Renaissance signaled a radical shift in world view. In the science, literature, and history of Western Europeans, God would no longer be the center of the universe. Since the dawn of history the world had been motivated by a theistic vision. Theism, you remember, argued for a world view in which God was in control of everything, and His moral precepts were critical to human conduct. Then, in the 15th century, Europeans entered a new epoch during which God and His moral code were being questioned. In a sense, the modern age had begun.

An impetus for this so-called great leap forward was a revival of Greek and Roman art and culture. However, this classical culture revival took decidedly new directions. The Renaissance embraced the artistic vision without embracing the theological vision of classical Greece and Rome, which had always been theistic (but not Christian) kingdoms. As the reader shall see, the Renaissance did not altogether reject theism, but for the first time, people began to question basic religious precepts.

After studying antiquity, Renaissance thinkers, scholars, and theologians concluded that their own cultural achievements rivaled those of Greece and Rome. They rivaled those of Moses and Jesus. This gave them reason to pause. When they paused, they concluded that they were after all the center of the universe. This sparked something like a cultural revival.

This cultural revival led Renaissance man to make two bold assumptions: first, everything that had happened during the Middle Ages had been bad; and second, what was happening during the Renaissance was much better.

The Renaissance began in Italy and eventually expanded into all of Europe. Several influences stimulated the growth of this movement. Humanism, which emphasized the worth of the individual above all other values, including God, drove European art, literature, and sciences in a new

The famous poet Dante Alighieri's statue in Piazza Santa Croce in Florence, Italy.

direction. Renaissance humanists believed it was possible to improve human society through classical education. They argued that there was practically nothing mankind could not know, and that in the pursuit of this expanded epistemology there would be a sort of utopia. Unfortunately, to Renaissance thinkers, the betterment of mankind did not necessarily mean an improvement in one's walk with God so much as it was advancement of scientific knowledge. To attain this laudable goal, mankind was again boldly encouraged to try to live without limits. Renaissance man thought that perhaps the fruit from the Tree of Life could be eaten without consequences after all, or so the spirit of the age foolishly invited him to believe. Three centuries later, poet T. S. Eliot warned, "Only the fool, fixed in his folly, may think he can turn the wheel on which he turns."

The Renaissance started in Italy, which, since it was not even a national state, could not hope to reclaim the political empire of Rome, but had lofty ambitions of reclaiming the cultural hegemony and intellectual superiority of ancient Rome. As the historian Jacob Burckhardt explains, "The Latin language . . . was easy to an Italian, and the numerous monuments and documents in which the country abounded facilitated a return to the past. With this tendency other elements—the popular character which time had now greatly modified, the political institutions imported by the Lombards from Germany, chivalry and other northern forms of civilization, and the influence of religion and the Church—combined to produce the modern Italian spirit, which was destined to serve as the model and ideal for the whole western world."

Dante Alighieri was Italy's greatest poet and also one of the most important writers in Western European literature during the late Middle Ages and the Renaissance. He is both a Middle Age theist and a Renaissance classicist. He merged the Christian vision with Greek motifs and myths.

He is best known for his monumental epic poem *The Divine Comedy*. It is an allegory (symbolic story), taking the form of a journey through hell, purgatory, and paradise. It is a modern piece of literature—written in Italian rather than Latin—but its themes are medieval. He was writing a book that any Italian could read. So, not only did he lend a voice to the emerging middle class of his own country, but, thanks to him, the Italian language replaced Latin as the literary language of Western Europe for several centuries.

While Augustine had, a millennium earlier, promoted the classics, which, during the Medieval period, most Christian writers had abandoned, Dante had a firm grasp of Christianity and the classics and brought them back into culture. This sonorous marriage was copied by Michelangelo and Da Vinci, who looked for Renaissance ways to interpret Christian themes. Later writers, such as John Milton, copied Dante's approach too.

The arts and literature remained, during Renaissance time, mostly God-centered (although there were some notable exceptions). Aristotelian in substance, Renaissance society had an intense interest in the physical world. **Epistemology**, not **ontology**, was the watchword of the era. Renaissance man was singularly interested in knowledge derived from concrete, measurable, sensory experience. Theology, then, took a major hit. Europeans looked to the telescope, rather than to God and His Word, for answers. This had a perverse twist that has lingered well beyond Renaissance days. Renaissance thinkers and scientists, who were not satisfied to remain in a scientific speculation mode, soon wandered into moral discourse and ethical discussions. This was an ominous development because henceforth a scientist felt credentialed to be a generalist, a scientist, priest, ethicist, and theologian all rolled into one.

Assignment

A. Scholar Jacob Burckhardt writes, "In the Middle Ages both sides of human consciousness—that which was turned within as that which was turned without—lay dreaming or half awake beneath a common veil. The veil was woven of faith, illusion, and childish prepossession, through which the world and history were seen clad in strange hues. Man was conscious of himself only as a member of a race, people, party, family, or corporation—only through some general category. In Italy this veil first melted into air; an objective treatment and consideration of the State and of all the things of this world became possible. The subjective side at the same time asserted itself with corresponding emphasis; man became a spiritual individual and recognized himself as such. In the same way the Greek had once distinguished himself from the barbarian, and the Arab had felt himself an individual at a time when other Asiatics knew themselves only as members of a race."

Paraphrase what Professor Burckhardt is saying.

B. In the 14th and 15th centuries many Italian scholars became aware of history. One group of Italian writers in the 14th century emphasized that their age resembled the great Roman civilization of the past. They tried to incorporate these perceived similarities into their civilization. What are the dangers of doing this?

THE RENAISSANCE: PART TWO

Another ominous world view development occurred. For the first time the individual was studied and admired separate from his or her environment. Human relationships became paramount—the test tube environment in which one learned truth. Art, once reserved for the depiction of religious subjects, expanded to include ordinary people and objects. Thus, in the Renaissance painting *The Venetian Lovers*, a man and a woman, for one of the first times, are pictured in a romantic human relationship. Quite tame by today's standards, this piece was extremely controversial in 16th-century Europe.

As in so many other areas of Renaissance culture, the individual and his relationships were being explored through art. These things became the source of reality. Man, not God, became the center of the universe.

Thus, the unique potential of the individual became significant. For example, Renaissance artists signed their works. This had never happened before. Medieval artists, in their desire to glorify God, remained largely anonymous. In Medieval times, a painter tried to make a theological statement through his painting. He drew attention away from himself and his art and focused the viewers' attention on God. In a painting by Medieval artist Dolci, Mary and the child are enjoying one another and presumably their special place in God's purposes with no cognizance of our presence. A halo around Mary's head signifies her role as Jesus' mother. Art and human life were created and lived to bring glory to God. Period.

A similar subject piece painted by Raphael during the Renaissance seems to have an entirely different purpose. Raphael's Madonna is not looking at the audience, nor is any other figure in the painting. All the characters appear to focus on the individual, and, while the concept of God may be present somewhere in this artistic thought, He is not the primary subject of this painting.

Scholar H. R. Rookmaaker suggested that Renaissance man was struggling with a fundamental dilemma: What is

The Venetian Lovers by Bordone, c1525 (PD-US, PD-Art).

truth? Was truth what people saw or what they knew was true whether they saw it or not? Medieval artists understood that although faith, hope, and love could not be painted literally, they were nonetheless real. Increasingly the answer, according to Renaissance man, would be that truth was in what could be seen, measured, and experienced.

Some Renaissance writers invited contemporaries to contemplate the subjective. The great **Petrarch**, for instance, abhorred **Aristotelian empiricism**. He urged his peers to explore the subjective, the human spirit, for reality. This, again, was an ominous beginning of what would become one of the most lethal world views of history: Romanticism.

All this conspired to place a great deal more emphasis on education. Most of the great European universities were founded at this time. The goal of education was to develop the individual's talents in all intellectual disciplines—art, science, and religion. He was to be a well-rounded, enlightened man. While the most ardent skeptic-scientist believed in God, there was a slight break in the seam. For the first time, human creation and its community was studied separately from God.

The Renaissance was not merely a revival of classical culture. It also stimulated and was stimulated by a growing entrepreneurial economy. By the 11th century, population growth and contact with other cultures through the Crusades had revived commercial trade. Crusaders brought home all sorts of exotic stories and goods. The cities of Italy, with their natural inland ports, were strategically located between Western Europe and the area along the eastern shore of the Mediterranean Sea. The merchants of Venice, Genoa, and Milan became wealthy barons of commerce and trade. They also were patrons of the arts who helped finance Italy's cultural events and achievements. Small entrepreneurial ventures became the Dell Computers of their age. Wealth was amassed almost instantly and in obscene amounts.

In the early 14th century, Florence became the banking center of Italy. The Medici bank loaned money to popes and kings. For the first time in history, money—not lineage or military power—was exerting its influence in geopolitical matters.

Small Portugal and then Spain ultimately ended Italian hegemony by opening up trade to Asia by rounding the African continent. It is no coincidence, however, that Columbus was Italian.

This new wealth created a new political force that demanded to be heard. Although there was nothing in continental Europe like the democracy that was evolving in England, there were new efforts to involve the middle class in decision making. Especially in the city-states of Milan and Genoa there was evidence of participatory politics. Above all, though, this secular middle class demanded that politics be separated from religion.

Thus, the leaders of the growing Italian city-states, as well as kings, had less need of the Catholic Church to maintain power as they had in the past. Leaders could now draw on the wealth of the growing middle class. For this and other reasons, the prestige of the Catholic Church declined. The Church had difficulty adjusting to the demands of a society based on commerce rather than hierarchal allegiances. The parish priest was replaced by the village mayor as the major sociopolitical influence. The Church also suffered when some of its leaders unwisely made bad choices in their personal conduct. Finally, the Church was indirectly blamed for the excesses and failures of the Crusades.

The reader must not think because of the previous

Madonna in Glory by Carlo Dolci, c1670 (CC BY-SA 3.0).

information that I regard the Renaissance as a bad thing. On the contrary, I realize that God was and is able to do great things for, in, and through mankind. Unfortunately, Renaissance people, perhaps more than ever before, were infected with a humanist amnesia and nostalgia in which they gave themselves—rather than God—credit for the great strides made during these two centuries.

The Renaissance was a time when people sensed that changes—good changes—were occurring. They sensed that they were creating a whole new culture. It was a period of intellectual ferment that prepared the ground for the thinkers and scientists of later centuries. Renaissance thinkers planted the seeds of later republicanism and liberty. They also planted the seeds of anarchy and despotism by separating the human will from the steadfast, perfect will of God. Perhaps the most positive thing the Renaissance left to history was the artistic beauty that defined Western culture for centuries to come.

Assignment

What ominous development occurred in Renaissance art?

HISTORICAL DEBATE

Until the 19th century no one referred to the period after the Middle Ages as "the Renaissance." Other eras were chronological—the Classical world, Ancient world, Middle Ages, modern times—but no period in history was descriptive—until the Renaissance.

The first historians to observe that there was something peculiar about this new era were Renaissance Italian historians themselves, who revelled in the new notoriety that a new era was bringing to their nascent homeland.

The Italian historians were concerned with the history of the world from their part of it, so they naturally began with the decline of Rome. Thus they divided history into two periods, ancient and modern.

Italian humanist historians broke with theological world history, and began to talk about history in terms of cultural and social phenomena. Copying the Roman Plutarch, the writers on cultural matters wrote biographies, not histories. In the prefaces and elsewhere, the biographers inserted historical summaries. These normally fixed the end of culture at the end of Rome; they dealt not at all with the barbarian age, but skipped directly to the rebirth of culture, which was usually in the recent past.

Other European nations got on board. In each case, these scholars wrote a Renaissance history with their country inevitably being the guardian of classical civilization. Erasmus, on the other hand, reminded his community that it was the Church, in particular the monastic tradition of the Church, that had preserved much of what Renaissance people were now enjoying.

Now the Middle Ages served as his whipping boy; it was the age of barbarians. Florence was the new Athens.

The Romantics of the 19th century valued national and nationalist history and loved the past for its religious and social content. They loved the idiosyncratic. It was they who first discovered positive value in the Middle Ages.

But it was the historians of art who first identified the Renaissance as a distinct historical period. Praising or condemning it, various writers saw in their own day a decline and recognized the Renaissance as a distinct phase that had ended sometime in the 16th century (E. L. Skip Knox, Boise State University).

Jacob Burckhardt was the first serious modern historian to discuss the Renaissance. Burckhardt created the modern conception of the Renaissance. He emphasized the spirit of self-discovery and self-fulfillment. He portrayed the Renaissance as the first era that truly recognized and respected human worth and individualism. He identified this period as the true beginning of modern times. He emphasized the dramatic break between the medieval and the modern, and for him secularism and even paganism were the hallmarks of the era.

Modern historians saw the period as an "age of reconciliation"—the reconciliation of the Ancient with the Medieval. Humanists tried to link the two into a larger synthesis. They strove to end "not only the dichotomy between paganism and Christianity but also that between heaven and earth, and to create a world of consistency and concord." This reconciliation was achieved in the early 16th century, and then was shattered by the Reformation (Knox).

Assignment

Some Renaissance scholars thought that the emergence of modern science lay in a view of nature that was based on the ideas of Christian biblical witness. Such a view of the universe was essentially supernatural and could not be studied objectively or by experimentation. They introduced the concept of the universe as an entity that could be approached objectively. What is wrong with this view?

The Return of the Prodigal Son by Rembrandt, c1663 (PD-US, PD-Art).

PETRARCH AND MACHIAVELLI

Petrarch (1304–1374)

The dominant intellectual movement of the Renaissance was humanism, a philosophy based on the idea that people acquire knowledge through reason instead of intuition, or through the Spirit of the Living God. The individual was paramount, and his value was innate rather than because he was created in the image of God. One high priest of humanism was Francesco Petrarch.

Petrarch was displeased by what he saw in the world. He felt that intellectual pursuits had not adequately dealt with the true needs of humanity. Petrarch was an incorrigible optimist. He believed in the possibility of a better future, and he hoped, above all, to better the world by the study of classical literature. He admired classical writing and considered it a remedy for contemporary ugliness.

An imaginary letter to Cicero:

To Cicero—You have heard what I think of your life and your genius. Are you hoping to hear of your books also; what fate has befallen them, how they are esteemed by the masses and among scholars? They still are in existence, glorious volumes, but we of today are too feeble a folk to read them, or even to be acquainted with their mere titles. Your fame extends far and wide; your name is mighty, and fills the ears of men; and yet those who really know you are very few, be it because the times are unfavorable, or because men's minds are slow and dull, or, as I am the more inclined to believe, because the love of money forces our thoughts in other directions. Consequently right in our own day, unless I am much mistaken, some of your books have disappeared, I fear beyond recovery. It is a great grief to me, a great disgrace to this generation, a great wrong done to posterity. The shame of failing to cultivate our own talents, thereby depriving the future of the fruits that they might have yielded, is not enough for us; we must waste and spoil, through our cruel and insufferable neglect, the fruits of your labors too, and of those of your fellows as well, for the fate that I lament in the case of your own books has befallen the works of many another illustrious man.

Marcus Tullius Cicero was a Roman philosopher and a statesman. He was Rome's greatest orator.

Machiavelli (1469–1527)

Niccolo Machiavelli, one of the most brilliant intellects of the Italian Renaissance, was born in Florence. His most famous and influential work was called *The Prince*. The book remains a most vivid and suggestive picture of political conditions in the Italy of the Renaissance. One scholar writes, "Of all Machiavelli's writings *The Prince* is the most famous, and deservedly, for it is the most characteristic. Few subjects of literary discussion have occasioned more controversy than the purpose of this celebrated book. Some have beheld in it a manual for tyrants, like the memoirs of Tiberius, so diligently perused by Domitian; others have regarded it as a refined irony upon tyranny, on the sarcastic plan of Swift's Directions to Servants, if so

Statue of Francesco Petrarca in Uffizi Alley in Florence, Italy.

FRANCESCO PETRARCA

humble an analogy be permissible. From various points of view it might alternately pass for either, but its purpose s accurately conveyed by neither interpretation. Machiavelli was a sincere though too supple a republican, and by no means desired the universal prevalence of tyranny throughout Italy. . . . His aim probably was to show how to build up a principality capable of expelling the foreigner and restoring the independence of Italy. But this intention could not be safely expressed, and hence his work seems repulsive, because the reason of state which he propounds as an apology for infringing the moral code appears not patriotic, but purely selfish. . . . With all his faults and oversights, nothing can deprive Machiavelli of the glory of having been the modern Aristotle in politics, the first, or at least the first considerable writer who derived a practical philosophy from history, and exalted statecraft into science."

A Passage from *The Prince* by Niccolo Machiavelli:

Everyone understands how praiseworthy it is in a Prince to keep faith, and to live uprightly and not craftily. Nevertheless, we see from what has taken place in our own days that Princes who have set little store by their word, but have known how to overreach men by their cunning, have accomplished great things, and in the end got the better of those who trusted to honest dealing. Be it known, then, that there are two ways of contending, one in accordance with the laws, the other by force; the first of which is proper to men, the second to beasts. But since the first method is often ineffectual, it becomes necessary to resort to the second. A Prince should, therefore, understand how to use well both the man and the beast. And this lesson has been covertly taught by the ancient writers, who relate how Achilles and many others of these old Princes were given over to be brought up and trained by Chiron the Centaur; since the only meaning of their having for instructor one who was half man and half beast is, that it is necessary for a Prince to know how to use both natures, and that the one without the other

has no stability. But since a Prince should know how to use the beast's nature wisely, he ought of beasts to choose both the lion and the fox; for the lion cannot guard himself from the toils, or the fox from wolves. He must therefore be a fox to discern toils, and a lion to drive off wolves. To rely wholly on the lion is unwise; and for this reason a prudent Prince neither can nor ought to keep his word when to keep it is hurtful to him and the causes which led him to pledge it are removed. If all men were good, this would not be good advice, but since they are dishonest and do not keep faith with you, you in return, need not keep faith with them; and no prince was ever at a loss for plausible reasons to cloak a breach of faith. Of this numberless recent instances could be given, and it might be shown how many solemn treaties and engagements have been rendered inoperative and idle through want of faith in Princes, and that he who was best known to play the fox has had the best success.

Assignment

A. What is Petrarch's point in writing to the dead Roman poet Cicero?

B. What advice does Machiavelli give potential rulers?

Statue of Niccolò Macchiavelli (Serie "the Great Florentines") by Lorenzo Bartolini, Uffizi gallery, Florence, Italy. Photo by Jebulon, 2011 (CC0 1.0).

NICCOLÒ MACCHIAVELLI

The Gothic styled Basilica of Saint Mary of the Flower
(the Duomo) is the cathedral church of Florence, Italy.
Construction began in 1296 and was completed in 1436.

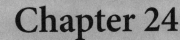
THE REFORMATION

First Thoughts . . .

In the middle of the 16th century, a Roman Catholic priest named Martin Luther became greatly distressed as he read in Paul's letter to the Roman Christians: "For in it [the gospel], the righteousness of God is revealed from faith for faith, as it is written, 'The righteous shall live by faith'" (Rom. 1:17). Luther wrote, "I greatly longed to understand Paul's Epistle to the Romans and nothing stood in the way but that one expression, 'the righteousness of God,' because I took it to mean that righteousness whereby God is just and deals justly in punishing the unjust. My situation was that, although an impeccable monk, I stood before God as a sinner troubled in conscience, and I had no confidence that my merit would assuage Him. Therefore I did not love a just angry God, but rather hated and murmured against Him. Yet I clung to the dear Paul and had a great yearning to know what he meant." It was from this prayerful beginning that a movement aimed at reforming the Roman Catholic Church began. It eventually culminated in the establishment of Protestantism, which spread all over the world and changed history forever.

Chapter Learning Objectives . . .

In chapter 24, we will begin with an overview of the Protestant Reformation. Next, we will examine the Zinzendorf 100-year prayer revival and its impact on history. Then, we will look at the Roman Catholic response to the Protestant Reformation. We will end by looking at theories developed by Max Weber, who argued that the Protestant Reformation was a seminal event in world cultural history.

As a result of this chapter you should be able to:

1. Analyze Martin Luther's influence on the Reformation.
2. Consider the importance of the printing press on the Reformation.
3. Discuss the power of prayer and its impact on history.
4. Evaluate whether the Protestant Reformation was necessary.
5. Test and weigh the veracity of the theories of Max Weber.
6. Synthesize the causes of the Reformation into a succinct theory.

THE PROTESTANT REFORMATION

The Protestant Reformation was one of the most important and radical social, political, and religious movements in all of world history. On the surface, this 16th-century religious revolution in the Christian church ended the ecclesiastical supremacy of the pope in Western Christendom and resulted in the establishment of Protestantism. But of course it did much more.

With the Renaissance that preceded and the French Revolution that followed, the Reformation put another nail into the coffin of the medieval way of life in Western Europe. As historian Max Weber argued, the Reformation initiated the beginning of modern history.

The key initial figure in the Reformation was Martin Luther, who started the Reformation on October 31, 1517, when he published his 95 Theses and then nailed them to the door of Castle Church in Wittenberg, Germany. In these theses (short polemics against perceived injustices) he opposed the manner in which indulgences (writs of forgiveness) were being sold in order to raise money for the building of Saint Peter's Cathedral in Rome.

It would be wrong to attribute the breakup of the medieval world and its consequent course solely to the genius of Luther, but surely he was a primary motivator. Historian John Dillinger writes, "The corporate world of Christendom, once exhibited in church, state, and culture alike, was being undermined as the result of a variety of factors. Such divergent movements as mysticism, with its emphasis upon the direct encounter with the divine, and nominalism, with its stress upon the concrete and discrete, inadvertently challenged the hierarchical and corporate claims of the Church.

The Martin Luther window at St. Matthew's Lutheran Church in Charleston, South Carolina. Photo by Cadetgray (CC BY-SA 3.0).

Humanists, with the enthusiasm of their new discoveries in the field of classical learning, favored the culture of Greece and Rome rather than the studied subtleties of the scholastic theologians. The empire itself was beset with the self-consciousness of rising ethnic and national feelings. The consequence was that the demands of the empire frequently had to be adjusted to the aggressive demands of such new groups, which, in German lands, were usually represented by princes and nobles. In the social context, the feudal system was challenged by the rise of a middle class interested in trade and commerce. Small towns became urban centers, and there was a new feeling of independence from the feudal lords. Peasants dissatisfied with their lot were ready to revolt, and did so in the period of the Reformation. The travels of Columbus and Magellan, the new ideas of Copernicus, and above all the spread of information through the printing press exposed new horizons of knowledge not heretofore available." Historian Thomas Lindsay writes, "The long struggle between the Medieval Church and the Medieval Empire, between the priest and the warrior, ended, in the earlier half of the thirteenth century, in the overthrow of the Hohenstaufens, and left the Papacy sole inheritor of the claim of ancient Rome to be sovereign of the civilized world. Strong and masterful Popes had for centuries insisted on exercising powers which, they asserted, belonged to them as the successors of St. Peter and the representatives of Christ upon earth." The Reformation seriously challenged that authority.

After the Revival of the Holy Roman Empire and the Roman Catholic Church by **Charlemagne**, popes and emperors fought for supremacy. Ultimately the Church won. There were, however, hard feelings. In German kingdoms in particular there was bitterness over the Pope's heavy hand.

Germany was not the only place.

The 14th-century English reformer John Wycliffe boldly—some thought foolishly—attacked the papacy itself, criticized indulgences, ridiculed pilgrimages, questioned the deification of saints, and vilified immoral priests. His greatest crime, according to the Church, was that he translated the Bible into English. The Roman Catholic Church leaders felt that neither this man, nor any man, should translate the Bible from its original Latin version (which after all had been translated from Greek). Some felt that the Church had a low view of Scripture; on the contrary, the Church had a high view of Scripture and did not wish to have men like Wycliffe translate it and present it to common people.

Wycliffe's teachings spread to the European continent, where they were embraced by reformer John Huss, who eventually was martyred. For this and other reasons—like the discontent of German princes—the continent was ripe for revolution when Luther nailed his 95 Theses on the Wittenberg door.

The Church reacted quickly. Authorities invited Luther to repent and to submit to church authority, but Luther only became bolder in his criticisms. Luther privatized faith and suggested that a believer could, and should, have a relationship with Christ outside of anything else—namely the Church. Luther suggested that Christians were saved by grace through faith—not by Church ordinances or other external practices. Luther, and later John Calvin, strongly argued for the concept of "the priesthood of all believers." This bold assertion argued that believers could experience expiation of their sins by direct confession rather than confession through a priest. Luther was excommunicated.

Life of Martin Luther and the heroes of the Reformation. Print shows Luther burning papal bill of excommunication, with vignettes from Luther's life and portraits of Huss, Savonarola, Wycliffe, Cruciger, Melanchton, Bugenhagen, Gustav Adolf, & Bernhard, duke of Saxe-Weimar by H. Breul, c1874 (PD-US).

At this point, Luther and his followers formally broke with the Church. In an effort at damage control, Holy Roman emperor Charles V, himself a pious Roman Catholic, assembled a group in 1521 at the Diet of Worms, and ordered Luther to repent. Luther refused again, and a warrant for his arrest was issued. For almost a year he remained in hiding, writing pamphlets expounding his principles and translating the New Testament into German. Although his writings were illegal, they were openly sold and were powerful instruments in turning the great German cities into centers of Lutheranism.

The reform movement was immensely popular, and when Luther left retirement, he returned to his home at Wittenberg as a revolutionary leader. Germany was deeply divided, and open warfare between Catholics and early Protestants broke out in 1524 with the beginning of the **Peasants' War**.

Luther's example inspired others.

Among those most glad to receive and propagate Luther's message was a young Englishman, William Tyndale, who, until he was martyred in 1536, fervently embraced Luther's theology. The early reform movement in Switzerland, contemporaneous with the Reformation in Germany, was led by the Swiss pastor Huldreich Zwingli.

In the generation after Luther and Zwingli, the dominant figure of the Reformation was John Calvin, a persecuted French scholar who in 1536 fled to Geneva, Switzerland. Calvin put meat on the bones of the Reformation by insisting on further reforms, including the enforcement of a strict moral discipline in the community by the pastors and members of the church. Calvin's church government was democratic and ultimately became the template of several secular democracies, including the United States of America.

Calvin, in kind, influenced other men. For example, John Knox, an ardent disciple of Calvin, established Calvinism as the national religion of Scotland.

Many large and small denominations formed during the Reformation. Besides the three great churches—Lutheran, Reformed, and Anglican—a smaller group, the Anabaptists, found many followers throughout Europe, particularly in Germany during the Reformation. Ironically, they were persecuted by everybody—Catholics, Lutherans, Zwinglians, and other Protestants—and many of them were put to death.

During the 16th and 17th centuries, the Roman Catholic Church tried to answer the Reformation with its own Counter-Reformation, but it was too little, too late. The world had already been forever changed.

Portrait of Young John Calvin. Artist unknown, c16th century (PD-US).

The Protestant Reformation was far more than a religious upheaval. The power and wealth lost by the feudal nobility and the Roman Catholic hierarchy passed to the middle classes and to new nationalistic monarchical rulers. Various regions of Europe gained political independence. The Protestant emphasis on personal responsibility encouraged participatory democracy. With emphasis on the priesthood of all believers and the primacy of the Word of God, universal literacy was encouraged.

Assignment

A. Without a doubt Martin Luther was a mighty, anointed man of God. We Christians all owe him a debt of gratitude. However, Luther had a weak spot: he was avowedly anti-Semitic. Luther writes, "Therefore be on your guard against the Jews, knowing that wherever they have their synagogues, nothing is found but a den of devils in which sheer self-glory, conceit, lies, blasphemy, and defaming of God and men are practiced most maliciously and veheming his eyes on them." While many pious Christians shared Luther's views, it surely is grievous that this great man wrote such things. Why? How should Christians react to statements like this?

B. Without the printing press, John Dillinger argues, Luther would have been just another little-known Christian martyr. Why do you agree or disagree?

NIKOLAUS VON ZINZENDORF

Nearly two centuries after Luther posted his 95 Theses, Protestantism had lost some of its fervor. As is often the case with religious revivals, spiritual enlightenment had been mitigated by exigencies of maintaining a resulting institution. Martin Luther was on fire; it was hard to maintain that fervor in the Lutheran Church. Now, onto the world stage entered Count Nikolaus von Zinzendorf, arguably the first "Jesus freak" of the modern age.

A wealthy Austrian noble, Zinzendorf was attracted to Christian piety, religious disciplines that emphasized prayer and sacrifice. He used his wealth to buy an estate that became a refuge to persecuted Protestants, especially the **Moravians**. Ten Moravian Protestants arrived before December and founded a settlement on the count's land. They named it Herrnhut—"the Lord's watch."

Zinzendorf preaching to people of Many Nations. Artist and date unknown (PD-US).

The community grew. In 1727 many in the community covenanted together of their own accord to meet often to pour out their hearts in prayer and hymns. The Holy Spirit was poured out on them all. Their prayers were answered in ways far beyond anyone's expectations. Many of them decided to set aside certain times for continued earnest prayer. Twenty-four men and 24 women covenanted together to continue praying in intervals of one hour each, day and night, each hour allocated by lots to different people. On August 27, this new regulation began. Others joined the intercessors and the number involved increased to 77. They all carefully observed the hour which had been appointed for them. The intercessors had a weekly meeting where prayer needs were given to them. The children, also touched powerfully by God, began a similar plan among themselves. Those who heard their infant supplications were deeply moved. The children's prayers and supplications had a powerful effect on the whole community.

That prayer meeting beginning in 1727 went on for 100 years. It was unique at that time. Known as the Hourly Intercession, it involved relays of men and women in prayer without ceasing made to God. More than one hundred missionaries left that village community in the next 25 years, all constantly supported in prayer (*Christian History* Magazine).

Assignment

Discuss an incident in your own life where your own prayers, or the prayers of others, changed your life.

THE CATHOLIC COUNTER-REFORMATION

Many Catholics shared the concerns of the Protestant reformers but were unwilling to abandon the Roman Catholic Church. The Catholic Reformation was a counter-force to nascent Protestantism. In fact, reform within the Catholic Church had started before Luther nailed his 95 Theses to the Wittenberg Door.

Catholic reformers, like Erasmus, knew that 15th-century society was changing. The Renaissance taught people to question and challenge authority, but the Catholic Church's hierarchy remained generally unresponsive.

St. Thomas Aquinas tried, through his published work *Summa Theologic*, to reform the Church by calling it back to a fusion of rationalism and theology.

Also, Catholics had their own pietistic priests. Master Eckhardt and Thomas à Kempis, for instance, both invited the Church to embrace the spiritual disciplines.

Between 1520 and 1530, there was a lot of common ground between Protestants and Catholics, but the emphasis was placed on their differences rather than their similarities. By 1550, the gap was unbridgeable, and as it widened, the policy of the Catholic Church was to become more aggressive. A new phase—the Counter-Reformation—began.

The Counter-Reformation denotes the period of Catholic revival from the **Council of Trent** (1545–1563) to the end of the **Thirty Years' War** in 1648. The Counter-Reformation was a comprehensive effort, composed of several major reforms. All these reforms encouraged new spiritual movements focusing on the devotional life and a personal relationship with Christ, including the Spanish mystics and the French school of spirituality (i.e., Jesuits).

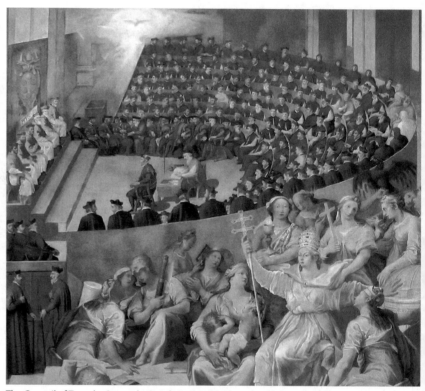

The Council of Trent by Pasquale Cati da Iesi, 1588. Photo by Anthony M., 2005 (CC BY 2.0).

Assignment

Was the Protestant Reformation necessary? Why or why not?

HISTORICAL ESSAY: MAX WEBER

In his seminal work *The Protestant Ethic and the Spirit of Capitalism*, Max Weber (below) argued that capitalism developed in the West because of the predominance of Protestantism. Weber reminded his community that Protestantism—not Catholicism—dominated the governments and culture of Western Europe during the times in which modern culture developed. The notion that God was pleased with hard work and frugal living assured a healthy maturation of society in a time when dislocation and poverty could have short-circuited the development of modernity. Weber wrote, "The emancipation from economic traditionalism appears, no doubt, to be a factor which would greatly strengthen the tendency to doubt the sanctity of the religious tradition, as of all traditional authorities. But it is necessary to note, what has often been forgotten, that the Reformation meant not the elimination of the Church's control over everyday life, but rather the substitution of a new form of control for the previous one. The Puritans, for instance, were hardly antinomian! They were intolerant of other religions and world views.

Passage from *The Protestant Ethic and the Spirit of Capitalism* by Max Weber:

Protestantism repudiated control which was very lax, at that time scarcely perceptible in practice, and hardly more than formal, in favor of a regulation of the whole of conduct which, penetrating to all departments of private and public life, was infinitely burdensome and earnestly enforced. The rule of the Catholic Church, 'punishing the heretic, but indulgent to the sinner', as it was in the past even more than today, is now tolerated by peoples of thoroughly modern economic character, and was borne by the richest and economically most advanced peoples on earth at about the turn of the fifteenth century. The rule of Calvinism, on the other hand, as it was enforced in the sixteenth century in Geneva and in Scotland, at the turn of the sixteenth and seventeenth centuries in large parts of the Netherlands, in the seventeenth in New England, and for a time in England itself, would be for us the most absolutely unbearable form of ecclesiastical control of the individual which could possibly exist. That was exactly what large numbers of the old commercial aristocracy of those times, in Geneva as well as in Holland and England, felt about it. And what the reformers complained of in those areas of high economic development was not too much supervision of life on the part of the Church, but too little. Now how does it happen that at that time those countries which were most advanced economically, and within them the rising citizen middle classes, not only failed to resist this unexampled tyranny of Puritanism, but even developed a heroism in its defense? For citizen classes as such have seldom before and never since displayed heroism. It was "the last of our heroisms", as Carlyle, not without reason, has said.

Assignment

Agree or disagree with Weber's statement and defend your argument.

Statue of Martin Luther, Wittenberg, Germany

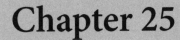

Chapter 25

THE FRENCH REVOLUTION

First Thoughts . . .

Less than a decade after the American Revolution, the French Revolution began. The French Revolution of 1789 began the Modern Era. In a sequence of upheavals, it saw the downfall of King Louis XVI, the rise of Robespierre, and the Reign of Terror, during which thousands were guillotined for political differences. Revolutionaries saw the Catholic Church as the enemy and promoted in its place a Cult of Reason. The Revolution emerged in part from the rationalism of the Enlightenment, which distrusted all established institutions. It inspired fear in European monarchs and aristocrats as well as conservative intellectuals like Edmund Burke in Britain, who mobilized his pen to fight the Revolution.

Chapter Learning Objectives . . .

In chapter 25 we will visit Dr. Guillotin's macabre creation. We will understand the causes and results of the French Revolution. Rarely are philosophers history makers, but in this chapter, we will visit: Immanuel Kant. Next, we will visit several other philosophers and evaluate the veracity of their world views. Finally, we will look more closely at the bloody excesses of the French Revolution and explore why these occurred.

As a result of this chapter you should be able to:

1. Analyze the causes and results of the French Revolution.
2. Discuss why bloody excesses occurred in the French Revolution.
3. Evaluate the impact of Immanuel Kant on world history.
4. Judge the world views of several 18th- and 19th-century philosophers.

BACKGROUND

France, on the eve of the French Revolution, was ruled by an absolute monarchy in the vein of an oriental despot. That in itself was intolerable in Western Europe, but it might be tolerated it things were going well in France. But they most assuredly were not. In fact, the whole country was approaching bankruptcy.

This had not always been the case. France had once been the richest and most powerful nation in Europe. Louis XIV (1643–1715) had been the envy of all other rulers in Europe. During his reign he had centralized the civil service, stimulated trade and industry, and moved his country into the industrial revolution.

Louis XIV and his predecessors squandered French resources in a long list of costly wars. Louis XIV and his son Louis XV (1715–1774) and grandson Louis XVI (1774–1793) had all fought wars that gained little but cost a great deal in men and material. France had suffered defeat in the Seven Years' War against Britain (1756–1763). At the same time, the French army, once feared by the whole Western Hemisphere, was crushed by the Germans. Even France's victories turned out to be defeats. The American Revolution was a victory for the Americans and a costly mistake for France. France paid much for little gain. Then there were the French monarchs—self-indulgent, wimpy kings who did not have the backbone of a Henry VIII or the vision of an Elizabeth I. Louis XVI was a particularly poor choice for a king. He had virtually no tact, no self-control, and absurd visions of grandeur. Louis XVI's wife, Marie Antoinette, exacerbated the problem even more. Her lavish spending represented all that was wrong with the French aristocracy.

On the eve of revolution, all sectors of French society had reason to be unhappy: The nobles wanted more power, the growing middle class needed tax relief, and the peasants needed almost everything.

France in 1789 had three classes, or estates. The majority of the population, called the Third Estate, was made up of the lower-middle-class store owners, day workers, and country peasants.

Portrait of Louis XVI by Antoine-François Callet, 1788 (PD-US).

The Second Estate—the nobility—was much smaller. It numbered a half million, with most of the nobility of unimportant rank. The First Estate comprised the clergy. The higher clergy were quite wealthy and powerful. The other priests lived among the poor.

The First Estate enjoyed all the privileges of patronage. They were at the top of the food chain. Woe to the Third Estate! The first two estates enjoyed privileges on the back of the Third Estate. Most galling of all, especially to the growing middle class, was that not only were the members of the First Estate—the richest of all—exempt from paying taxes, but, by virtue of their rank, whether they were competent or not, they were also the only members of society who could hold positions of importance.

Negative things powered the Revolution engine, but new and revolutionary ideas were entering the picture. Revolutionary thinkers such as Voltaire and Rousseau offered a new path. Seeing their American allies overcoming tyranny, they asked, "Why shouldn't France do the same?" They challenged the absolute right to rule, and presented ideas of equal rights and the abolition of the class system. All of this appealed to the French middle and lower classes, who envisioned a better life for themselves through drastic change.

Voltaire and Rousseau advanced the notion that reason was a higher power than a monarch's claim to divine right; that through the brotherhood of man, equal rights and responsibilities should replace privileges; and that people should be able to support themselves through opportunity and education rather than by inherited titles. The allure of this viewpoint to the working classes was obvious.

The year 1788 was a very bad year for France. It was a time of lost opportunity. The economy collapsed. The king did not take advantage of this opportunity to introduce reforms and gain the support of the people. He could have taxed the nobility and reduced the pressure on the middle class. One side note: At the same time, the Wesleyan Revival that was sweeping England, France experienced no such revival. Revivals often bring upheaval, but can also cause participants to take stock of their relationships with God and one another. France could have used a Wesleyan Revival in 1788.

Marie Antoinette with her children and Madame Élisabeth, when the mob broke into the Tuileries Palace on 20 June 1792. Artist unknown (PD-US).

Under pressure, King Louis summoned the Estates-General (the French version of Parliament). His reluctance to do so, in face of acute hardship, encouraged further criticism of the Ancient Regime and provided further evidence against absolutism in France. He did not know it, but this was the beginning of the end for Louis XVI. On June 17, the Third Estate decided to break the deadlock on the voting issue and to declare themselves the representative body of France (the National Assembly), disregarding the king's opinion. Louis was alarmed at this and decided to close down their assembly hall. Rather than deterring them, this led them to take the infamous Tennis Court Oath. They vowed to continue protesting until they had a constitution.

On that fateful day, absolute rule ended in France and a Constitutional Monarchy (much like the British model) began. Louis XVI was forced to recognize the National Assembly. Overnight, the middle class had taken control of the government. It was not enough and it would not last long. There was to be no peaceful Magna Carta in France. The French Revolution had begun in earnest.

Assignment

Louis XVI did not want to be king. He was not equipped to be a good king. He became king by default. He was a man of Christian morals, yet he was a poor ruler. How could Louis have been expected to live up to the reputation of his father and grandfather, who had ruled France when it was prosperous and strong? Do you think Louis XVI was a victim of circumstances or a major cause of the French Revolution? Why?

"Cleric, Knight, and Workman": the three estates in a French medieval illumination. Artist unknown (PD-US).

FIRES OF REVOLUTION

France's National Assembly had an ugly beginning with the storming of the Bastille on July 14, 1789. This proved to be a significant event in the revolution. The Bastille Prison was regarded as a symbol of political oppression, the place where people were sent when they opposed the Ancient Regime. A huge crowd stormed the bastion, freed its prisoners, and then indiscriminately hanged aristocrats, government officials, and army officers from lampposts. A new phase of the French Revolution—a violent phase—had begun.

In the countryside, peasants then stormed and looted country estates and church monasteries. French aristocrats fled the country in wholesale fashion. Foreign nations were alarmed. The Austrian emperor and the Prussian king threatened war if Louis XVI was harmed.

On July 13, 1789, the Paris Commune (Municipal Council) and the National Guard were formed. They were "mobs" with a chip on their shoulders. They indiscriminately served justice on the guilty and innocent alike. Using fear tactics, they ultimately began to restore order. The military units of the National Guard became responsible to the Municipal Council, and there was one tertiary police force in charge.

Meanwhile, the National Assembly met and all forms of feudalism were abolished. This meant that tenant farmers were not legally bound, as medieval serfs, to their land and to their masters. At least the peasants were satisfied. City dwellers would get their satisfaction later.

On August 26, 1789, the National Assembly issued the **Declaration of the Rights of Men**. This document proclaimed the sovereignty of the people.

In October 1789, the king and his family were taken prisoner. Two years later they tried to escape to Austria, but were captured and returned to Paris. The king lived to see all his power disappear with the **Constitution of 1791**.

Once again, war brought on yet another national crisis.

Portrait of Maximilien de Robespierre. Artist unknown, c1790 (PD-US, PD-Art).

Austria led a coalition to punish France's new revolutionary government. To meet the threat, a small group called the Committee of Public Safety began to rule. It had nine members. They had unlimited power to do anything to save the Republic from internal and external perils. They exercised control over every aspect of French life.

Within the Committee of Public Safety a revolutionary tribunal was also set up. The Revolutionary tribunal, led by the infamous **Maximilien Robespierre**, tried all "enemies of the state" and murdered thousands of citizens. When the

Execution of Louis XVI in what is now the Place de la Concorde, facing the empty pedestal where the statue of his grandfather, Louis XV, had stood by Isidore-Stanislas Helman, Graveur; Antoine-Jean Duclos, Graveur; and Charles Monnet, illustator (PD-US).

danger of war had passed, Robespierre himself was executed. The Convention then abolished the Committee of Public Safety and the Revolutionary Tribunals. Then, almost as an afterthought, King Louis XVI and his wife, Marie Antoinette, were beheaded in 1793.

A group of five men, known as the "Directory," ruled from 1795 to 1799. The period between 1795 and 1799 was marked by attempted coups. However, the Directory was able to continue in government, as it had the backing of the military. A final successful rebellion was led by Napoleon Bonaparte, who joined with three of the Directors in a conspiracy to take control.

Thus began the series of Napoleonic Wars through which Napoleon ultimately became emperor. France had traded one dictator—Louis XVI—for another—Napoleon.

Napoleon gave France what it wanted—a "friendly dictator." He insisted on human rights (his Napoleonic Code became a model for civil law in many countries), but he often enforced them at swords' points.

Assignment

The French Revolution introduced a new type of personality: the self-confident, idealistic revolutionary. Maximilien Robespierre symbolized its extremes: laudable humanist ideology and cold-blooded murder. He not only encouraged the Reign of Terror, he created an ideological basis for its existence. What is most disconcerting about this era, and this man, is that Robespierre was seen by contemporaries as virtuous—a righteous man, bringing the vengeance of the Lord on scoundrels and rascally enemies of the Revolution. What causes a Judeo-Christian society, whose church attendance is almost 100 percent, to execute thousands of people in the name of justice? How can this "Christian" country have leaders like Robespierre?

IMMANUAL KANT

At the heart of the French Revolution was a philosophy developed by German philosopher Immanual Kant. The French Revolution, at its heart, emphasized the subjective—liberty, fraternity, and equality. These are abstract concepts whose reality was rooted in experience (vs. objective cognitive truth such as the Bible).

Kant argued that reality was experience. If one could not experience something with his senses, then it was not real. It was a small step from the absence of consequences in David Hume's theory to the subjectiveness in Kant's. Whereas Descartes argued that there was knowledge that existed before experience (e.g., mathematics), and Hume argued that people could have experience separate from any knowledge, Kant argued that reality was experience. But not everything was experience. Knowledge could not completely step away from experience, but there was some knowledge—called a priori knowledge—that could not be gained by experience. For example, Kant said that "bachelors are unmarried" is an a priori statement because the word "bachelor" means "unmarried male," whether the speaker meant this truth or the hearer experienced this truth. Truth, then, was limited to irreducible human-created structures. Morality and ethics would never be a priori truth. With only a priori knowledge, Kant argued, morality was based on man's ability to act rationally, not on any ipso facto phenomenon. The human mind actively shapes sensations into ideas by selecting and coordinating them according to certain ordering principles, e.g. space and time. Thus, space and time are random principles, because the mind cannot organize sensations without reference to these categories.

Yet human reason gives us no access to the "thing-in-itself": We have access only to our experience of the thing. There is no objective reality, then, in Kantian philosophy.

Assignment

A. Immanuel Kant was identified by some of his Christian contemporaries as being a serious threat to Christianity. Why?

B. Why is Kant's philosophy so popular today?

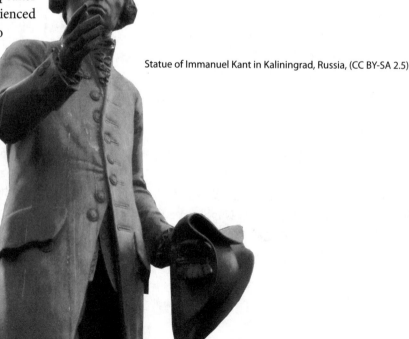

Statue of Immanuel Kant in Kaliningrad, Russia, (CC BY-SA 2.5)

THE WEALTH OF NATIONS

Adam Smith is famous for his book *The Wealth of Nations,* written in 1776, which had a profound influence on modern economics and consequently concepts of individual freedom. Smith laid the intellectual framework for the free market. Smith argued that self-interest guides the most efficient use of resources in a nation's economy, with public welfare coming as a by-product. Called laissez-faire convictions, Smith argued that state and personal efforts to promote social good are ineffectual compared to unbridled market forces.

Passage from chapter five of *The Wealth of Nations* by Adam Smith:

Every man is rich or poor according to the degree in which he can afford to enjoy the necessaries, conveniencies, and amusements of human life. But after the division of labour has once thoroughly taken place, it is but a very small part of these with which a man's own labour can supply him. The far greater part of them he must derive from the labour of other people, and he must be rich or poor according to the quantity of that labour which he can command, or which he can afford to purchase. The value of any commodity, therefore, to the person who possesses it, and who means not to use or consume it himself, but to exchange it for other commodities, is equal to the quantity of labour which it enables him to purchase or command. Labour, therefore, is the real measure of the exchangeable value of all commodities.

The real price of every thing, what every thing really costs to the man who wants to acquire it, is the toil and trouble of acquiring it. What every thing is really worth to the man who has acquired it and who wants to dispose of it, or exchange it for something else, is the toil and trouble which it can save to himself, and which it can impose upon other people. What is bought with money, or with goods, is purchased by labour, as much as what we acquire

Adam Smith by James Tassie, 1787 (PD-US).

by the toil of our own body. That money, or those goods, indeed, save us this toil. They contain the value of a certain quantity of labour, which we exchange for what is supposed at the time to contain the value of an equal quantity. Labour was the first price, the original purchase money that was paid for all things. It was not by gold or by silver, but by labour, that all the wealth of the world was originally purchased; and its value, to those who possess it, and who want to exchange it for some new productions, is precisely equal to the quantity of labour which it can enable them to purchase or command (www.gutenberg.org/).

Assignment

Why was the concept of laissez-faire so important to the development of the modern nation?

Marie-Antoinette with the Rose by Élisabeth Vigée-Lebrun, 1783 (PD-US, PD-Art).

Chapter 26

NATIONALISM

First Thoughts . . .

A "nation-state" was a country whose territory had defined borders and whose principally similar ethnic people were organized by either race or cultural background. Generally in a nation-state, everyone spoke the same language and shared the same set of cultural values. During the period from 1820 to 1871, nation-states achieved mature status in Europe. Nationalism clearly became the basis for the organization of Western civilization. This development not only ended the last vestiges of feudalism, but also set the stage for the replacement of religious wars by national political wars that proved costly and devastating to the Western world.

Chapter Learning Objectives . . .

In chapter 26, we will examine 19th-century Europe and observe the rise of France, Germany, Czechoslovakia, and Italy—nation-states that replaced Bavaria, Bohemia, Alsace-Lorraine, and Burgundy. Next, we will examine the great nationalist revolutions of 1848. We will compare and contrast several competing world views. Finally, we will examine how nationalism and the national state forever changed the political complexion of Europe.

As a result of this chapter you should be able to:

1. Analyze the rise of nationalism in Europe.
2. Evaluate the 1848 revolutions that wracked Europe.
3. Discuss the warring world views that emerged in Europe during this period.
4. Investigate the inevitable rise of Absolutism out of Nationalism.

THE RISE OF NATIONALISM

Nations have been around for a very long time, though they have taken different shapes at different points in history. In the middle of the 19th century they suddenly appeared all over Europe.

What is a nation? One historian defines a nation as "an imagined political community—and imagined as both inherently limited and sovereign. It is imagined because the members of even the smallest nation will never know most of their fellow-members, meet them, or even hear of them, yet in the minds of each lives the image of their communion." Millions of strangers rally around a flag, an idea, and a charismatic leader.

"For the development of nationhood from many different cultures and ethnicities, by far the most important factor is that of an extensively used vernacular literature" (Benedict Anderson). A long struggle against an external threat may also have a unifying, significant effect, as that which occurred in France at the end of the 18th century.

An ethnicity is a group of people with a shared cultural identity and spoken language. Different ethnic groups can exist in one nation, but somehow they must find a way to unify. Outside threats and a common language all conspire to make a people unite as a nation.

Benedict Anderson, in *Imagined Communities*, writes, "A nation is a far more self-conscious community than an ethnic group. Formed from one or more ethnicities, and normally identified by a literature of its own, it possesses or claims the right to political identity and autonomy as a people, together with the control of specific territory, comparable to that of biblical Israel and of other independent entities in a world thought of as one of nation-states."

Often a nation is formed by geographical barriers. The Pyrenees Mountains separate France from Spain, and the Atlantic Ocean separates England from everyone else.

Professor Anderson concludes, "A nation-state is a state which identifies itself in terms of one specific nation whose people are not seen simply as 'subjects' of the sovereign but as a horizontally bonded society to whom the state in a sense belongs. There is thus an identity of character between state and people. In some way the state's sovereignty is inherent within the people, expressive of its historic identity. In it, ideally, there is a basic equivalence between the borders and character of the political unit upon the one hand and a self-conscious cultural community on the other. In most cases this is a dream as much as a reality. Most nation-states in fact include groups of people who do not belong to its core culture or feel themselves to be part of a nation so defined. Nevertheless almost all modern states act on the blind assumption that they are nation-states."

The Bible provides the original model for a nation. The nation of Israel was a people of destiny in a particular geographical area, serving the same God.

In summary, most nations develop on the basis of common ties of religion and language. However, many exceptions exist—among them, the United States.

How did the modern nation arise? The beginnings of modern nationalism started at the end of the Middle Ages when the nation-state had more allure than other social orders. The cultural life of Europe was based on a common inheritance of ideas and attitudes transmitted in the West through Latin and, originally, a common religion, Roman Catholic Christianity. The pope was the head of every European nation. The breakup of feudalism, the growth of competing social and economic systems, and the Reformation conspired to encourage the growth of nations.

A great leap forward for nationalism was the French Revolution and subsequent Napoleonic conquests. France became a uniform and united national territory, with common laws and institutions. French armies spread the new good news of nationalism throughout lands they conquered, which included almost every European country. Universal suffrage and literacy also helped. Although language became a barrier between nations, within a nation it was as binding as glue. A whole set of national symbols, folklore, and holidays arose to stimulate nationalism.

The Revolution of 1848 marked the awakening of various peoples to national consciousness. In that year both the Germans and the Italians originated their movements for unification and for the creation of nation-states. Although the attempts at revolution failed in 1848, the movements gathered strength in subsequent years. After much political agitation and several wars, an Italian kingdom was created in 1861 and a German empire in 1871.

The growth of nationalism in another important area—Central Europe—had a great impact on later history. Peoples living in the Balkan Peninsula desired to break away from the ailing Austro-Hungarian Empire for most of the last part of the 19th century.

One clear result of the nationalistic revolutions of 1848 was the creation of an Italian nation. Previously, Italy's peninsula included several small but powerful city-states (Genoa, Milan, and Naples). On March 17, 1861, the kingdom of Italy was proclaimed, with Victor Emmanuel II as king. Rome and Venice remained outside the kingdom. However, the patriot Garibaldi organized a march on Rome. Fearing foreign intervention, the Italian government reluctantly stopped Garibaldi. France still controlled Rome. In 1866, Italy became the ally of Prussia in the Seven Weeks' War against Austria, and, at the war's end, acquired Venice. In 1870, French defeats in the Franco-Prussian War caused France to withdraw from Rome, finally freeing the Italians to enter the city. In July 1871, Rome became the capital of a united Italy.

France, which was already a nation, was also rocked by the Revolution of 1848.

Giuseppe Garibaldi. Artist unknown, c1861 (PD-US).

Assignment

"Nationalism involves a strong identification of society and the state. Often, it is the belief that an ethnic group has a right to statehood, or that citizenship in a state should be limited to one ethnic group. It can also include the belief that the state is of primary importance, or the belief that one state is naturally superior to all other states. It is also used to describe a movement to establish or protect a homeland (usually an autonomous state) for an ethnic group. In some cases the identification of a national culture is combined with a negative view of other races or cultures. Nationalism is sometimes reactionary, calling for a return to a national past, and sometimes for the expulsion of foreigners. Other forms of nationalism are revolutionary, calling for the establishment of an independent state as a homeland for an ethnic underclass.

Given the above definition, how can Christians, who are first and foremost "citizens of heaven," participate in an earthly national state?

THE REVOLUTION OF 1848

By 1848, many liberal Frenchmen, for whom the Napoleonic days were distant memories, were afraid that they might lose their rights. They joined mobs in the streets of Paris. Ultimately a new constitution was written. The 1848 constitution affirmed the hallowed revolutionary ideals of Liberty, Equality, and Fraternity. The French Second Republic was proclaimed.

Republics were likewise emerging all over Europe. Monarchs still existed but, increasingly, following the British model, they were more symbolic than real leaders. Prime ministers, presidents, and chairmen ruled with a represented body undergirded by a written constitution. Allied to these egalitarian movements were the growing national identities of states.

The same was true all over Europe. Germans, Poles, Italians, and Spaniards all had experienced the heady feeling of belonging not merely to a church or to an ethnic group but to a nation. They liked the feeling. Now Bavarians called themselves German. Burgundians called themselves French. The Flemish were Belgium.

At the same time the desire for natural rights and freedom could and would be sacrificed for nationalistic purposes. For instance, in France, the most egalitarian nation in Europe, Louis Napoleon Bonaparte, nephew of Napoleon I, overwhelmingly defeated the incumbent in a national election. It was not enough for the popular young Napoleon. President Bonaparte overthrew the republic with ease in the violent coup d'état of December 2, 1851. He assumed dictatorial powers and renamed himself Napoleon III. He also extended his term of office to ten years. Despite continued pockets of opposition, clear evidence of widespread popular support encouraged him a year later to convert the Second Republic into the Second Empire. After 1860, Napoleon III began a series of liberal reforms that resulted in a constitutional monarchy in 1870. Nonetheless, a new pattern emerged: When asked to choose between their rights and the nation, citizens uniformly chose the latter.

Bonaparte at the Bridge of Arcole by Antoine-Jean Gros, Palace of Versailles c1801 (PD-US, PD-Art).

What did Europe look like in the middle part of the 19th century?

France, in spite of its energetic domestic scene, was very much a second-rate European power. This was to be confirmed in the Franco-Prussian War of 1871 where the nascent Germany soundly thrashed the French Republic in a short war.

The semblance of a German nation, as a part of the Holy Roman Empire, emerged before the first millennium AD. The first German king of note was Otto I. Elected in 936, Otto combined extraordinary forcefulness, dignity, and military prowess with great diplomatic skill and genuine religious faith. Germany was several independent German states, including Hanover, Prussia, and Bavaria, among others.

The warrior King Frederick I, known as Frederick Barbarossa, ruled from 1152 to 1190. Regarding himself as the successor of Charlemagne, he spent most of his reign trying to restore imperial glory to Germany and Italy. He almost succeeded.

The Reformation, some scholars argue, created Germany. Germany embraced Protestantism, which became the unifying factor in many divergent areas. Before long, Prussia dominated other German states. The Hohenzollern family controlled the kingdom of Prussia. Unlike the English, the Hohenzollerns enjoyed uncontested male heirs from 1640 to 1786. This brought great stability to Germany. Frederick William of Prussia, known as the Great Elector, reigned from 1640 to 1688. His grandson Frederick the Great was a Renaissance warrior.

However, it was not until the Napoleonic Wars that Germany started to unite. Napoleon I's aggression had the unintended effect of pushing German states together and arousing a sense of German national identity. This nation would defeat France half a century after the Battle of Waterloo.

To a much lesser degree than in France, Germany experienced national revolts in 1848. The only thing the revolts accomplished was the strengthening of the monarchy.

At that point, a bigger-than-life individual—**Otto von Bismarck**—entered German history. Bismarck remained one of the most significant political figures of modern Germany. He contributed significantly to the creation and shaping of the modern German state as Prussian minister, president, and imperial chancellor from 1862 to 1890.

Bismarck's view of Germany was based on territory rather than on language and culture. He wanted to establish a Reich, or Greater Germany. He succeeded so well that no one could deny that Germany was a unified state when it defeated France in 1871.

The Franco-Prussian War was a truly modern, nationalistic war that would eventually plague the 20th century. In the Franco-Prussian War of 1870–1871, France was defeated by the German states under the leadership of Prussia. The underlying causes of the conflict were the determination of Bismarck to unify Germany under Prussian control and, as a step toward this goal, to eliminate French influence in Europe. However, Napoleon III, emperor of France from 1852 to 1870, wanted a war by which he could regain the

Frederic I Barbarossa and his sons King Henry VI and Duke Frederick VI. Medieval illumination from the Chronic of the Guelphs, Weingarten Abbey, c1179 (PD-US, PD-Art).

prestige lost as a result of defeats suffered at the hands of Prussia in the Austro-Prussian War of 1866. In addition, the military strength of Prussia, as revealed in the war with Austria, constituted a threat to French dominance on the continent of Europe. France lost this war completely. It was a humiliating defeat.

But France and Prussia were not the only European powers. Like a sleeping bear, Russia was awakening and reaching for empire. Russia was looking more and more to the West for its identity. Russia was the largest nation on earth and in many ways the most backward.

Russia had experienced stable leadership for three centuries under the Romanovs. During Romanov rule, the dominant theme was the state's determination that Russia become and remain a great European power. By the mid-18th century, Russia was militarily and economically powerful, but at the cost of despotic rule. Russians had virtually no rights and lived in a feudalistic regime.

Franz Joseph I of Austria by I. Ranzi, 1855 (CC BY 3.0).

In the early 19th century, France's emperor, Napoleon I, invaded Russia and was defeated. Russia was then Europe's most powerful empire. It could not remain that way long. Other European countries became more powerful as their economies experienced the vast changes of the Industrial Revolution, which began in England and took a number of generations to spread across Europe. The Industrial Revolution did not reach Russia until the late 19th and early 20th centuries—100 years after it had begun in England.

The Crimean War (1853–1856), in which Russia was defeated by France and Britain, showed that smaller industrialized countries could whip mighty Russia. The Nationalist revolutions of 1848 did not touch Russia at all.

As Prussia's fate was tied to the Hohenzollern family, Austria's fate was closely linked to the Hapsburgs, who provided stable leadership for five centuries. By the early 19th century, the Hapsburgs were the most stable royal family in Europe, and they were firmly in control of a joint Austrian-Hungarian Empire.

In March 1848, a revolutionary movement arose among the many people groups in Austria. Germans, Magyars, Slavs, Italians, and Serbs turned against the Hapsburg regime. A constitutional monarchy satisfied the rebels, and Franz Joseph I assumed leadership. Eventually, however, Joseph removed all liberal reforms except the dissolution of serfdom.

Nationalism remained in Austria, however, and would prove to be its undoing because it was one cause of World War I. In the 1850s Austria faced the problems of protecting the empire from nationalism encouraged by its neighbors. Russia, for instance, aided Russian ethnic groups in Austria-Hungary. Austria-Hungary carved out a tenuous kingdom in central Europe. Franz Joseph, realizing that he needed a strong ally to maintain his nation, turned to Germany. Germany and Austria began a 75-year alliance that made the two nations practically inseparable but ultimately destroyed both nations during World War I.

In summary, nationalism and democratic movements were often emerging in Europe hand in hand. When they were at odds, though, inevitably Europeans chose their nation before their rights.

Assignment

A. The Revolution of 1848 was an international event and, apart from the world wars, the only such event in the West. But it did not affect all of Europe. At least two states, England and Russia, were unaffected. What made these two countries different from the others?

B. The Manifesto of the Communist Party was drafted as its party program by Karl Marx and Frederick Engels in Brussels at the order of the second congress of the League of Communists December 2–8, 1847. In this document, Marx and Engels argued that European nations were dominated by selfish rulers called bourgeois who dominated the workers or proletariat. In their opinion, only revolution would make things right. To many Europeans the revolutions of 1848 appeared to confirm many of the conclusions offered in the Manifesto. Why?

C. By 1848 there was a definite propensity in Europe to solve problems through revolutions. Memories of the French Revolution caused people to look again to the mass rally to change governments. Revolutions in 1848 spoke its language, used its symbols, idealized its heroes, and even copied its institutions. However, as Karl Marx argued: "The 1848 Revolution could do no better than parody either 1789, or the revolutionary tradition from 1793 to 1795." In what ways were the European revolutions of 1848 different from the French Revolution?

HEGEL, MARX AND PROUDHON

G. W. F. Hegel (1770–1831)

Hegel held that truth had no application if there were not opposites warring for its reality. Although he never held a political office and was not even alive during the revolutions of 1848, he probably did more to stimulate revolution than any other living person. Hegel, a decidedly modern philosopher, vigorously attacked everything scientific. He believed strongly in the dialectic and in polarity. For instance, if there was no evil, there was no good. There could be no good in the universe if there was no evil in the same universe. From the struggle between these polarities, or in the dialectic, there emerged truth. Hegel began with a thesis (a position put forward for argument). Opposed to this was a contradictory statement or antithesis. Out of their opposition came a synthesis that embraced both. Since the truth lay only in the whole system, this first synthesis was not yet the truth of the matter, but became a new thesis, with its corresponding antithesis and synthesis, and so on. Truth, then, was not absolute and was always open to interpretation. Truth lay in the "search" of the "system."

Excerpt from Hegel:

> The essence of the modern state is that the universal be bound up with the complete freedom of its particular members and with private well-being, that thus the interests of family and civil society must concentrate themselves on the state. It is only when both these moments subsist in their strength that the state can be regarded as articulated and genuinely organized.

Karl Marx (1818–1883)

One disciple of G. W. F. Hegel was Karl Marx. Marx, the father of Communism, applied Hegelian theory to society. The proletariat fought the bourgeoisie, and in this struggle the proletariat was cleansed and prepared for its ultimate call to rule. To the deterministic, atheistic Marx, Christianity

G. W. F. Hegel by Sophus Williams, 1884 (PD-US)..

was a fairy tale created to placate weak people.

Passage from Karl Marx:

> The history of all hitherto existing society is the history of class struggles. Freeman and slave, patrician and plebeian, lord and serf, guild-master and journeyman, in a word, oppressor and oppressed, stood in constant opposition to one another, carried on an uninterrupted, now hidden, now open fight, a fight that each time ended, either in a

revolutionary reconstitution of society at large, or in the common ruin of the contending classes. In the earlier epochs of history, we find almost everywhere a complicated arrangement of society into various orders, a manifold gradation of social rank. In ancient Rome we have patricians, knights, plebeians, slaves; in the Middle Ages, feudal lords, vassals, guild-masters, journeymen, apprentices, serfs; in almost all of these classes, again, subordinate gradations. The modern bourgeois society that has sprouted from the ruins of feudal society has not done away with class antagonisms. It has but established new classes, new conditions of oppression, new forms of struggle in place of the old ones. Our epoch, the epoch of the bourgeoisie, possesses, however, this distinct feature: it has simplified class antagonisms. Society as a whole is more and more splitting up into two great hostile camps, into two great classes directly facing each other—bourgeoisie and proletariat. From the serfs of the Middle Ages sprang the chartered burghers of the earliest towns. From these burgesses the first elements of the bourgeoisie were developed. The discovery of America, the rounding of the Cape, opened up fresh ground for the rising bourgeoisie. The East-Indian and Chinese markets, the colonization of America, trade with the colonies, the increase in the means of exchange and in commodities generally, gave to commerce, to navigation, to industry, an impulse never before known, and thereby, to the revolutionary element in the tottering feudal society, a rapid development.

Pierre-Joseph Proudhon (1809–1865)

Proudhon instituted the last serious philosophical attempt to undermine the human will as a determining factor in human decision-making.

This anarchist revolutionary, strong on practice, weak on theory, believed that mankind was neither good naturally nor bad because of circumstances. Mankind, to Proudhon, was wrongly made–a dud, so to speak. It was not mankind's fault that it had so much trouble–it was God's fault for making him this way. Therefore, in Proudhon's words, mankind's "destiny is perpetually to re-create his ideal in himself," translates roughly to "Sinner, save yourself." Since mankind could rely on no outside source to ameliorate him, governments, religions, and any other external authority were superfluous.

Pierre-Joseph Proudhon et ses Enfants by Gustave Courbet, 1865 (PD-US, PD-Art).

Quote from Pierre-Joseph Proudhon:

"Justice, as we can see from the example of children and savages, is the last and slowest to grow of all the faculties of the soul; it needs an energetic education in struggle in adversity."

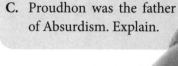

Assignment

A. While Hegel was certainly no Christian, his view of "maturity and truth emerging from a struggle" would be appealing to a Christian. Why?

B. Clearly, Marx was a determinist Hegelian. What is that?

C. Proudhon was the father of Absurdism. Explain.

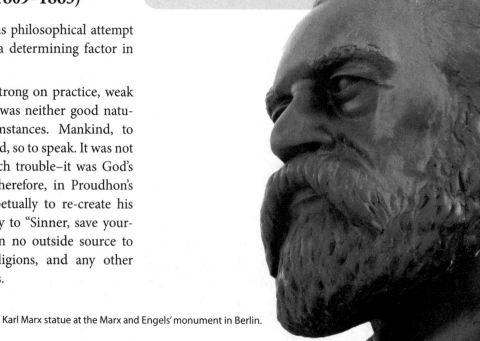

Karl Marx statue at the Marx and Engels' monument in Berlin.

A RUSSIAN ZIONIST MAKES THE CASE FOR A JEWISH HOMELAND

Leo Pinsker (1882)

That hoary problem, subsumed under the Jewish question, today, as ever in the past, provokes discussion. Like the squaring of the circle it remains unsolved, but unlike it, continues to be the everburning question of the day. That is because the problem is not one of mere theoretical interest: it renews and revives in everyday life and presses ever more urgently for solution.

This is the kernel of the problem, as we see it: the Jews comprise a distinctive element among the nations under which they dwell, and as such can neither assimilate nor be readily digested by any nation.

Hence the solution lies in finding a means of so readjusting this exclusive element to the family of nations, that the basis of the Jewish question will be permanently removed. . . .

A fear of the Jewish ghost has passed down the generations and the centuries. First a breeder of prejudice, later in the conjunction with other forces we are about to discuss, it culminated in Judeophobia.

Judeophobia, together with other symbols, superstitions, and idiosyncrasies, has acquired legitimacy among all the peoples of the earth with whom the Jews had intercourse. Judeophobia is a variety of demonopathy with the distinction that it is not peculiar to particular races but is common to the whole of mankind, and that this ghost is not disembodied like other ghosts but partakes of flesh and blood, must endure pain inflicted by the fearful mob who imagines itself endangered.

Judeophobia is a psychic aberration. As a psychic aberration it is hereditary, and as a disease transmitted for two thousand years it is incurable. . . .

The Jews are aliens who can have no representatives, because they have no country. Because they have none, because their home has no boundaries within which they can be entrenched, their misery too is boundless. The general law does not apply to the Jews as true aliens, but there are everywhere laws for the Jews, and if the general law is to apply to them, a special and explicit bylaw is required to confirm it.

Since the Jew is nowhere at home, nowhere regarded as a native, he remains an alien everywhere. That he himself and his ancestors as well are born in the country does [not] alter this fact in the least.

When we are ill-used, robbed, plundered, and dishonored, we dare not defend ourselves, and, worse still, we take

Kindergarten at Rishon-Le'zion, Education in Israel, c1898 (PD-US).

Israeli flag on a windy day.

it almost as a matter of course. When our face is slapped, we soothe our burning cheek with cold water; and when a bloody wound has been inflicted, we apply a bandage. When we are turned out of the house which we ourselves built, we beg humbly for mercy, and when we fail to reach the heart of our oppressor we move on in search of another exile.

If we would have a secure home, give up our endless life of wandering and rise to the dignity of a nation in our own eyes and in the eyes of the world, we must, above all, not dream of restoring ancient Judaea. We must not attach ourselves to the place where our political life was once violently interrupted and destroyed. The goal of our present endeavors must be not the "Holy Land," but a land of our own. We need nothing but a large tract of land for our poor brothers, which shall remain our property and from which no foreign power can expel us. There we shall take with us the most sacred possessions which we have saved from the shipwreck of our former country, the God-idea and the Bible. It is these alone which have made our old fatherland the Holy Land, and not Jerusalem or the Jordan. Perhaps the Holy

Land will again become ours. If so, all the better, but first of all, we must determine—and this is the crucial point—what country is accessible to us, and at the same time adapted to offer the Jews of all lands who must leave their homes a secure and undisputed refuge, capable of productivization (piedmont.k12.ca.us/phs/faculty/).

Assignment

Most people would reject the notion of a "Christian homeland" or a "Buddhist homeland." Are you persuaded that there is a need for a "Jewish homeland"? Why or why not?

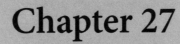

Chapter 27

THE RUSSIAN REVOLUTION

First Thoughts . . .

"The Bolsheviks slavishly imitated speech and gesture of the French Jacobins, just as the Jacobins in turn had imitated the heroes of ancient Rome. But they forgot that the French Revolution itself was drowned in bloody defeat precisely because of its terrorism" (Minister of Justice). The Russian Revolution of 1917 is also called the Bolshevik Revolution or the October Revolution. In 1917 there were actually two revolutions in Russia. One was the February Revolution in which the czar abdicated his throne and the Provisional Government took power. The other was the October Revolution in which the Provisional government was overthrown by the Bolsheviks.

Chapter Learning Objectives . . .

In chapter 27, we will examine closely the origin of the Russian Revolution. We will observe its evolution from a worker's revolt to one of the most heinous political regimes of all time. Finally, we will close by looking at aberrant world views that emerged from and alongside the nihilism that the Russian Revolution became.

As a result of this chapter you should be able to:

1. Judge the effectiveness and success of the Russian Revolution.
2. Evaluate if the violence engendered in the Russian Revolution was necessary.
3. Trace the events of 1917 that precipitated the October Revolution.
4. Assess the impact of Beauvoir's writings on history.
5. Discuss what impact Dewey's philosophy had on American education.

PRE-REVOLUTIONARY RUSSIA

The Russian Revolution began on March 8, 1917. On this day a Provisional Government replaced czarist Russian autocratic rule for the first time in history. No one knew it, but Russia had begun a cataclysmic journey that would not end for more than 80 years.

A more violent version, the second revolution, called the October Revolution, opened on October 24 and 25. It was organized by the Bolshevik (i.e., Communist) Party against the Provisional Government. It permanently changed Russian society and then the whole world.

Some saw the Russian Revolution as a long overdue victory for common people (the proletariat), arguing that it created a grassroots democracy that transformed the workplace and abolished the typical lot of all workers everywhere. Others saw the Russian Revolution as an unmitigated disaster, an orgy of bloodthirsty murder and violence against humanity. Who was correct? You judge.

The underlying causes of the Russian Revolution were complicated and deeply rooted in Russia's history. For centuries, the Romanovs, Russia's royal family, ruled the country with an iron hand. Most of the population lived under severe economic and social stress. During the 19th and early 20th centuries, things became almost unbearable. Finally, various movements aimed at overthrowing the despotic government were undertaken by Russian citizens. Two of these unsuccessful movements were the 1825 revolt against Nicholas I and the revolution of 1905 against Nicholas II, both of which were attempts to establish a constitutional monarchy. Russia's defeat in World War I (1914–1918) only added to popular discontent. In 1917, these events ultimately resulted in the fall of the government and the establishment of the Bolshevik Party.

The Russian masses had had enough. From the time of Peter the Great, the monarchy increasingly used its autocratic bureaucracy to impose its will on Russians in random and often terrorizing ways. On top of that, Western technology and liberal ideas were adopted without accompanying liberal

Russian tsar Nicholas II of Russia with the order of St. Vladimir by Russian painter H. Manizer, 1905 (PD-US, PD-Art).

politics, which frustrated the Russian middle class. Ultimately the Bolshevik Revolution was a middle-class uprising.

The university too became a seat of revolutionary activity. By 1917, the Russian intelligentsia had a philosophy, an empowered middle class, and a declining economy, all of which conspired to bring about revolution.

The reforms by Alexander II brought the emancipation of the serfs and opened the way for industrial development. Industrialization concentrated people in urban centers, where the exploited working classes became receptive audiences for radical ideas. One wonders whether the Russian Revolution could have occurred if Russia had remained a primarily agricultural, backward nation.

By 1903, Russia was divided into several political groups. In a repressive regime like czarist Russia, the growing worker class had no legitimate way to express its will. This resulted in an aborted revolution in 1905 that exacerbated further the tenuous cause of peace in Russia.

This was not enough, however. The immediate cause of the February Revolution of 1917 was the collapse of the czarist regime under the gigantic strain of World War I. The underlying cause was the aforementioned weak economic condition of the country, which made it unable to sustain the war effort against powerful, industrialized Germany. Also, now there was an empowered middle class who wanted change.

Russian manpower was virtually inexhaustible. Russian industry, however, lacked the capacity to arm, equip, and supply the 15 million men who were sent into the war.

They died in droves. Factories were few and insufficiently productive, and the railroad network was inadequate. Repeated mobilizations, moreover, disrupted industrial and agricultural production. Again, this irritated the endangered middle class.

The Russian infrastructure cracked. The food supply decreased and many starved. Basic civil services disappeared. The transportation system was disorganized. Russian casualties were greater than those sustained by any army in any previous war. These reverses were attributed by many to the alleged treachery of Queen Alexandra and her circle, of which the peasant monk Grigory Yefimovich Rasputin was the dominant influence.

Finally the Russian middle class was fed up. When the Duma, the lower house of the Russian parliament, protested against the inefficient conduct of the war and the arbitrary policies of the imperial government, the czar—Emperor Nicholas II—and his ministers simply brushed it aside. This was a fatal mistake.

Grigorij Rasputin. Photographer unknown, c1914 (PD-US).

Late in December a group of aristocrats, led by Prince Feliks Yusupov, assassinated Rasputin in the hope that the emperor would then change his course. The emperor responded by showing favor to Rasputin's followers at court. Talk of a palace revolution in order to avert a greater impending upheaval became widespread, especially among the upper ranks.

Assignment

From its inception, why was the Russian Revolution doomed to fail to meet its goals to empower the masses?

THE REVOLUTION UNFOLDS

Russians felt that they had nowhere to turn except to revolution. On February 23, meetings and demonstrations occurred in Petrograd. On February 25, the strike became general throughout the capital. On February 26, the troops of the Petrograd garrison were called out to suppress the uprising. When the workers and soldiers came face to face in the streets, the troops wavered when ordered to fire, allowing the workers to pass through their lines. Nicholas II dissolved the Duma.

On February 27, the revolution triumphed. Within 24 hours the entire garrison, approximately 150,000 soldiers, joined the revolution, and the united workers and soldiers took control of the capital. By March 1, Russia was ruled by Soviets, or a group of leaders. The military submitted to this new order.

The Petrograd Soviet could have easily assumed complete power, but it did not want to damage the war effort. There was now a vacuum of leadership until Vladimir Ilyich Lenin was secretly escorted by the German government from Switzerland to Russia. Lenin quickly became a powerful force in Russia.

Before the Revolution reached its climax, however, there was still an attempt at a temporary government. On February 27, the provisional committee of the Duma announced that it would handle restoration of order, and on February 28, it placed its commissars (representatives) in charge.

Nicholas abdicated the throne on March 2, 1917. Ultimately the Provisional Government, which could not build a coalition, failed as well, and by October, Russia was ready for the catastrophic Communist Revolution that transformed the country.

Meanwhile, the war in Europe was going badly for Russia too. A final, humiliating peace was made in Brest-Litovsk on March 3, 1918, by which Russia agreed to stop fighting the Central Powers (Germany, Austria-Hungary, Ottoman Empire, and Bulgaria) in World War I (1914–1918). Russia lost Finland, Poland, Estonia, Livonia, Kurland, Lithuania, the Ukraine, and Bessarabia.

Lenin was committed to the assumption of full power by the Soviets, immediate termination of the war, planned and organized seizure of the land by the peasants, and control of industrial production by the workers. Communist (Bolshevik) propaganda argued for "peace, land, and bread." Leon Trotsky (left, PD-US),

The Bolshevik. Boris Mikhailovich Kustodiev, 1920 (PD-US, PD-Art).

arriving from America, helped Lenin push the Revolution forward. Trotsky was the consummate organizer whose gifts moved Lenin's program forward. Lenin could not have brought about a full-scale revolution without Trotsky's help.

Peace would not come, however, without the shedding of much blood. A civil war between the Communists and the Conservatives lasted from 1918 until 1920. It was a hard fight. Lenin began a terror campaign in which suspected anti-Communists, known as Whites, were executed. Although most people were hostile to the Communists, they did not want a return of the monarchy either, so they supported the Bolsheviks.

In 1921, Lenin established the New Economic Policy to strengthen the country, which had been drained by seven years of turmoil and economic decline. On December 30, 1922, the Union of Soviet Socialist Republics (USSR) was formally established when the ethnic territories of the former Russian Empire were united with the Russian Soviet Federated Socialist Republic (RSFSR).

Women's Regiment from Petrograd relaxing, drinking tea, and eating in front of their tents. Photographer unknown, c1918 (PD-US).

Assignment

A. The Bolshevik policy of Red Terror promoted the use of mass execution and fear as a tactic to be implemented ruthlessly. Acts of violence were glorified. Latsis, the head of the infamous Cheka (secret police), wrote, "In civil war there are no courts of law for the enemy. It is a life or death struggle. If you do not kill, you will be killed. Therefore kill, that you may not be killed." The Bolsheviks argued that the terror and violence they practiced was necessary, and that the results justified the means. Were they correct?

B. Trace the events of 1917 that precipitated the October Revolution.

Lenin statue in Kineshma, next to the Volga River. Photo by Ferran Cornellà, 2007 (CC BY-SA 3.0).

ALEXANDER KERENSKY

Alexander Kerensky was a Russian revolutionary leader who headed the Provisional Government from March 1917 until the Bolshevik takeover in October 1917. Kerensky was a Marxist socialist, but a moderate one. In July 1917, after the overthrow of the czar and the establishment of a provisional republican government, Kerensky was appointed provisional prime minister of Russia.

Kerensky recognized the dangers of Communism to both his country and to the world. One of his first acts as prime minister was the suppression of the Bolshevik Party. At the same time, Kerensky was being assailed on the right by Monarchists who sought to bring back the czar. Kerensky's failure to ameliorate the economic and military situation of the country doomed his provisional government to failure. The failure of Kerensky's government, along with the Bolshevik Revolution, put Lenin in power. Kerensky was an honorable man who tried to make the best of a bad situation.

Assignment

Some see the Russian Revolution as a long overdue victory for the masses. They argue that it created a grassroots democracy that transformed the workplace and improved the condition of all workers everywhere. Others see the Russian Revolution as an unmitigated disaster, an orgy of bloodthirsty murder and violence against humanity. Who is correct?

Kerensky at the National Press Club by Harris & Ewing, 1938 (PD-US).

BEAUVOIR AND DEWEY

Simone de Beauvoir (1908–1986)

As Russia went up in flames, Beauvoir and Dewey were staging a revolution of sorts in femininity and education.

Simone de Beauvoir, an advocate of "free love," completely rejected the biblical understanding of marriage, which she saw as an oppressive institution.

Beauvoir was an influential feminist theorist and a key 20th-century spokesperson for Existentialism, a movement in philosophy that emphasized individual freedom, human experience, and subjective choice. She believed that people, especially women, must take control of the meanings that others (e.g., husbands and fathers) placed on their lives.

A passage from a letter by Simone de Beauvoir:

> You see it has never been very easy for me to live, though I am always very happy. I like so much to live and I hate the idea of dying one day. And then I am awfully greedy. I want everything from life, to have many friends and to have loneliness, to work much and write good books, and to travel and enjoy myself, to be selfish and to be unselfish. You see, it is difficult to get all I want. And then when I do not succeed I get mad with anger.

John Dewey (1859–1952)

John Dewey's educational theory completely transformed American education. Dewey argued that the traditional quest to learn a corpus of information based on permanent truths was a futile activity because there was no such truth. There were no immutable structures of reality. Dewey argued in favor of fatalism, which posited that nothing about the world could be logically conclusive. The only reality was experience and then practice. Truth, to Dewey, was merely the theories to which we all subscribed and mutually agreed to call "truth." Dewey's "truth" was a reflection of circumstances and contingencies. Dewey rejected all organized religion (especially Christianity) that purported to know the whole and complete truth. Dewey had no problem with people living in this sort of "fairyland," as long as they did not force their delusions on anyone else.

A passage from *Democracy and Education* by John Dewey:

> We have seen that a community or social group sustains itself through continuous self-renewal, and that this renewal takes place by means of the educational growth of the immature members of the group. By various agencies, unintentional and designed, a society transforms uninitiated and seemingly alien beings into robust trustees of its own resources and ideals. Education is thus a fostering, a nurturing, a cultivating process. All of these words mean that it implies attention to the conditions of growth. We also speak of rearing, raising, bringing up [children]—words which express the difference of level which education aims to cover. Etymologically, the word education means just a process of leading or bringing up. When we have the outcome of the process in mind, we speak of education as shaping, forming, molding activity—that is, a shaping into the standard form of social activity. . . . We are concerned with the general features of the way in which a social group brings up its immature members into its own social form.

Assignment

A. Many people feel that Beauvoir was the mother of feminism. What is the basic flaw of feminism?

B. Why did Dewey's philosophy have such a devastating effect on American education?

Celebrating Russian Revolution, Vladivostok. Photographer and date unknown (PD-US).

Chapter 28

GERMAN HISTORY

First Thoughts . . .

While America was developing its nascent democracy, Germany was flirting with despostism. Many people who grew up in the early to mid-20th century vividly remembered Germany's role in World War I, its enthusiastic acceptance of Nazi rule in 1932, its despicable role in the Holocaust—the systematic extermination of six million Jews before and during World War II. But that is not the Germany we meet in previous centuries. While always dominated politically by militaristic regimes, Germany nonetheless birthed Beethoven, Bach, Schiller, and Goethe. In fact, it was perhaps the most sophisticated nation on the face of the earth in the mid-20th century. How did this humane, civilized country become so inhumane during the mid-1900s? How much responsibility must be borne by the heroic leader Otto von Bismarck? After the defeat of the Weimar experiment, did the catastrophic defeat of Nazi Germany in 1939–1945 finally put the nation back on the track of democratic and humanitarian values?

Chapter Learning Objectives . . .

In chapter 12 we will look at German history briefly and reflect on how such a civilization could produce the Holocaust. Next, we will look at several seminal historical figures and their impact on German history. Finally, we will see how Bismarck created the first unified German nation.

As a result of this chapter you should be able to:

1. Evaluate what is distinctive about the Germanic culture.

2. Discuss the impact of Charlemagne on history.

3. Explain how Frederick the Great hindered German unification.

4. Explain how Bismarck created the first unified German nation.

5. Explain how Germany, the nation that produced Schiller, Goethe, Bach, and Beethoven, could also have produced Hitler, Eichmann, Heydrich, and others who started World War II and created the Holocaust.

THE GERMAN PEOPLE

More than 1,500 years ago, a fierce and fair-haired Celtic people roamed Europe. The ancestors of these fierce Teutonic warriors may have come from Northern Europe. The Romans later called them the Germani. As these Germanic tribes migrated southward and westward, they clashed with the Romans. In 113 BC, German tribes invaded the Mediterranean regions.

The Roman general Gaius Marius defeated them in 102 and 101 BC. The concept of Germany as a distinct region can be traced to Roman commander Julius Caesar, who referred to the unconquered area east of the Rhine as Germania, thus distinguishing it from Gaul (France), which he had conquered. This was a geographic expression, as the area included both Germanic tribes and Celts. The victory of the Germanic tribes in the Battle of the **Teutonburg Forest** (AD 9) prevented annexation by the Roman Empire.

Following the fall of the Roman Empire, the Franks subdued the other West Germanic tribes. When the Frankish Empire was divided among Charlemagne's heirs, Otto I became the first emperor of what historians refer to as the Holy Roman Empire, the medieval German state

In the High Middle Ages, the dukes of the empire gained power at the expense of the emperors, who were elected by the princes and crowned by the pope. The Northern states became Protestant in the early 16th century, while the Southern states remained Catholic. Protestants and Catholics clashed in the **Thirty Years' War** (1618–1648), which left vast areas depopulated. The peace of Westphalia, which ended the war, effectively marked the end of the Holy Roman Empire and the beginning of the modern nation-state system. Unification was followed by an industrial revolution. By 1900, Germany's economy was by far the largest in Europe (and second only to the U.S. in the world). Defeated in the First World War (1914–1918), Germany faced territorial losses and war reparations. Emperor Wilhelm II abdicated and democracy was introduced under the Weimar Republic.

The Ratification of the Treaty of Münster by Gerard ter Borch the Younger, 1648 (PD-US, PD-Art).

The Great Depression, which began in 1929, led to great support of the Nazi party. In 1932, the Nazis, under German dictator Adolf Hitler, gained power. The Nazis imposed a totalitarian regime and followed an expansionist foreign policy that led to World War II. After allied forces defeated Nazi Germany in World War II, the country was divided into democratic West Germany and communist East Germany. In 1990, East Germany was reunited with West Germany. In recent years, Germany has become increasingly integrated into the European Union, notably through its effort to create a unified market and adoption of the euro, a Europe-wide currency, in 2002.

Assignment

Who were the Germans and what distinctives did they bring to Central Europe?

CHARLEMAGNE

Charlemagne was German. He was self-educated but could barely read. But he could speak old Teutonic and literary Latin, and understood Greek.

In 771, 29-year-old Charlemagne became king of the Holy Roman Empire. Two years later he received from Pope Hadrian II an urgent appeal for aid against barbarians who were invading the Papal States. Charlemagne defeated them.

Now the ferocious Charlemagne conducted 18 campaigns (772–804). Once, when he conquered the Saxons, he invited them to repent and to join the Church, but 4,500 were beheaded in one day.

The next great challenge came from Islamic rulers in Spain. Charlemagne confronted them in the passages of the Pyrenees. In one such pass, at Roncesvalles in Navarre (778), a force of Basques pounced down upon the rear guard of the Franks, and slaughtered nearly every man in it; there the noble Hruodland died, who would become three centuries later the hero of France's most famous poem, the Song of Roland.

Charlemagne now governed a kingdom from the Pyrenees to the Alps. How did one man competently govern so vast and varied a realm? He guarded his kingdom with firm military organization and fervent religious zeal. . . He could vision large purposes, and could will the means as well as wish the ends.

He made military service a condition of owning property. Around the king gathered a court of administrative nobles and priests. The sense of public participation in the government was advanced by semiannual assemblies of property owners. The King himself would meet with them and listen to their concerns.

The empire was divided into counties, each governed in spiritual matters by a bishop, and in secular affairs by a count. A local assembly of landholders convened twice or thrice a year in each provincial capital to pass upon the government of the region, and serve as a provincial court of appeals.

Church window in the Dom of Cologne, Germany, depicting Charlemagne. The window, made in the Royal Glass Painting Manufactory in Munich, was installed in 1856.

Charlemagne had the most enlightened government that Europe had known. Never had a monarch so completely ruled the private lives of his subjects. Charlemagne created laws for agriculture, industry, finance, education, and religion as well as for government and morals. Charlemagne struggled to protect free landholding against spreading serfdom, but he only had partial success.

Reading and writing were top priorities of his regime. Concerned by the illiteracy of his time, when hardly any but ecclesiastics could read, and by the lack of education among the lower clergy, he called in foreign scholars to restore the schools of the Empire. He himself studied Latin furiously, but continued to speak German at his court; he compiled a German grammar, and collected specimens of early German poetry.

Today he is regarded not only as the founding father of both French and German monarchies, but also as the father of Europe: His Empire united most of Western Europe for the first time since the Romans, and the Charlemagne renaissance encouraged the formation of a common European identity (Will Durant).

Einhard was a dedicated servant of Charlemagne and his son Louis the Pious; his main work is a biography of Charlemagne. This excerpt is from that biography:

Charles was large and strong, and of lofty stature, though not disproportionately tall (his height is well known to have been seven times the length of his foot); the upper part of his head was round, his eyes very large and animated, nose a little long, hair fair, and face laughing and merry. Thus his appearance was always stately and dignified, whether he was standing or sitting; although his neck was thick and somewhat short, and his belly rather prominent; but the symmetry of the rest of his body concealed these defects. His gait was firm, his whole carriage manly, and his voice clear, but not so strong as his size led one to expect. His health was excellent, except during the four years preceding his death, when he was subject to frequent fevers; at the last he even limped a little with one foot. Even in those years he consulted rather his own inclinations than the advice of physicians, who were almost hateful to him, because they wanted him to give up roasts, to which he was accustomed, and to eat boiled meat instead. In accordance with the national custom, he took frequent exercise on horseback and in the chase, accomplishments in which scarcely any people in the world can equal the Franks. He enjoyed the exhalations from natural warm springs, and often practised swimming, in which he was such an adept that none could surpass him; and hence it was that he built his palace at Aixla-Chapelle, and lived there constantly during his later years until his death. He used not only to invite his sons to his bath, but his nobles and friends, and now and then a troop of his retinue or body guard, so that a hundred or more persons sometimes bathed with him.

He used to wear the national, that is to say, the Frank, dress-next his skin a linen shirt and linen breeches, and above these a tunic fringed with silk; while hose fastened by bands covered his lower limbs, and shoes his feet, and he protected his shoulders and chest in winter by a close-fitting coat of otter or marten skins. Over all he flung a blue cloak, and he always had a sword girt about him, usually one with a gold or silver hilt and belt; he sometimes carried a jeweled sword, but only on great feast-days or at the reception of ambassadors from foreign nations. He despised foreign costumes, however handsome, and never allowed himself to be robed in them, except twice in Rome, when he donned the Roman tunic, chlamys, and shoes; the first time at the request of Pope Hadrian, the second to gratify Leo, Hadrian's successor. On great feast-days he made use of embroidered clothes, and shoes bedecked with precious stones; his cloak was fastened by a golden buckle, and he appeared crowned with a diadem of gold and gems: but on other days his dress varied little from the common dress of the people.

Charles was temperate in eating, and particularly so in drinking, for he abominated drunkenness in anybody, much more in himself and those of his household; but he could not easily abstain from food, and often complained that fasts injured his health. He very rarely gave entertainments, only on great feast-days, and then to large numbers of people. His meals ordinarily consisted of four courses, not counting the roast, which his huntsmen used to bring in on the spit; he was more fond of this than of any other dish. While at table, he listened to reading or music. The subjects of the readings were the stories and deeds of olden time: he was fond, too, of St. Augustine's books, and especially of the one entitled *The City of God*.

Assignment

Summarize Charlemagne's rise to power in the early Middle Ages.

FREDERICK THE GREAT

Frederick the great, king of Prussia, was an enigma. On one hand he was a great Prussian patriot. On the other hand, he was not interested in German unification.

Frederick the Great unwisely placed Bavaria outside the Pan-German alliance with the Austro-Hungarian Empire and in effect doomed Germany to a century-long conflict with its neighbor. Not until the final Prussian victory over Austria in 1866 was the long contest for leadership in Central Europe finally resolved. A central, unified Germany was impossible because of Austro-Hungarian intrigue.

The truth is, Frederick had no appreciation for, and simply did not desire to reign over, a unified German kingdom. He showed no sympathy toward, and no understanding of, the embryonic German nationalism. Partly because of the reign of Frederick the Great, German unification was late to develop.

Frederick was interested in the East. He joined with Russia to determine the fate of Poland. As one historian explained, "For generations to come, this was to be a factor turning Prussia's attention to Eastern Europe and making it less Western in some of its political attitudes than otherwise have been the case. Yet in many ways, Frederick deserved the admiration that later generations, especially in Germany, increasingly felt for him. For all his social and intellectual conservatism he sympathized with the enlightened intellectual currents and political strivings of the age and with their tolerant and humanitarian aspects. Building on the foundations laid by his father, he consolidated a Prussian

ethos of duty, effort, and discipline that, despite some serious negative features, was to become for several generations one of the major political traditions of Europe."

"He who defends everything defends nothing."
—Fredericka

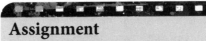

Assignment

How did Frederick the Great hinder German unification?

233

OTTO VON BISMARCK

Bismarck remains one of the most significant political figures of modern Germany.

Bismarck entered politics in 1847 as an ultra-conservative champion of Prussian noble interests. When revolutions swept across Europe and reached Berlin the following year, his first impulse was to arm the peasants of his estate in defense of king and country. At the same time, he was a pragmatist and had an uncanny ability to draw Germans of all persuasions into this camp. . . . For instance, the 1848 revolution was a liberal revolution with cries of liberty and freedom. Bismarck astutely observed that drawing these causes into the cause of nationalism would ultimately benefit all, especially Prussia—the most dominating of German states. Nationalism, to Bismarck, ultimately meant the elevation of his own state, Prussia, to national prominence among all German states in a unified confederation.

As Prime Minister of Prussia from 1862–1890, he oversaw the unification of Germany. He designed the German Empire in 1871, becoming its first Chancellor and dominating its affairs until his dismissal in 1890. His powerful rule gained him the nickname "The Iron Chancellor."

After his death, German nationalists made Bismarck their hero, building hundreds of monuments glorifying the symbol of powerful personal leadership. Historians praised him as a statesman of moderation and balance who was primarily responsible for the unification of the German states into a nation-state. He used balance-of-power diplomacy to keep Europe peaceful in the 1870s and 1880s. He created a new nation with a progressive social policy, a result that went beyond his initial goals as a practitioner of power politics in Prussia. Bismarck, a devout Lutheran who was obedient to his king, promoted government through a strong, well-trained bureaucracy with a hereditary monarchy at the top.

On the other hand, Bismarck's empire of 1871 deliberately restricted democracy, and the anti-Catholic and anti-Socialist legislation that he introduced unsuccessfully in the 1870s and 1880s left a devastating legacy of distrust

Otto Fürst von Bismarck by AD.BRAUN & Cie Dornach, 19th century (PD-US).

and fragmentation in German political culture.

On constitutional issues, Bismarck was a Hegelian, meaning power and its distribution was more important to him than ideology.

"Bismarck's view of Germany was based on territory rather than on language and culture. Central Germany belonged to Germany. Austria and other countries could exist, but only if they were satellites of Germany" (J. H. Hoffman).

Assignment

Why was Bismarck the perfect politician to unify the German states?

Chapter 29

CENTRAL AND SOUTH AMERICAN HISTORY

First Thoughts . . .

Beginning in the 16th century, on another continent, the people and natural resources of South America were repeatedly exploited by foreign conquistadors, first from Spain and later from Portugal. These competing colonial nations claimed the land and resources as their own and divided the land into colonies. European infectious diseases (smallpox, influenza, measles, and typhus)—to which the native populations had no immune resistance—and systems of forced labor decimated the native population. At the same time, Spain was committed to converting their native subjects to Christianity, and was quick to purge any native cultural practices that hindered this goal. Eventually, South America and, later, Central America gained their independence. Today many troubling issues still plague our neighbors to the South!

Chapter Learning Objectives . . .

In chapter 29 we will examine Central and South American native peoples. Then we will discuss European colonization and its impact on the peoples and the lands of Central and South America. Next, we will evaluate why Bolivar and other nationalist leaders could not create a multistate nation (like the U.S.A.). We will then examine how progress can be balanced with indigenous peoples' needs. Finally, we will discuss illegal immigration and how it impacts America.

As a result of this chapter you should be able to:

1. Compare and contrast the Aztecs, Mayas, and Incas.

2. Discuss the legacy Spain and Portugal deposited in the New World.

3. Explain why Bolivar and other leaders were unable to create a large confederation of South American states.

4. Evaluate whether Jim Elliot was inspired or reckless when he flew into the jungle to share Christ with the violent Huaorani people.

5. Speculate upon how progress can be balanced with indigenous peoples' needs.

6. Consider ways Americans can deal with illegal immigration.

NATIVE AMERICANS

The first inhabitants of South America were probably descendants of Asians who had crossed the Bering Strait. These native peoples were nomadic hunters, wandering from place to place, raising and subsisting on herds of animals. The development of agriculture probably first took place along the coast of Peru.

Agriculture and civilization advanced most rapidly in the valleys of the **Andes Mountains**. The most magnificent civilization was that of the Inca Empire, which arose in about the 13th century AD. Beyond the Andes, most of the natives were still at a primitive cultural level at the end of the 15th century. In 1492, the Europeans arrived, and from the beginning, Native Americans were viewed suspiciously and with curiosity. They were misunderstood and certainly unappreciated. They were considered foreigners in their own land.

In 1646, a Christian convert asked the Massachusetts missionary John Eliot: "Why do you call us Indians?" Ultimately, this was because Columbus mistakenly believed he had arrived in the East Indies. Even though Europeans realized that Columbus had not reached the East Indies, the name "Indian" continued to be used.

The term was a European-imposed concept—no Native American called himself "Indian." Besides, there was not a single monolithic Native American culture. They were acutely conscious of their differences and virtually never united together for a single purpose. The Hurons were enemies of the Iroquois as surely as the French were enemies of the English.

Surprisingly, there was a contradictory stereotype too. According to this stereotype, the Native Americans embodied innocence and freedom, lacking private property, yet possessing health and eternal youth. Arthur Barlowe, who visited Roanoke Island off the coast of North Carolina in 1584, described the Native Americans as nature's nobility: "We found the people most gentle, loving and faithful, void of all guile and treasure, and such as live after the manner of the golden age."

But if some Europeans regarded Native Americans with fascination, most looked at them with fear. The "bloodthirsty savage" who stood in the way of progress and civilization was the stereotype of choice.

The most important view, by far, was the notion that Europeans could not live side-by-side with Native Americans. Englishman William Penn tested this theory, with some initial success, but even in Pennsylvania, eventually Europeans and Native Americans became enemies. It would be two centuries before General Phil Sheridan would pronounce that "the only good Indian was a dead Indian." Rest assured, though, in the 18th century many, if not most, Europeans felt that way.

The story in Central and South America, unfortunately, was far more sordid. The Spanish Conquistadors and subsequent settlers instituted a draconian policy of "conversion or death" that made most Native Americans eternal enemies. That policy, however, was somewhat ameliorated in the latter part of the 18th century when King Charles III of Spain instituted a series of humanitarian missions along the Californian coast, under the auspices of the Roman Catholic Franciscan Order. A series of outposts/missions were established that brought advanced agricultural practices and aid that greatly improved the lives of most Native Americans. This was, regrettably, the exception.

Assignment

What were some Native American stereotypes shared by many Europeans?

Caption: The new indian war. Now, no sarcastic innuendoes, but let us have a square fight. Drawing by Thomas Nast, *Harper's Weekly*, December 21, 1878 (PD-US).

EUROPEAN SETTLERS

The first European known to have reached South America was Christopher Columbus, in 1498, during his third voyage from Spain to the New World. Several years earlier, Spain and Portugal had arrogantly created a **line of demarcation**, where, in faith, these two countries had divided the new world among themselves. Spanish and Portuguese conquistadors soon followed Columbus to establish colonies and to search for silver and gold.

In the 1530s, Francisco Pizarro sailed south from Panama to conquer the Incas of Peru. From there, the Spaniards explored the surrounding territory. An expedition under Sebastián de Belalcázar moved north and subdued the Inca kingdom at Quito (now Ecuador). His forces then pushed into southwest Colombia. Expeditions were also sent south into Chile and east, across the Andes, into Brazil. During the expedition to Brazil, Francisco de Orellana made his way to the mouth of the Amazon River.

Hostile Indians and inhospitable jungles slowed conquest of the northern coastal region of South America and Central America, known as the Spanish Main. A few coastal settlements were established in the early 1500s, but the interior was not penetrated until decades later.

Meanwhile, in 1500, the Portuguese explorer Pedro Alvares Cabral discovered Brazil, which was on the Portuguese side of the Line of Demarcation. Few attempts were made to explore the interior, however.

Unlike British colonies, which often were private entrepreneurial enterprises, Spanish South America was ruled as the king's private property. From the 16th to the early 19th centuries, it was governed by a complex administrative system in which viceroys were the king's representatives and the highest authorities in the colonies.

As in most European colonies, Native Americans were converted, enslaved, and annihilated, particularly in New Spain. Vast fortunes were made and some were lost. But, generally speaking, Spanish rule was uneventful until the 19th century.

In Portuguese South America, the king granted large areas to nobles, who were responsible for colonization. Early settlement was limited to the coast. In the mid-16th century, Brazil, like New Spain, was united under a single colonial administration. During the 17th and 18th centuries, the interior was penetrated by missionaries and by farmers seeking land, but was not interesting to most Portuguese. Intermarriage among all people groups and races assured that no rigid class system developed in Brazil.

Assignment

What legacy did Spain and Portugal deposit in the New World?

Statue of Christopher Columbus located in Old San Juan Puerto Rico.

SOUTH AMERICAN INDEPENDENCE

Generally speaking, Spanish Roman Catholic missionaries were a powerful force for good in the colonial era. They established many missions among the Indians. These missions provided medical care and care giving for millions of Native Americans and European settlers. The **Jesuits**, in particular, were involved in good works.

The Spanish and Portuguese were not the only countries interested in South America. By the end of the 17th century, English, French, and Dutch traders were regularly trading with South American Natives. In fact, they acquired, through treaties and warfare, their own colonies, especially in the Caribbean Sea.

Spanish colonialists began to want more independence. Remember, the Spanish colonies were not democracies like the English colonies. Uprisings against the Spanish colonial governments became frequent toward the end of the 18th century.

By 1810, revolutionary movements were underway in most of Spanish South America. Complete independence was finally achieved in 1825, after a series of bloody wars. The two great leaders of the revolution were Simón Bolívar and José de San Martín.

Brazil achieved independence from Portugal in 1822,

Battle of Bailén by José Casado del Alisal, date unknown (PD-US).

almost without bloodshed. England, France, and Holland continued to hold their small South American colonies by granting human and political rights that were by that time endemic to the mother country.

Simón Bolívar envisioned a confederation of all of Spanish South America, much like the United States, with one federal government overseeing individual states. All efforts at consolidation failed, however, and nine weak nations were created. In fact, to Bolivar's horror, many border wars erupted among the new nations, and obviously a South American federation was out of the question.

Not until the middle of the 20th century did all South American countries throw off European rule. Political instability plagued most South American countries throughout the 19th century and into the 20th. Revolutions were frequent, and the constant turmoil led to the rise of dictatorships. Social inequalities dating from the colonial period continued. Growing pressure from the laboring and middle classes for social and political reforms became widespread. Economic problems, especially inflation, were common in the period following World War II and added to the unrest.

South America's population increased rapidly during the 1950s and 1960s. Many rural laborers moved to the cities to search for jobs. Land reforms were undertaken

Soldiers guarding the altar at a Jesuit's monastery. Photographer and date unknown (PD-US).

in several countries; large estates were broken up to provide more of the rural population with land. Economic difficulties and a heightened sense of nationalism led several countries to take control of foreign-owned industries. In the 1960s and 1970s most nations were at one time or another under military rule. During the 1980s a number of countries replaced military rule with democratic rule, and by the mid-1990s all had some form of democratically elected governments. An exception is Venezuela, which today is still ruled by a dictator.

Economic problems—particularly those caused by the huge national debts owed to foreign banks and countries by many South American nations—continued into the 1990s. By the late 1990s, however, the economies of some countries, including Chile and Argentina, recovered and experienced strong economic growth.

Assignment

Why were Bolivar and other leaders unable to create a large confederation of South American states?

Statue of Simon Bolivar in Washington, DC.
Photo by Jyothis, 2009 (CC BY-SA 3.0)

JIM ELLIOT

Philip James Elliot (October 8, 1927 – January 8, 1956) was an evangelical Christian missionary to Ecuador who, with four others, was killed while attempting to evangelize the Auca people in Ecuador. Elliot professed faith in Jesus at the age of six and grew up in a home where obedience and honesty were encouraged.

In the fall of 1945, Elliot entered Wheaton College. Elliot's interest in missions solidified during his years at Wheaton. He soon followed the pattern of other "faith missionaries" by not seeking to be sponsored by a denomination. Elliot, who, along with his roommate David Howard, was a member of the campus organization Student Foreign Missions Fellowship, spoke to an Intervarsity Christian Fellowship group on the role of the Holy Spirit in missions. During the summer of 1947, after his second year of college, Elliot and his friend Ron Harris did mission work in Mexico. He stayed there for six weeks, working with and learning from a local missionary family. At the end of the following year, he attended Intervarsity's International Student Missionary Convention, where he met a missionary to Brazil. That experience confirmed his missionary calling to tribal work in South America.

Elliot and friend Pete Fleming arrived in Ecuador on February 21, 1952, with the purpose of evangelizing Ecuador's Auca Indians. They first stayed in Quito to study Spanish, and then moved to the jungle, where they took up permanent residence at the Shandia mission station. On October 8, 1953, he married fellow Wheaton alumna and missionary Elisabeth Howard (his college roommate's sister). Their only child, Valerie, was born February 27, 1955. While working with the Quichua Indians, Elliot was called to share Christ with the violent Huaorani Indians, known at that time as the Aucas.

He and four other missionaries, Ed McCully, Roger Youderian, Pete Fleming, and their pilot, Nate Saint, made contact from their airplane with the Huaoranis using a loudspeaker and a basket to pass down gifts. After several

Demonstration of a typical Ecuadorian blowgun by Julia Rubinic, 2007 (CC BY 2.0).

months, the men decided to build a base a short distance from the Indian village, along the Curaray River. There they were approached one time by a small group of Huaoranis and even gave an airplane ride to one curious Huaorani whom they called "George." Encouraged by these friendly encounters, they began plans to visit the Huaoranis, without knowing that George had lied to the others about the missionaries' intentions. Ten Huaorani warriors killed Elliot and his four friends on January 8, 1956.

Elliot's famous journal entry from October 28, 1949, stated, "He is no fool who gives what he cannot keep to gain that which he cannot lose."

The story has a happy ending. Some of the wives and a sister of the martyrs went back to Ecuador to continue their ministry; the Aucas became Christians; and that one of the Huaoranis who killed the missionaries traveled with the son of one of the martyred men to tell how he and other Huaoranis came to Christ because of the Christians' love and forgiveness.

Assignment

Was Elliot inspired or reckless when he flew into the jungle to share Christ with the violent Huaorani people?

Chapter 30

SCANDINAVIAN HISTORY

First Thoughts . . .

Five hundred years before Columbus discovered South America, Vikings, Scandinavians, discovered North America. Though marked by certain geographical, linguistic, and cultural differences, Denmark, Iceland, Norway, and Sweden are united by a common bond and a shared history. They share religions, historical events, political ideas, economic practices, intellectual movements, and technological innovations that have made them what they are. For one thing, they share the Vikings—a most enigmatic people group that, while being notoriously aggressive and ruthless, also practiced the first serious democracy in Northern Europe. Essentially a prehistoric culture, Scandinavians created one of the most effective and enduring legal systems in world history.

Chapter Learning Objectives . . .

In chapter 30, we will examine in depth the Vikings. Next, we will examine the history and present situation of several Scandinavian countries. Finally, we will predict Scandinavia's future.

As a result of this chapter you should be able to:

1. Speculate as to why the Vikings were so successful in their initial subjugation of cultures in Northern Europe but ultimately failed to have a lasting cultural impact.
2. Compare the Vikings' democracy with the ancient Greek democracy in Athens.
3. Explain how prehistoric Viking society was able to sustain a democracy.
4. Contrast Scandinavian history with German history.
5. Contemplate upon the future of Scandinavia.
6. Review Scandinavian history.

OVERVIEW

Peter Stearns once quizzed, "Why does a civilization begin to ascend within the ranks of the various societies of the world, gaining new power and importance?" (Peter Stearns, *World History in Brief*. NY: Longman, 2010. p. 267). For one thing, the culture had to have a heroic nature, often popular among nomadic food gatherers. Next, advances of technology were also necessary. Scandinavia, and its people groups, manifested both fairly early in its history.

Think of Scandinavia's history and what comes to mind? Rapacious Vikings in innovative ships bravely plying Northern seas. While Viking reputation for violence and barbarianism is a significant part of Scandinavian history, it ignores the relative neutrality of its nations, countries who rose from distinct differences in tribe, culture, and religion.

The earliest evidences of human settlement in Scandinavia are evident right after the Great Flood. These early peoples developed a sophisticated living through hunting and fishing, with some evidence of agrarianism in present-day Sweden. Not much is known about the 200-year period (c. 850 AD to 1050 AD) of the Vikings. The few written accounts we do have come from their victims: England, Scotland, Germany, Russia, Ireland, which from 1018 to 1035 fell completely into Viking hands. These accounts, of course, are not very flattering. The legendary seafaring adventurousness of these peoples belonged primarily to the Norwegian Vikings, whose settlements dotted the North Atlantic and included Iceland, the Orkney and Shetland Islands, Greenland and North America (though no permanent settlements were maintained in America). Viking conquests made extensive inroads by land as well. Conquests and trade routes to the East led to the eventual origin of the Russian state, and created links to Constantinople and the Mediterranean.

Literature appeared with the introduction of Christianity during the Middle Ages. As the first Scandinavian country to embrace Roman Catholicism, Denmark has historical records dating back to 829. Because of its geographical proximity to Western Europe, Denmark led the rest of Scandinavia in shaping its society toward a European model. For a while Denmark dominated Scandinavia.

This union was broken in 1521–53, in a revolt led by Gustavus Vasa, which led to the establishment of a separate Swedish nation. After the Swedish revolt, Norway remained allied with Denmark and remained so until 1814. Thus, the historical monarchies of Denmark and Norway on the one side, and Sweden and Finland on the other were established. But they were never really serious enemies and cooperated in many common endeavors. The Napoleonic wars proved especially damaging to Denmark's empire, weakening that country's influence in Sweden, and led to Sweden annexing Norway in 1807. Eventually, the Swedish-Norwegian union ended and Norway became independent in 1905. Likewise, Finland, who ceded to Russia in 1845, won independence in 1918 because of Russia's weakened condition after World War 1.

This short overview reminds us again of Scandinavia's unique place on the stage of history. Perhaps no region in the world so effectively cooperated among themselves in a common cause of peace. A Scandinavian proverb reminds us, "Go often to the house of thy friend; for weeds soon choke up the unused path." Scandinavians lived this maxim.

Assignment

Scandinavian countries, with very few historical exceptions, have cooperated together in common causes to bring peace and harmony. Historians have emphasized the common heritage and geographical similarities that the Scandinavian countries share as possible causes. Yet, China and Japan share a common heritage and geography but are mortal enemies. Germany and France both emerged from the Holy Roman Empire and the Charlemagne Empire before that. Yet they fought war after war in the 19th and 20th centuries. Why are Scandinavians different?

VIKING LIFE

Around AD 1000, Danish Vikings, also known as Norseman, sailed from Greenland to North America and set up a village on the tip of what is now Newfoundland. These people were far removed from so much legend about Viking lore. For one thing, they did not wear horned helmets!

The Viking people came from the lands now known as Denmark, Norway, and Sweden. From AD 800 to AD 1100, they raided Western Europe from Ireland to Russia. Though they were a very warlike people, nonetheless they had strong families and a well-developed culture. The Vikings were the first Europeans to settle in North America, though their presence faded within 50 years.

To their thriving culture, a man's honor was essential. Therefore, Vikings were generally hospitable and supported friends in need. If, on the other hand, they were offended, their wrath was horrific. Thus, revenge was a serious, prevalent component of this social system that placed great importance on maintaining personal honor.

Most Vikings were farmers who lived in hall-like houses in small countryside villages near **fjords**, or in valleys farther inland. Due to a relatively short growing season, these farms specialized in hardy perennials that weathered cool summer nights and a short growing season.

The Vikings lived in collective or extended families. If a farmer kept workers, servants, or slaves, they also usually lived in the family house. When the oldest son in the family took over the farm, he became the chief of the family and it became his duty to run the farm.

The duty of the wife was to run the house in such a way that the family had enough food during the long, dark winter. She made butter and cheese, dried fish and meat, and smoked fish and meat as well. She would also have knowledge about herbs in order to make medicine for ill or wounded family members. She was also the leader when the family held private religious rites inside the house.

Viking girls were expected to marry when they were 12 to 15 years old. It was then expected that a new bride would

Viking Girl, vintage opera photograph. Photographer unknown, c1900.

be able to run the household and do the work belonging to women on the farm. The arrangement of the wedding (to determine whom a son or daughter should marry) was the duty of the family chief or king rather than the young person's father. Normally, a young person had no right to choose a mate according to his or her own wishes.

Assignment

Viking society was prehistoric (lacking writing and reading). How can a society flourish without reading and writing?

BRIEF OVERVIEW OF EACH NATION: PART ONE

Denmark

Denmark is a Scandinavian country in Northern Europe and the main member of the Kingdom of Denmark, which includes more than the Denmark peninsula in Northern Europe. It is the southernmost of the Nordic countries, southwest of Sweden and south of Norway, and bordered to the south by Germany.

Denmark is a constitutional monarchy with a parliamentary system of government. This means that Denmark, like England, has a monarch (king or queen) but is ruled by a representative body (e.g., parliament). Denmark has a state-level government and local governments in 98 municipalities. Denmark has been a member of the European Union since 1973, and is a founding member of NATO.

NATO, the North Atlantic Treaty Organization, was founded after World War II to check Soviet Union expansionism.

With a mixed market capitalist economy and a large welfare state, Denmark ranks as having the world's highest level of income equality. It also has the best business climate in the world. Also, in spite of its strategic location, Denmark has been able to maintain its neutrality for 60 years.

The national language, Danish, is similar to the languages of Sweden and Norway, with which it shares strong cultural and historical ties. 82 percent of all inhabitants of Denmark, and 90.3 percent of the ethnic Danes, are members of the Lutheran state church. As of 2009, 526,000 people (9.5 percent of the Danish population) were either immigrants or

descendants of recent immigrants. Most of these (54 percent) have their origins in Scandinavia or elsewhere in Europe, while the others originate mainly from a wide range of Asian countries.

Norway

The Kingdom of Norway is a Nordic country in Northern Europe occupying the western portion of the Scandinavian Peninsula. It is one of the most sparsely populated countries in Europe. The majority of the country shares a border to the east with Sweden; its northernmost region is bordered by Finland to the south and Russia to the east; and Denmark lies south of its southern tip across the Skagerrak Strait. The capital city of Norway is Oslo. Norway's extensive coastline, facing the North Atlantic Ocean and the Barents Sea, is home to its famous fjords.

After World War II, Norway experienced rapid economic growth, due, during the first two decades, to the Norwegian shipping and merchant marine and domestic industrialization, and, from the early 1970s, to the exploitation of large oil and natural gas deposits discovered in the North Sea and the Norwegian Sea. Today, Norway ranks as the third wealthiest country in the world in monetary value, with the largest capital reserve per capita of any nation. Norway is the world's fifth largest oil exporter, whose petroleum industry accounts for around a quarter of its GDP.

Following the ongoing financial crisis of 2007–2010, bankers have deemed the Norwegian krone to be one of the most solid currencies in the world.

Norway has rich resources of oil, natural gas, hydroelectric power, forests, and minerals, and has been the second-largest exporter of seafood (in value, after the People's Republic of China). Other major industries include shipping, food processing, shipbuilding, the metal industry, chemicals, mining, fishing, and the pulp and paper products from forests. Norway maintains a Scandinavian welfare model with universal healthcare, subsidized higher education, and a comprehensive social security system.

Norway is a constitutional, hereditary monarchy and parliamentary democracy.

Assignment

Contrast the national development of Denmark and Norway with that of Germany. Why were these Scandinavian countries able to stay neutral for so many years?

Panorama of Copenhagen, Denmark

BRIEF OVERVIEW OF EACH NATION: PART TWO

Sweden

Sweden is a Nordic country on the Scandinavian Peninsula in Northern Europe. Sweden has land borders with Norway to the west and Finland to the northeast, and has also water borders with Denmark, Germany, and Poland to the south, and Estonia, Latvia, Lithuania, and Russia to the east.

Sweden is the third-largest country in the European Union in terms of area. Sweden emerged as an independent country during the Middle Ages. In the 17th century, the country expanded its territories to form the Swedish Empire. The empire grew to be one of the great powers of Europe in the 17th and early 18th centuries. Most of the conquered territories outside the Scandinavian Peninsula were lost during the 18th and 19th centuries, however. The eastern half of Sweden, present-day Finland, was lost to Russia in 1809. The last war in which Sweden was directly involved was in 1814, when Sweden by military means forced Norway into a personal union, which lasted until 1905. Since then, Sweden has been at peace, having adopted a foreign policy of nonalignment in peacetime and neutrality in wartime.

Today, Sweden is a constitutional monarchy with a parliamentary system of government.

Stockholm, Sweden

Blue Lagoon, famous Icelandic spa and geothermal power plant

Iceland

Iceland is a European island country located in the North Atlantic Ocean fairly close to Greenland. The interior mainly consists of a plateau characterized by sand fields, mountains, and glaciers, while many glacial rivers flow to the sea through the lowlands. Iceland is warmed by the Gulf Stream and has a temperate climate despite its high latitude just outside the Arctic Circle.

Iceland was settled in AD 874 when the Norwegian chieftain Ingólfur Arnarson became the first permanent Norwegian settler on the uninhabited island. Others had visited the island earlier and stayed over winter. Over the following centuries, it was part of Norway and later Denmark. In 1994, the nation became party to an agreement that established the European Economic Area, thus allowing it to diversify from fishing to economic and financial services.

In 2007, it was ranked as the most developed country in the world by the United Nations' Human Development Index, and the fourth most productive country per capita. Icelandic culture is based on the nation's Norse heritage and its status as a developed and technologically advanced society. Most Icelanders are descendants of Norse (particularly from Western Norway) settlers. The country's cultural heritage includes traditional cuisine, poetry, and medieval Icelanders' sagas.

Iceland's history shows that the country was settled by Norwegian and Celtic immigrants during the late ninth and tenth centuries AD, and as such, the country of Iceland has the oldest functioning legislative assembly (established in 930) in the world. At points, Iceland was ruled by Norway and Denmark. Later, about 20 percent of the island's population immigrated to North America. Denmark granted Iceland limited home rule in 1874, and Iceland finally became completely independent in 1944.

Assignment

Speculate upon the future of Scandinavia.

Ingólfr Arnarson, the first permanent Norwegian settler in Iceland by Johan Peter Raadsig, 1850 (PD-US).

Iceland, from the NASA Visible Earth image gallery. Photo by Jeff Schmaltz, 2004 (NASA).

Chapter 31

WORLD WAR I: A WORLD TRAGEDY

First Thoughts . . .

World War I is the most difficult war of the 20th century to explain. There was no clear-cut issue, no clear-cut victor. On June 28, 1914, Archduke Francis Ferdinand (heir to the Austrian-Hungarian throne) was assassinated during a visit to Sarajevo. At the time of the assassination, Austria-Hungary and Serbia were involved in a serious dispute. The Austrian-Hungarian government was convinced that Serbia was behind the assassination and used the event as an excuse to crush its enemy. Upon declaration of war a chain reaction began leading most of Europe to war. Most Americans were reluctant to get involved, but powerful forces including German unlimited submarine warfare pulled the nation into battle. In 1917 American soldiers had joined Europeans in the trenches of war. When the guns finally quieted, President Wilson launched a campaign for a peace treaty and a new organization that would prevent such a tragedy from ever happening again. It failed and a much worse catastrophe was lurking over the horizon.

Chapter Learning Objectives . . .

We will begin with an overview of World War I. Then we will examine briefly the war itself. Then we will observe the peace and reflect upon the problems it caused. Finally, we will look at contemporary witnesses of the carnage.

As a result of this chapter you should be able to:

1. Discuss the causes of World War I.
2. Analyze why casualties were so high in World War I.
3. Evaluate how effective the Versailles Treaty was.
4. Reflect on how contemporaries handled the horror that was World War I.
5. Discuss the culpability of all the participants in World War I.
6. Offer contemporary legacies of World War I.

OVERVIEW

The First World War created the modern world. A conflict of unprecedented ferocity, it abruptly ended the relative peace and prosperity of the Victorian era, unleashing such demons of the 20th century as mechanized warfare and mass death. It was the training ground for Adolf Hitler and prepared him for his macabre work ahead. It also helped to usher in the ideas that have shaped our times—modernism in the arts, new approaches to psychology and medicine, radical thoughts about economics and society—and in so doing shattered the faith in rationalism and liberalism that had prevailed in Europe since the Enlightenment (John Keegan, *The First World War.* NY: Alfred A. Knopf, 2001. p. 3).

It is truly a mystery how a civilization at the height of its achievement could have propelled itself into such a ruinous conflict. Many historians argue that by an astonishing failure of diplomacy and communication, a bilateral dispute grew to engulf an entire continent.

But perhaps nothing was more horrible than the military battles in this war. No 1914 army could anticipate, much less imagine, what was ahead of them. Verdun, the Somme, and Gallipoli one after another brought terrible, unparalleled carnage. Around 715,000 men died in the Battle of Verdun. That is more—10 percent more—than all the men killed in the American Civil War—and this was only one battle!

By the end of the war, three great empires—the Austria-Hungarian, the Russian, and the Ottoman—had collapsed. The devastation extended over the entirety of Europe, and still profoundly informs the politics and culture of the continent today. And perhaps the greatest irony and tragedy of this needless war was that it was to be fought all over again 20 years later. But this time, 30 million, not 10 million, were to die in World War II.

The tragic conflagration that was World War I was precipitated by the assassination of Archduke Franz Ferdinand, heir to the Austro-Hungarian throne, in Sarajevo on June

Archduke Franz Ferdinand of Austria. Photo by Carl Pietzner, c1914 (PD-US).

28, 1914. Ferdinand's death at the hands of the Black Hand, a Serbian nationalist secret society, set in motion a mindlessly mechanical series of events that culminated in the world's most costly world war to date.

In truth, no assassination, even of a future monarch, could precipitate the death of 10 million people without other mitigating circumstances. These "circumstances" included entangling alliances and war plans.

Dardanelles Fleet. More photos of World War I. Photographer unknown, c 1915 (PD-US).

England, France, and Italy were united to defend Russian borders, of all things! Germany, likewise, was obligated to defend Austria-Hungary's border. In addition, Germany had a war plan, called the Schlieffen Plan. The so-called Schlieffen Plan, devised by former Army Chief of Staff Alfred von Schlieffen, had been carefully written to deal with a two-front war scenario. The plan, which very nearly succeeded, outlined a plan to conquer France, to knock her out of the war, on a "Western Front," within five weeks—before, the Germans calculated, Russia could effectively mobilize for war on the "Eastern Front" (which they estimated would take six weeks to two months).

The allies, of course, knew this, and made plans to initiate the war—that is, mobilize their troops—before Germany could consummate the Schlieffen Plan.

Austria-Hungary's reaction to the death of their heir was three weeks in coming. With German support, it issued an ultimatum to Serbia that, in the extent of its demand that the assassins be brought to justice, effectively nullified Serbia's sovereignty. Serbia refused. Russia supported its ally, Serbia. And the die was cast.

Assignment

In the midst of so much progress and optimism, how could the tragedy that is World War I occur?

Latin bridge (prev. Princip bridge) in Sarajevo. Site of the assassination of Archduke Franz Ferdinand, which started WW I. Photographer and date unknown (CC BY-SA 3.0).

THE WAR

The first month of combat consisted of bold attacks and rapid troop movements on both fronts. All the armies were fighting a modern war with 19th century tactics. For example, no army fully grasped the impact of the machine gun. Brightly garbed, idealistic young men attacked in formation and were slaughtered by machine guns. Casualties were usually 10–20 percent, and in some case, 80 percent. Since armies recruited "buddy regiments," whole towns of young men were killed.

In the west, implementing the Schliefflen Plan, Germany attacked first Belgium and then France. In the east, Russia attacked both Germany and Austria-Hungary. In the south, Austria-Hungary attacked Serbia. Since the attack took too long, the German commander swung too far south too soon, and moved in front of Paris. The Battle of the Marne ensued. Following the Battle of the Marne (September 5–9, 1914), the western front became entrenched in central France and remained that way for the rest of the war. The fronts in the east also gradually locked into place too.

Late in 1914, the Ottoman Empire was brought into the fray as well, after Germany tricked Russia into thinking that Turkey had attacked it. As a result, much of 1915 was dominated by Allied actions against the Ottomans in the Mediterranean. First, Britain and France launched a failed attack on the Dardanelles. This campaign was followed by a disastrous British invasion of the Gallipoli Peninsula.

The middle part of the war, 1916 and 1918, was dominated by continued trench warfare in both the east and the west. Soldiers fought from dug-in positions, striking at each other with modern weapons and chemical weapons. Though soldiers died by the millions, neither side had any real success. It was legal, wholesale slaughter.

Despite the stalemate on both fronts in Europe, two important developments in the war occurred in 1917. In early April, the United States, angered by attacks upon its

British Vickers machine gun in action near Ovillers during the Battle of the Somme in 1916. The crew are wearing gas masks. Photo by Lt. J.W. Brooke, 1916 (PD-US).

ships in the Atlantic, and other inflammatory events, declared war on Germany. Then, in November, the Bolshevik Revolution prompted Russia to pull out of the war. Germany was free to fight its one front war.

Although both sides launched renewed offensives in 1917 and 1918 in an all-or-nothing effort to win the war, both efforts failed. Eventually, the governments of both Germany and Austria-Hungary began to lose control as both countries experienced multiple mutinies.

The war ended in the late fall of 1918, after the member countries of the Central Powers signed armistice agreements one by one.

Assignment

Why were casualties so high during World War I?

THE AFTERMATH

After such a devastating war, the victorious Western Powers acted as if they had won a great war, that there was no unconditional surrender. In fact, it was an armistice, with no clear-cut winner. The allies imposed a series of harsh treaties upon the defeated nations. These treaties stripped the Central Powers of substantial territories and imposed significant reparation payments. Seldom before had the face of Europe been so fundamentally changed. As a direct result of the war, the German, Austria-Hungarian, Russian, and Ottoman Empires ceased to exist. Whole sections of Germany now became Poland, Czechoslovakia, and France. Germany would not forget her humiliation.

In January 1918, ten months before the end of World War I, U.S. President Woodrow Wilson had written the "Fourteen Points." Eight of these points dealt specifically with territorial and political settlements associated with the victory of the Allies, including the idea of national self-determination for ethnic populations in Europe. The last proposed a **League of Nations** to arbitrate international disputes. Wilson hoped his proposal would bring a "peace without victory."

When German leaders signed the armistice in the Compiègne Forest on November 11, 1918, many of them believed that the Fourteen Points would form the basis of the future peace treaty, but when the heads of the governments of the United States, Great Britain, France, and Italy met in Paris later to discuss treaty terms, the European contingent of the "Big Four" rejected this approach. Germany, with some justification, felt betrayed by the Allies.

Perhaps the most humiliating portion of the treaty for defeated Germany was Article 231, commonly known as the "War Guilt Clause," which forced the German nation to accept complete responsibility for starting World War I. As such, Germany was liable for all material damages. At the same time, the German military was severely curtailed.

For the populations of the defeated powers—Germany, Austria, Hungary, and Bulgaria—the respective peace treaties

Woodrow Wilson. Photo by Harris & Ewing, c1912 (PD-US).

appeared an unfair punishment, and their governments, whether democratic as in Germany or Austria, or authoritarian, in the case of Hungary and Bulgaria, quickly violated the agreement.

Nothing justifies the horror that will follow in World War II, but the Versailles Treaty did not help. The Versailles Treaty became the rallying cry of German nationalists and the Nazi Party that ultimately initiated World War II.

Assignment

How did the Versailles Treaty cause World War II? What would have been a better treaty?

CONTEMPORARY ACCOUNTS

Vernon Bartlett, an English Soldier

It is a monotonous time, that hour of waiting until darkness falls, for gossip is scarce in the trenches, and the display of fireworks in the shape of German star shells has long since ceased to interest us—always excepting those moments when we are in front of our trench on some patrol. Away to the left, where the artillery have been busy all day, the shelling slackens as the light fades, and the rifle shots grow more and more frequent. Presently the extra sentries are posted—one man in every three—the disgusted working parties are told off to their work of filling sandbags or improving the communication trenches, and the long, trying night begins.

All down the line the German bullets spin overhead or crack like whips against our sandbags, sending little clods of earth down into the trench; all down the line we stand on our firing platforms, and answer back to the little spurts of flame which mark the enemy trench; sudden flashes and explosions tell of bombs or grenades, and star shells from both sides sweep high into the air to silhouette the unwary and to give one something to fire at, for firing into the darkness with the probability of hitting nothing more dangerous than a tree or a sandbag is work of but little interest.

I wander on my rounds to see that all the sentries are on the alert, and, suddenly, nearly fall over a man lying face downwards along the bottom of the trench. "Here, you can't sleep here, you know; you give no one a chance to pass," I say, and, for answer, I am told to "shut up," while a suppressed but still audible giggle from Private Harris warns me that the situation is not as I had imagined. The figure in the mud gets up and proves to be an officer of the Engineers, listening for sounds of mining underneath us. "I think they're at it again, but I'm not certain yet," he says cheerfully as he goes off to his own dug-out. I, in turn, lie down in the mud with my ear pressed to the ground, and I seem to hear, far beneath me, the rumble of the trolleys and the sound of the pick, so that I am left for the rest of the night in the uncomfortable expectation of flying heavenwards at any moment.

At last the order to stand to arms is given again, and the new day comes creeping sadly over the plain of Flanders. What looked like a great hand stretched up appealingly to heaven becomes a shattered, broken tree; the uniform veil of grey gives place to grass and empty tins, dead bodies lying huddled up grotesquely, and winding lines of German trenches. The sky goes faintly blue, and the sun peeps out, gleaming on the drops of rain that still hang from our barbed wire, and on the long row of bayonets along the trench.

The new day is here, but what will it bring? The monotony may be broken by an attack, the battalion may be relieved. Who knows? Who cares? Enough that daylight is here and the sun is shining, that periscopes and sleep are once more permitted, that breakfast is at hand, and that some day we shall get back to billets.

—Vernon Bartlett.
Mud and Khaki: Sketches from Flanders and France. London: Simpkin, Marschall, Hamilton, Kent, and Co., Ltd., 1917.

Ellen N. La Motte, an American Nurse

Rochard died today. He had gas gangrene. His thigh, from knee to buttock, was torn out by a piece of German shell. It was an interesting case, because the infection had developed so quickly. He had been placed under treatment immediately too, reaching the hospital from the trenches about six hours after he had been wounded. To have a thigh torn off, and to reach first-class surgical care within six hours, is practically immediately. Still, gas gangrene had developed, which showed that the Germans were using very poisonous shells. At that field hospital there had been established a surgical school, to which young men, just graduated from medical schools, or old men, graduated long ago from medical schools, were sent to learn how to take care of the wounded. After they had received a two months' experience in this sort of war surgery, they were to be placed in other hospitals, where they could do the work themselves. So all those young men who did not know much, and all those old men who had never known much, and had forgotten most of that, were up here at this field hospital, learning. This had to be done, because there were not enough good doctors to go round, so in order to care for the wounded at all, it was necessary to furbish up the immature and the senile. However, the Médecin Chef in charge of the hospital and in charge of the surgical school was a brilliant surgeon and a good administrator, so he taught the students a good deal. Therefore, when Rochard came into the operating room, all the young students and the old students crowded round to see the case. It was all torn away, the flesh from that right thigh, from knee to buttock, down to the bone, and the stench was awful. The various students came forward and timidly pressed the upper part of the thigh, the remaining part, all that remained of it, with their fingers, and little crackling noises came forth, like bubbles. Gas gangrene. Very easy to diagnose. Also the bacteriologist from another hospital in the region happened to be present, and he made a culture of the material discharged from that wound, and afterwards told the Médecin Chef that it was positively and absolutely gas gangrene.

So Rochard died, a stranger among strangers. And there were many people there to wait upon him, but there was no one there to love him.

—Ellen N. La Motte,

The Backwash of War: The Human Wreckage of the Battlefield as Witnessed by an American Hospital Nurse. NY: G. P. Putnam's Sons, 1916. Pp. 52-55.

Despite the brutality of WWI finally ending with the Treaty of Versailles, within 20 years the world would again be embroiled in conflict - this time WWII - leading to massive death tolls on and off the battlefield such as these in the cemetery overlooking Omaha Beach in Normandy, France.

Erich Maria Remarque, a German Soldier

But now, for the first time, I see you are a man like me. I thought of your hand-grenades, of your bayonet, of your rifle; now I see your wife and your face and our fellowship. Forgive me, comrade. We always see it too late. Why do they never tell us that you are poor devils like us, that your mothers are just as anxious as ours, and that we have the same fear of death, and the same dying and the same agony. Forgive me, comrade; how could you be my enemy? . . .

I am young, I am twenty years old; yet I know nothing of life but despair, death, fear, and fatuous superficiality cast over an abyss of sorrow. I see how peoples are set against one another, and in silence, unknowingly, foolishly, obediently, innocently slay one another.

—Erich Maria Remarque,
All Quiet on the Western Front, Ch. 9–10

Assignment

Pretend that you are the pastor responsible to minister to Mr. Remarque, Ms. La Motte, and Mr. Bartlett. What can you say to them to encourage them?

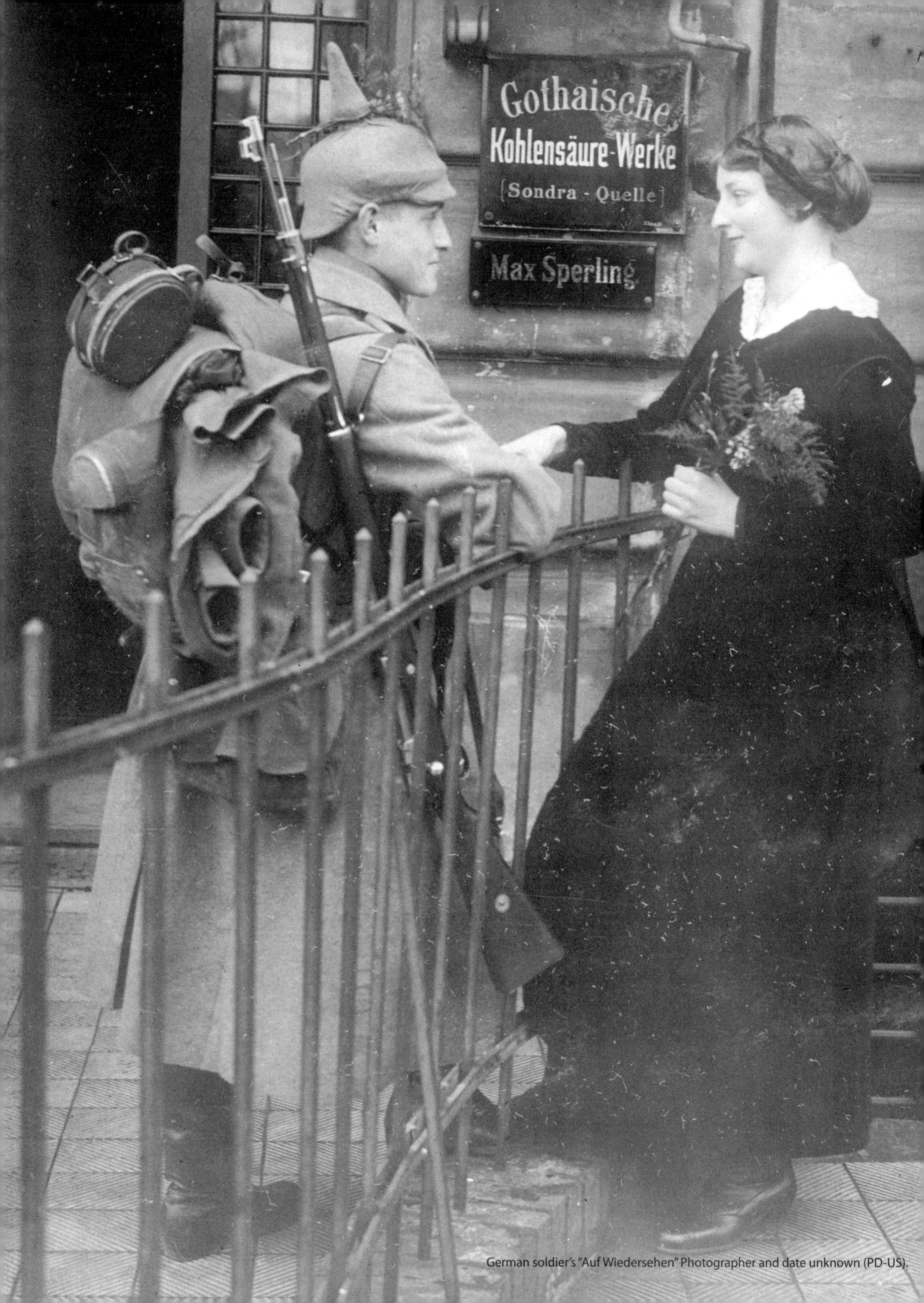

Gothaische
Kohlensäure-Werke
(Sondra - Quelle)

Max Sperling

German soldier's "Auf Wiedersehen" Photographer and date unknown (PD-US).

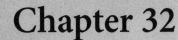

Chapter 32

THE JAZZ AGE

First Thoughts . . .

The lifestyles of young men and women in the 1920s were as shocking to their parents as the 1960s "hippie" generation were to post–World War II. In reaction to uncontrollable forces around them, including immigration, a consumer revolution, and Prohibition, Americans sought answers in places once considered out of bounds, both morally and physically. Ellen Welles Page, a young woman writing in *Outlook* magazine in 1922, tried to explain why this was:

> Most of us, under the present system of modern education, are further advanced and more thoroughly developed mentally, physically, and vocationally than were our parents at our age. . . . We have learned to take for granted conveniences, and many luxuries, which not so many years ago were as yet undreamed of. [But] the war tore away our spiritual foundations and challenged our faith. We are struggling to regain our equilibrium. . . . The emotions are frequently in a state of upheaval, struggling with one another for supremacy.

In their attempt to come to terms with their place in this new world, Americans tested their new boundaries with more and more outrageous forms of behavior. Wilder music, faster cars, and shorter skirts were just a few symptoms of this strange postwar era called the Jazz Age.

Chapter Learning Objectives . . .

We will review the Scopes Trial and show how it caused many Christians to withdraw from American society. Next, we will observe the great social experiment called Prohibition. We will examine the rise of the Ku Klux Klan. Finally, we will observe America entering the consumer age.

As a result of this chapter you should be able to:

1. Review the events surrounding the Scopes Trial.

2. Evaluate the effectiveness of Prohibition.

3. Understand the rise of the Ku Klux Klan.

4. Analyze the rise of consumer culture in America.

THE SCOPES TRIAL

In the summer of 1925, a young schoolteacher named John Scopes stood trial in Dayton, Tennessee, for violating the state law against the teaching of evolution. Two of the country's most famous attorneys faced off in the trial. William Jennings Bryan, 65 years old and a three-time Democratic presidential nominee, prosecuted; 67-year-old Clarence Darrow, who was a staunch agnostic and who had defended Nathan Leopold and Richard Loeb the year before, represented the defense. Bryan declared that "the contest between evolution and Christianity is a duel to the death."

The five-year-old American Civil Liberties Union had taken out newspaper advertisements offering to defend anyone who flouted the Tennessee law. George Rappelyea, a Dayton, Tenn., booster, realized that the town would get enormous attention if a local teacher was arrested for teaching evolution. He enlisted John Scopes, a science teacher and football coach, who arranged to teach from George Hunter's Civic Biology, a high school textbook promoting Charles Darwin's arguments in *The Descent of Man.*

The trial had a carnival-like atmosphere. For 12 days in July 1925, 100 reporters sent dispatches.

Attorney Clarence Darrow. Photographers Harris & Ewing, 1915 (PD-US).

The trial judge had prohibited the defense from using scientists as witnesses. So, on the trial's seventh day, the defense team called Bryan to testify as an expert on the Bible. Darrow subjected Bryan to a withering cross-examination. He got Bryan to say that Creation was not completed in a week, but over a period of time that "might have continued for millions of years."

Reporters characterized Bryan as a religious maniac, but in actuality, Bryan's position was solid. He opposed the mandated teaching of evolution in public schools because he thought the people should exercise local control over school curricula. He also opposed Darwin's theory of evolution because he thought it was bad science.

The day after this exchange, Darrow changed his client's plea to guilty. Scopes was convicted and fined $100. However, the conviction was thrown out on a technicality by the Tennessee Supreme Court (that the judge, and not the jury, had determined the $100 fine). In 1967, the Supreme Court struck down Tennessee's anti-evolution law for violating the

William Jennings Bryan. Photographers Harris & Ewing, 1915 (PD-US).

To the secular world, however, the Scopes Trail symbolized the conflict between science and theology, faith and reason, individual liberty and majority rule. The object of intense publicity, the trial was seen as a clash between city sophistication and country naivete. As the reader can guess, the evangelical fundamentalists were characterized as the bad guys.

Assignment

Why did evangelical Christians withdraw from American society after the Scopes Trial?

John Scopes taken one month before the Tennessee v. John T. Scopes Trial. From the Smithsonian Institution Archives. Photo by Watson Davis, 1925 (PD-US).

Constitution's prohibition against the establishment of religion.

Five days after the trial's conclusion, Bryan died of exhaustion.

The Scopes Trial, to many evangelical Christians, was the cultural turning point in American history. It was undeniable evidence that the United States had moved dangerously away from its Christian roots. Evangelical Christians knew they were in a culture war. There was a mass exodus from American society as evidenced by the founding of a plethora of evangelical colleges.

The Rhea County Courthouse in Dayton, Tennessee, site of the Scopes Trial. Photo by Calvin Beale, 2006 (PD-US).

PROHIBITION

At midnight, January 16, 1920, breweries, distilleries, and saloons closed their doors.

Prohibition sought to reduce drinking by eliminating the businesses that manufactured, distributed, and sold alcoholic beverages. The Eighteenth Amendment to the U.S. Constitution took away the license to do business from the brewers, distillers, vintners, and the wholesale and retail sellers of alcoholic beverages. Prohibition proponents were concerned about the effects of alcoholism on American families.

The strength of Prohibition grew, especially after the formation of the Anti-Saloon League in 1893. The League, and other organizations such as the Woman's Christian Temperance Union, succeeded in enacting local prohibition laws. Eventually the prohibition campaign was a national effort. Henry Ford joined the effort because he thought the ravages of drunkenness would weaken the American labor community.

The problem was real. Alcoholism was rampant. It was not uncommon to find one saloon for every 150 or 200 Americans, including those who did not drink. Enterprising saloonkeepers sometimes introduced gambling and prostitution into their establishments in an attempt to increase profits.

Prohibition supporters had no delusions about the human heart. They had no intention of legislating morality. They knew this was impossible. The prohibition leaders believed that once the license to do business was removed from the liquor traffic, churches would enjoy an opportunity to persuade Americans to give up drink. The blight of saloons would disappear from the landscape, and saloonkeepers would no longer be allowed to encourage people, including children, to drink alcoholic beverages. There would be a level playing field, so to speak, and America would be the beneficiary.

The truth is it really worked. The best evidence available to historians shows that consumption of alcohol declined dramatically under prohibition. In the early 1920s, consumption of alcohol was about 30 percent of the pre-prohibition level. Consumption grew somewhat in the last years of prohibition, as illegal supplies of liquor increased and as a new generation of Americans disregarded the law. Nevertheless, it was a long time after repeal before consumption rates rose to their pre-prohibition levels. The death rate from alcoholism was cut by 80 percent by 1921 from pre–World War I levels, while alcohol-related crime dropped markedly. Deaths from cirrhosis of the liver for men fell from 29.5 per 100,000 in 1911 to 10.7 per 100,000 in 1929. Prohibition was indeed good for America.

It was repealed because enforcing the law was simply impossible. Smuggling and bootlegging were widespread. The legal system did not take the law seriously. In New York, 7,000 arrests for liquor law violations resulted in 17 convictions. The noble experiment ended at 3:32 p.m., December 5, 1933, when Utah became the 36th state to ratify the 21st Amendment, repealing Prohibition.

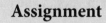

Assignment

Was Prohibition a "noble experiment" or a misguided effort to use government to shape morality?

THE CONSUMER ECONOMY

Before the 1920s people produced most of their clothing and food. They entertained themselves and spent a great deal of time reading and talking. That changed from 1919 to 1941.

People in the 1920s were the first to wear exact-size clothing. A historian explains, "They were the first to play electric phonographs, to use electric vacuum cleaners, to listen to commercial radio broadcasts, and to drink fresh orange juice year round. In countless ways, large and small, American life was transformed during the 1920s, at least in urban areas. Cigarettes, cosmetics, and synthetic fabrics such as rayon became staples of American life. Newspaper gossip columns, illuminated billboards, and commercial airplane flights were novelties during the 1920s. The United States became a consumer society."

In 1913, the 50-year-old Henry Ford revolutionized American manufacturing by introducing the automated assembly line. By using conveyor belts to bring automobile parts to workers, he reduced the assembly time for a Ford car from 12½ hours in 1912 to just 1½ hours in 1914. Declining production costs allowed Ford to cut automobile prices—six times between 1921 and 1925. The cost of a new Ford was reduced to just $290. To lower employee turnover and raise productivity, Ford introduced a minimum wage of $5 in 1914—twice what most workers earned—and shortened the workday from nine hours to eight hours. Alfred Sloan, the president of General Motors from 1923 to 1941, built his company into the world's largest automaker, not by refining the production process, but by adopting new approaches to advertising and marketing. Sloan summed up his philosophy with these blunt words: "The primary object of the corporation was to make money, not just to make cars." If Henry Ford demonstrated the efficacy of mass production, Sloan revealed the importance of merchandising in a modern consumer society.

Cars revolutionized life. On one hand, the automobile

Portrait of Henry Ford. Photo by Hartsook, 1919 (PD-US).

promoted family togetherness through evening rides, picnics, and weekend excursions. On the other hand, automobiles created squabbles between parents and teenagers over use of the vehicle and encouraged an apparent decline in church attendance resulting from Sunday outings.

Mass-produced clothing was another important innovation in the world's expanding consumer economy. During World War I, governments created standard clothing sizes to help the nation's garment industry meet the demand for military uniforms. Standard sizes meant that it was now possible to mass produce ready-to-wear clothing.

Ernest A. Franke drives his "Lizzie" to the White House to show Henry Ford. Washington, D.C., April 27. His 1921 Model T Ford polished to a mirror like finish. Photographers Harris & Ewing, 1938 (PD-US).

During the 1920s, the chain store movement completely changed retailing. Chains of stores multiplied across the country, like Woolworth's. The largest grocery chain, A&P, had 17,500 stores by 1928. The mass economy had come.

Assignment

A historian observed, "A fundamental shift took place in the American economy during the 1920s. The nation's families spent a declining proportion of their income on necessities—food, clothing, and utilities—and an increasing share on appliances, recreation, and a host of new consumer products. As a result, older industries, such as textiles, railroads, and steel, declined, while newer industries, such as appliances, automobiles, aviation, chemicals, entertainment, and processed foods, surged ahead rapidly." Speculate upon the problems of a consumer, driven economy.

Even the public's eating habits changed. People consumed less bread and potatoes and more candy. Instead of preparing food at home, an increasing number of people purchased prepared foods. The nation's first million-dollar advertising campaign—for Uneeda Bisquits in a waterproof box—demonstrated advertising's power. Almost every household had a box of Uneeda Biscuits. Ad campaigns created new eating and entertainment habits. This was a sign of the emerging mass media campaigns that would revolutionize social history.

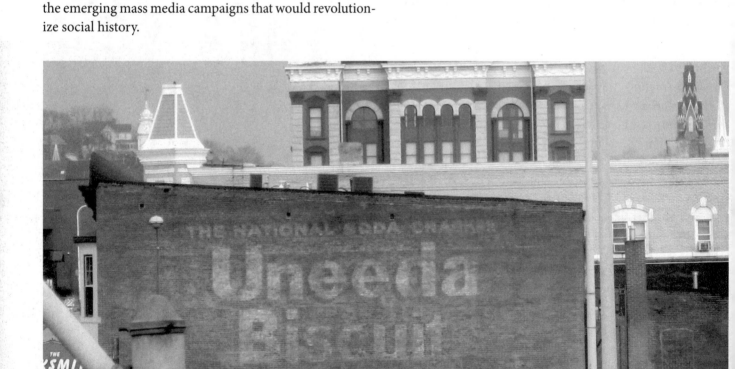

Early 20th-century Uneeda Biscuit Ghost sign, Dubuque, Iowa. Photo by Bill Whittaker, 2009 (CC BY-SA 3.0).

THE KU KLUX KLAN

A new version of the Ku Klux Klan emerged during the early 1920s. African Americans were no longer the only targets of the KKK. Roman Catholics, Jews, and foreigners were now targets as well.

The Klan grew astronomically in the 1920s. Contributing to the Klan's growth was a post-war depression in agriculture and the migration of African Americans into Northern cities.

During the early 1920s, the Klan helped elect 16 U.S. Senators, many Representatives, and local officials. By 1924, when the Klan had reached its peak, it controlled 24 of the nation's 48 state legislatures. That year it succeeded in blocking the nomination of Al Smith, a New York Catholic, at the Democratic National Convention.

The reader must not think that Klan members were simple, uneducated, unsophisticated people. The three million members of the Klan included small-business owners, independent professionals, clerical workers, and farmers. Many were urban, highly educated men, and even some women.

Assignment

Why did the Klan experience such astronomical growth in the 1920s?

Ku Klux Klan. Photo by Herbert A. French, c1921 (PD-US).

Henry Ford, standing, and Barney Oldfield in 1902, with the Ford 999 racing automobile. Photographer unknown, 1902 (PD-US).

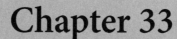

Chapter 33

WORLD WAR II AND BEYOND

First Thoughts . . .

World War II ushered in a new world order, bringing an end to Hitler's Third Reich, Mussolini's fascist dictatorship in Italy, and an aggressive Japanese empire in the Pacific. For the part it played in the Allies' victory, the United States earned a new powerful and coveted role on the world stage. Americans commonly refer to World War II as "the Good War," a conflict in which the forces of good triumphed over the forces of evil.

Chapter Learning Objectives . . .

In chapter 33, we will examine in depth World War II and the Cold War that followed. We will witness the triumph of American-led democracy. Great men of God like Dietrich Bonhoeffer will also inspire us.

As a result of this chapter you should be able to:

1. Identify the causes of World War II.
2. Analyze the causes and results of the Holocaust.
3. Discuss the roots of the Cold War and the reasons the Allies ultimately won this conflict.
4. Ponder Bonhoeffer's contrasting of cheap grace and costly grace.
5. Understand why Germany, firmly in control of Europe in 1940, eventually lost World War II in 1945.

WORLD WAR II

There are many excellent resources on the causes of World War II. One of the best is by historian Jen Rosenberg, who describes the beginning of World War II in Europe as follows:

As passage by Jen Rosenberg:

Adolf Hitler wanted more land, especially in the east, to expand Germany according to the Nazi policy of Lebensraum. Hitler used the harsh limitations that were set against Germany in the Versailles Treaty as a pretext for Germany's right to acquire land where German-speaking people lived. Germany successfully used this reasoning to envelop two entire countries without starting a war. Why was Germany allowed to take over both Austria and Czechoslovakia without a fight? The simple reason is that Great Britain and France did not want to repeat the bloodshed of World War I. They believed, wrongly as it turned out, they could avoid another world war by appeasing Hitler with a few concessions (such as Austria and Czechoslovakia). Great Britain and France had not clearly understood that Hitler's goal of land acquisition was much, much larger than any one country. After having gained both Austria and Czechoslovakia, Hitler was confident that he could again move east, this time acquiring Poland without having to fight Britain and France. To eliminate the possibility of the Soviet Union fighting if Poland were attacked, Hitler made a pact with the Soviet Union—the Nazi-Soviet Non-Aggression Pact. So that Germany did not officially seem the aggressor (which it was), Hitler needed an excuse for entering/attacking Poland. It was Heinrich Himmler who came up with the idea; thus the plan was code named Operation Himmler.

   On the night of August 31, 1939, Nazis took an unknown prisoner from one of their concentration

Hitler at Nazi party rally, Nuremberg, Germany, Heinrich Hoffman Collection, c1928 (PD-US).

camps, dressed him in a Polish uniform, took him to the town of Gleiwitz (on the border of Poland and Germany), and then shot him. The staged scene with the dead prisoner dressed in a Polish uniform was supposed to appear as a Polish attack against a German radio station. Hitler used the staged attack as the excuse to invade Poland.

The burning wreckage of the U.S. Navy battleship USS *Arizona* (BB-39) at Pearl Harbor, Hawaii. Photo by United States Navy, 1941 (PD-US).

At 4:45 on the morning of September 1, 1939 (the morning following the staged attack), German troops entered Poland. The sudden, immense attack by the Germans was called a Blitzkrieg ("lightning war"). The German air attack hit so quickly that most of Poland's air force was destroyed while still on the ground. To hinder Polish mobilization, the Germans bombed bridges and roads. Groups of marching soldiers were machine-gunned from the air. But the Germans did not just aim for soldiers, they also shot at civilians. Groups of fleeing civilians often found themselves under attack. The more confusion and chaos the Germans could create, the slower Poland could mobilize its forces.

Using 62 divisions, six of which were armored and ten mechanized, the Germans invaded Poland by land. Poland was not defenseless, but they could not compete with Germany's motorized army. With only 40 divisions, none of which were armored, and with nearly their entire air force demolished, the Poles were at a severe disadvantage—Polish cavalry were no match for German tanks. On September 1, the beginning of the German attack, Great Britain and France sent Hitler an ultimatum—withdraw German forces from Poland or Great Britain and France would go to war against Germany.

On September 3, with Germany's forces penetrating deeper into Poland, Great Britain and France both declared war on Germany.

World War II had begun.

Though war had begun in Europe, 1939 Depression-era America was not yet ready to fight. Preoccupied with domestic problems, Americans had no intention of entering another European War as we had in 1917. Let the Europeans fight their own war! These "**Isolationists**" were, without a doubt, the majority of Americans.

The outbreak of World War II in Europe proved to be an important turning point in the development of American foreign policy. This was a shift back to the America of the 1870s (see Foreign Expansion Unit) that now wished to be left alone and out of European politics. Most American sympathies, however, lay with the underdogs—Great Britain and France—and it was difficult to remain neutral, especially after France fell in 1940 and Great Britain was about to fall. German submarine warfare also complicated matters. Still, in 1941, America officially was neutral.

The situation in Asia was no better. In the early 1930s, Japan began her conquest of China and vigorously continued her efforts in 1937 with an attack called "the rape of Nanking." President Roosevelt responded slowly to Japanese threats. His domestic problems were all he

Jews captured and forcibly pulled out from dugouts by the Germans during the Warsaw Ghetto uprising. Photo by John Stroop, 1943 (PD-US).

could bear, and besides, from the beginning, Roosevelt saw Hitler as a greater threat. Roosevelt supported nonviolent means to control Japanese aggression. By 1941, America had imposed an embargo on certain goods—notably scrap iron. These measures persuaded Japan to take a great gamble.

Japan could retreat from her attempted world conquest and lose face, or she could take a bold gamble and attack the U.S. She chose the latter course of action.

On December 7, 1941, air force bombers from the Japanese Empire attacked the American Naval base at Pearl Harbor. The next day, December 8, 1941, the same day the U.S. declared war on Japan, Germany declared war on America. Now the whole world was at war!

The Japanese attack on American soil at Pearl Harbor motivated America in a way no one expected. America brought her entire industrial might to bear against the powers of the Axis—Japan, Italy, and Germany. It took four years to do so, but, by August 1945, the Allied Forces had defeated the Axis and ended World War II.

From 1941 to 1945, millions of Americans who had never traveled far from home found themselves in military service halfway around the world, in places like Hamburg, Manila, Honolulu, and Casablanca. This world war changed America in ways no one had ever predicted. We had become a permanent member of the world community. Isolationism was not an option.

One group who experienced this change was the Japanese Americans. During the early years of the war, most Americans were afraid that Japan or Germany might invade the United States. Such thoughts seem ludicrous to us today, but to our parents and grandparents, it was a real possibility. The federal government felt that it needed to relocate thousands of Japanese Americans, so it resettled them in inland internment camps, far from the Pacific coast. This was a tragic mistake, but at the time, the decision had widespread support from most Americans.

The war required a massive effort on the part of all

Crematory in Majdanek German Nazi concentration camp near Lublin.

Assignment

What were the causes of World War II?

Americans. More than 12 million Americans served in the armed forces. The total of our dead, wounded, or missing was one million (Fenton, et al., p. 624). Americans who were not called by the military had to adjust to a strikingly different life at home. The federal government strictly regulated the economy. Food, fuel, and other strategic raw materials were rationed. Women replaced their soldier-husbands in factories and other workplaces. America would never be the same again.

In fact, the world would never be the same again. More than 46 million people died in World War II. Six million of these casualties were Jewish people murdered by the Nazis during the Holocaust..

The word *holocaust* literally means "massive destruction by fire." The word *Shoah*, meaning "widespread disaster", is the modern Hebrew equivalent. The Holocaust was the systematic extermination of approximately six million Jews by the Nazis and their collaborators. Between the German invasion of the Soviet Union in the summer of 1941 and the end of the war in Europe in May 1945, Nazi Germany and its accomplices strove to murder every Jew under their domination. They very nearly succeeded. Today there are virtually no Jewish people living in Poland; before World War II there were millions. Almost all the Jewish children of Europe—four out of five (80 percent)—died. The Jews were not the only victims; other individuals and groups were persecuted and murdered during this period, but the Jews were the only group that the Nazis sought to destroy entirely (Yad Vashem & Wiesenthal Center).

By the end of the Second World War in 1945, the Nazi regime and its accomplices had physically annihilated about 11.5 million people: 6 million Jews and 5.5 million "undesirable others"—mentally ill, disabled, political opponents, homosexuals, Slavs, Gypsies, Jehovah's Witnesses, and Pentecostals.

Electrical fence around Auschwitz concentration camp

POSTMODERNISM

Postmodernism is a tendency in contemporary culture characterized by the rejection of objective truth and a common cultural narrative. In other words, in postmodernism every sacrosanct ethic is in question. Before postmodernism the Golden Rule, for instance, was universally accepted as a desirable moral trait. Not in postmodernism—everything is on the chopping block

Postmodernism emphasizes the role of language, power relations, and motivations; in particular it attacks the use of classifications such as male versus female, straight versus gay, white versus black, and imperial versus colonial. Postmoderns avoid "categories," which by definition limit reality.

Postmodernism has influenced many cultural fields, including literary criticism, sociology, linguistics, architecture, visual arts, and music. Recently the author heard former President Bill Clinton respond in a postmodern way to a question posed to him by reporters. President Clinton told reporters that one of Clinton's colleagues had mistakenly destroyed valuable but un-flattering Clinton archival material.

"President Clinton," the assertive reporters continued, "how do we know that your friend did not destroy this material to protect you?"

"My friend is a good man and he would not do that," President Clinton re-sponded with a smile.

"Why should we believe you, Mr. President?" the reports retorted.

President Clinton was visibly upset. "Why? Because I am telling you it is true."

This reader believes absolutely that former Pres-ident Clinton really thought that the public should be-lieve him because "he said it was true." Reality to a postmodern man is very much tied up in the subjective language that he generates.

Most scholars argue that postmodernism began in the 1990s, after the end of the Cold War. Postmodernist thought is an intentional departure from modernist approaches that embraced empiricism and science. The term "postmodernism" comes from its critique of the "modernist" scientific mentality of objectivity and progress associated with the Enlightenment.

Assignment

In postmodernism there is no right or wrong, no doctrine. What implications can this have for Christianity?

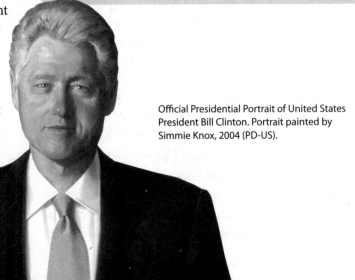

Official Presidential Portrait of United States President Bill Clinton. Portrait painted by Simmie Knox, 2004 (PD-US).

THE MODERN FAMILY

Can an expectant mother obtain an abortion without her husband's permission? Who gets custody in a divorce battle? Should same-sex marriage partners be allowed to adopt? Does a father have the right to give his children his last name even if his wife objects? Should a teenager, unhappy with her parents' restrictions on her smoking, dating, and choice of friends, be allowed to have herself placed in a foster home? Should a childless couple be permitted to hire a "surrogate mother" who will be artificially inseminated and carry a child to delivery? These are among the questions that the nation's courts have had to wrestle with as the nature of American family life has, in the course of a generation, been revolutionized (according to historian Steven Mintz).

Social historians point out that during the 1950s, the television show *Leave It to Beaver* characterized the American family. In 1960, over 70 percent of all American households were like the Cleavers: made up of a breadwinner father, a homemaker mother, and their two kids. Today, "traditional" families with a working husband, an unemployed wife, and one or more children make up less than 15 percent of the nation's households.

Profound changes have reshaped American family life in recent years. In a decade, divorce rates doubled. The number of divorces today is twice as high as in 1966 and three times higher than in 1950. The rapid upsurge in the divorce rates contributed to a dramatic increase in the number of single-parent households or what used to be known as broken homes. The number of households consisting of a single woman and her children has tripled since 1960. A sharp increase in female-headed homes has been accompanied by a startling increase in the number of couples cohabitating outside of marriage. The number of unmarried couples living together has quadrupled since 1970 (Steven Mintz).

In summary, according to Tom W. Smith, National Opinion Research Center, while still a central institution in American society, marriage plays a less dominant role than it once did. The proportion of adults who have never been married rose from 15 percent to 23 percent between 1972 and 1998. When the divorced, separated, and widowed are added in, three-quarters of adults were married in the early 1970s, but only 56 percent were by the late-1990s.

According to social historians, the decline in marriage comes from three main sources. First, people are delaying marriage. Between 1960 and 1997 the median age at first marriage rose from 22.8 to 26.8 years for men and from 20.3 to 25.0 years for women. Second, divorces have increased. The divorce rate more than doubled from 9.2 divorces per year per 1,000 married women in 1960 to a divorce rate of 22.6 in 1980. This rise was at least in part caused by increases in female, labor-force participation, and decreases in fertility mentioned below. The divorce rate then slowly declined to 19.8 in 1995. The drop in the divorce rate in the 1980s and 1990s has been much slower than the rapid rise from the 1960s to the early 1980s, and as a result, the divorce rate in the 1990s is still more than twice as high as it was in 1960. Even with the slight recent moderation in the divorce rate, the proportion of ever-married adults who have been divorced doubled from 17 percent in 1972 to 33–34 percent in 1996/98. In some areas of the country (e.g., Southern California) the divorce rate is over half. This means that over half of American children are being raised in single-family or blended-family homes. Third, people are slower to remarry than previously. While most people divorced or widowed before the age of 50 remarry, the length of time between marriages has grown. Fourth, both the delay in age at first marriage and in remarriage is facilitated by an increase in cohabitation. Cohabitation represented only 1.1 percent of couples in 1960 and 7.0 percent in 1997.

The cohabitation rate is still fairly low overall because most cohabitations are short term, typically leading to either a marriage or a break-up within a year. But cohabitation has become the norm for both men and women as their first form of union and after divorces. For women born in 1933–1942 only 7 percent first lived with someone in a cohabitation rather than in a marriage, but for women born in 1963–1974, 64 percent started off cohabiting rather than marrying. The trend for men is similar. Among the currently divorced, 16 percent are cohabiting, and of those who have remarried, 50 percent report cohabiting with their new spouse before their remarriage.

Along with the decline of marriage has come a decline in childbearing. The fertility rate peaked at 3.65 children per woman at the height of the Baby Boom in 1957 and then declined rapidly to a rate of 1.75 children in 1975. This is below the "replacement level" of about 2.11 children that is needed for a population to hold its own through natural increase. The rate then slowly gained ground to 2.0–2.1 children in the early 1990s. In 1972 the average adult had had 2.4 children, and this number slipped to a low of 1.8 children in the mid-1990s. Likewise, while only 45 percent of households had no children under 18 living at home in 1972, this climbed to 62 percent in 1998. Thus, the typical American household currently has no minor children living in it. Accompanying this decline in childbearing and childrearing was a drop in preferences for larger families. In 1972 56 percent thought that the ideal number of children was three or more. By 1996–98 only 39 percent thought that three or more represented the ideal number of children. However, there was also little or no increase in a preference for small families. Over the last three decades just 3–5 percent have favored families with zero to one children.

Moreover, during the last generation, childbearing increasingly became disconnected from marriage. In 1960 only 5.3 percent of births were to unmarried mothers, while by 1996 over 32 percent of all births were outside of marriage. The rate of increase has been much greater for whites than for blacks. For whites the percentage of unmarried births has expanded more than ten-fold from 2.3 percent of all births in 1960 to 25.7 percent in 1996, while the African-American level grew by over three-fold from 21.6 percent in 1960 to 70.4 percent in 1994. While in 1972 73 percent of children were being reared by two parents in an uninterrupted marriage, this fell to 49 percent in 1996 and was a 52 percent in 1998. Thus, the norm of the stable, two-parent family was close to becoming the exception for American children rather than the rule.

Assignment

Identify trends that are occurring in the modern family.

DIETRICH BONHOEFFER

German pastor Dietrich Bonhoeffer was one of the most powerful Christian martyrs of the 20th century. The son of a noted physician, Bonhoeffer was born in Breslau, Prussia. When Hitler assumed power in Germany, Bonhoeffer was in the United States. Knowing that Hitler was bad news for Germany, Bonhoeffer, at the risk of his own life, returned home. An outspoken opponent of Adolf Hitler and his rise to power in 1933, Bonhoeffer joined the Confessing Church, which resisted Nazism. After World War II started, Bonhoeffer joined in the political resistance to Hitler that led to his imprisonment in April 1943 in Berlin and his death by hanging at the Nazi concentration camp at Flossenbüürg on April 9, 1945.

A passage from *Cost of Discipleship* by Bonhoeffer:

Cheap grace is the deadly enemy of our Church. We are fighting today for costly grace. Cheap grace means grace sold on the market like cheapjacks' wares. The sacraments, the forgiveness of sin, and the consolations of religion are thrown away at cut prices. Grace is represented as the Church's inexhaustible treasury, from which she showers blessings with generous hands, without asking questions or fixing limits. Grace without price; grace without cost! The essence of grace, we suppose, is that the account has been paid in advance; and, because it has been paid, everything can be had for nothing. . . . Cheap grace means grace as a doctrine, a principle, a system. It means forgiveness of sins proclaimed as a general truth, the love of God taught as the Christian "conception" of God. An intellectual assent to that idea is held to be of itself sufficient to secure remission of sins. . . . In such a Church the world finds a cheap covering for its sins; no contrition is required, still less any real desire to be delivered from sin. Cheap grace therefore amounts to a denial of the living Word of God, in fact, a denial of the Incarnation of the Word of God. . . . Cheap grace means the justification of sin without the justification of the sinner. Grace alone does everything they say, and so everything can remain as it was before. "All for sin could not atone." Well, then, let the Christian live like the rest of the world, let him model himself on the world's standards in every sphere of life, and not presumptuously aspire to live a different life under grace from his old life under sin. . . . Costly grace is the gospel that must be sought again and again and again, the gift that must be asked for, the door at which a man must knock. Such grace is costly because it calls us to follow, and it is grace because it calls us to follow Jesus Christ. It is costly because it costs a man his life, and it is grace because it gives a man the only true life. It is costly because it condemns sin, and grace because it justifies the sinner. Above all, it is costly because it cost God the life of his Son: "ye were bought at a price," and what has cost God much cannot be cheap for us. Above all, it is grace because God did not reckon his Son too dear a price to pay for our life, but delivered him up for us. Costly grace is the Incarnation of God. Costly grace is the sanctuary of God; it has to be protected from the world, and not thrown to the dogs. It is therefore the living word, the Word of God, which he speaks as it pleases him. Costly grace confronts us as a gracious call to follow Jesus. It comes as a word of forgiveness to the broken spirit and the contrite heart. Grace is costly because it compels a man to submit to the yoke of Christ and follow him; it is grace because Jesus says: "My yoke is easy and my burden is light."

Assignment

In your own words, explain the difference between cheap grace and costly grace.

Statue of Dietrich Bonhoeffer at the Gallery of 20th Century Martyrs at Westminster Abbey.

Chapter 34

SOUTH AFRICA

First Thoughts . . .

If the history of South Africa is in large part one of increasing racial divisiveness, it is also the story of—eventually—a journey through massive obstacles towards the creation, from tremendous diversity, of a single nation whose dream of unity and common purpose is now capable of realization. Like Kumalo in *Cry the Beloved Country*, South Africa suffered deeply. By the end of the novel Kumalo lost a brother, a sister, and a son. But he has gained a daughter-in-law, a nephew, and a grandchild as yet unborn. Once, when much younger, he had considered taking a job that would pay better than the priesthood. But suffering ennobles him. He grows into every bit as much a man of God. Instead of becoming a bitter old man, he acquires the vision to bring real change and hope to his community. Today, apartheid is dead, but it exacted a great price on the land. Let us hope that this new generation can face new challenges—like the HIV/AIDS epidemic—and bring lasting and permanent change to the land.

Chapter Learning Objectives . . .

In chapter 34, we will examine South African history in-depth. Then, we will look at the Boer people. Next, we will examine the AIDS epidemic that is afflicting all of Africa. Finally, we will end by looking at four philosophers that have ushered in the modern age.

As a result of this chapter you should be able to:

1. Discuss the history of South Africa.
2. Analyze the impact of the Boer people on South Africa.
3. Evaluate the causes of the African HIV/AIDS epidemic.
4. Discuss five philosophers who greatly impacted the postmodern world.

SOUTH AFRICAN HISTORY

Around 2,500 years ago Bantu peoples started migrating across sub-Saharan Africa from the Niger River Delta. The San People of Southern Africa and the Bantu-speakers lived mostly peacefully together, although since neither had any method of writing, researchers know little of this period.

From around AD 1200 a trade network began to emerge. Additionally, the idea of sacred leadership emerged —concept that transcends English terms such as "kings" or "queens." Sacred leaders were elite members of the community, types of prophets, people with supernatural powers and the ability to predict the future. A Western euphemism for this leadership would be "witch doctors."

In 1488 Portuguese explorer Bartolomeu Dias rounded the Cape of Good Hope first. Although the Portuguese basked in the nautical achievement of successfully navigating the cape, they showed little interest in colonization. The Portuguese had little competition in the region until the late 16th century, when the English and Dutch began to challenge the Portuguese along their trade routes.

The Dutch East India Company established the first permanent European settlement. The Dutch, however, were never keen on establishing a permanent colony in South Africa.

By 1800, Dutch power began to fade and the British moved in to fill the vacuum. They seized the Cape in 1795 to prevent it from falling into the hands of Napoleonic France, then briefly relinquished it to the Dutch (1803) before definitively conquering it in 1806.

At the tip of the continent the British found an established colony with 25,000 slaves, 20,000 white colonists, and 1,000 freed black slaves. Power resided solely with a white élite in Cape Town, and differentiation on the basis of race was deeply entrenched. Outside Cape Town and the immediate hinterland, isolated black and white pastoralists populated the country.

A new militant group emerged: the Boers. The Boers were a group of mostly Dutch settlers, now called Afrikaners, who moved out of the cities to avoid British control. The gap between the British settlers and the Boers further widened with the abolition of slavery in 1834, a move that the Boers generally regarded as against the God-given ordering of the races. Yet the British settlers' conservatism stopped any radical social reforms, and in 1841 the authorities passed a Masters and Servants Ordinance, which perpetuated white control. Meanwhile, numbers of British immigrants increased rapidly in Cape Town, in the area east of the Cape Colony (present-day Eastern Cape Province), in Natal. The discovery of diamonds and the subsequent discovery of gold led to a rapid increase in immigration of fortune seekers from all parts of the globe, including Africa itself.

Meanwhile a Zulu tribe war very nearly killed all Europeans in South Africa.

Assignment

Why was South Africa slow to attract European colonists?

South African Zulu Dancer

THE AFRICAN SLAVE TRADE

Portuguese traders established trading posts along the coast of Africa in 1445, followed by the French and English; the African slave trade began not long after, which over the following centuries would debilitate the region's economy and population.

Slave trading was a huge industry and immensely profitable. Along the west coast of Africa, from the Cameroons in the south to Senegal in the north, Europeans built 60 forts that served as trading posts. European traders could become outrageously wealthy after only one cargo of slaves.

Africans were brought to these forts by Africans. European traders waited at these forts for slaves; African traders transported slaves from the interior of Africa. Slaves were traded more than once, often in slave markets. African merchants became very wealthy abducting fellow Africans.

The African slave-trade - slaves taken from a ship captured by H.M.S. "Undine", artist unknown, 1884 (PD-US).

After kidnapping potential slaves, merchants cruelly forced them to walk in slave caravans to the European coastal forts, sometimes as far as 1,000 miles. Merchants learned that it was more profitable to allow weaker captives to die along the way than chance that their cargo would remain unsold at the European forts. Thus thousands of African captives never survived the arduous journey to the coast, and many others died on the journey across the sea.

Shackled and under nourished, only half the people survived these death marches. Those who reached the coastal forts were put into underground dungeons where they would stay—sometimes for as long as a year—until they were boarded on ships.

In the Spanish Caribbean islands and Portuguese Brazil by the mid-1500s, colonists had turned to the quick and highly profitable cultivation of sugar, a crop that required intense labor. European colonists found an answer to their pressing labor shortage by importing enslaved workers from Africa.

By 1619, more than a century and a half after the Portuguese first traded slaves on the African coast, European ships had brought a million Africans to plantations in the Americas. Trade through the West African forts continued for nearly 300 years. The Europeans made more than 54,000 voyages to trade in human beings and sent at least 10 to 12 million Africans to the Americas. This African diaspora was the most massive forced migration in world history.

Assignment

Describe the devastation of the African slave trade.

AIDS/HIV EPIDEMIC

HIV/AIDS is a major public health concern and cause of death in Africa. Although Africa is inhabited by just over 14.7 percent of the world's population, it is estimated to have more than 88 percent of people living with HIV and 92 percent of all AIDS deaths in 2007.

Without the kind of health care and medicines that are available in developed countries, large numbers of people in Africa will develop full-blown AIDS. They will not only be unable to work, but will also require significant medical care. This will likely cause a collapse of economies and societies. Thanks to former President George W. Bush, millions of Africans will receive vaccines and have real hope of survival. But millions will also no doubt die.

A sociologist explained, "Society's fittest, not its frailest, are the ones who die—adults spirited away, leaving the old and the children behind. You cannot define risk groups: everyone who is sexually active is at risk. Babies too [are] unwittingly infected by mothers. Barely a single family remains untouched. Most do not know how or when they caught the virus, many never know they have it, many who do know don't tell anyone as they lie dying."

In 1959 scientists identified the AIDS virus. Only in the mid-1980s did a scientist at the National Institutes for Health, with a high profile reputation in cancer research, claim to have proven the link between HIV and AIDS. Although disputed at the time by a handful of scientist, in their desperation to find a cure, the world stopped looking for the virus and began trying to find a treatment or vaccine. It is now generally accepted that HIV is a descendant of a Simian Immunodeficiency Virus because certain strains of SIVs bear a very close resemblance to HIV-1 and HIV-2, the two types of HIV.

In the 26 African nations with the highest prevalence, average life expectancy is 48.3 years—6.5 years less than it would be without the disease. For the 11 countries in Africa with prevalence rates above 13 percent, life expectancy is 47.7 years—11.0 years less than would be expected without HIV/AIDS.

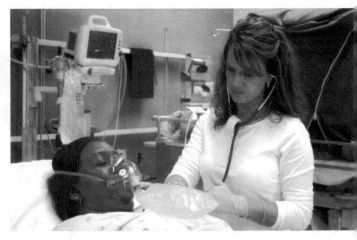

The social impact of HIV/AIDS is most evident in the continent's orphan crisis. Approximately 12 million children in sub-Saharan Africa are estimated to be orphaned by AIDS. These children are overwhelmingly cared for by relatives, including especially grandmothers, but the capacity of the extended family to cope with this burden is stretched very thin and is, in places, collapsing.

In the mid-1980s, HIV and AIDS were virtually unheard of in southern Africa; it is now the worst-affected region in the world. Of the 11 southern African countries—Angola, Namibia, Zambia, Zimbabwe, Botswana, Malawi, Mozambique, South Africa, Lesotho, Swaziland, Mada-gascar—at least six estimate an infection rate of over 20 percent.

There is some reason for hope. Millions of Africans are being successfully treated with medical interventions. Lifestyle decisions are also being influenced by expensive and extensive public relations campaigns. Nonetheless, the AIDS epidemic, like no other historical event, has reshaped African society in permanent and significant ways (ABC News).

Assignment

What are the causes and the solution to the African AIDS/HIV epidemic?

WITTGENSTEIN AND RUSSELL

Ludwig Wittgenstein (1889–1951)

"If a person could not speak it, it was not real," Wittgenstein was famous for saying.

Wittgenstein was the Albert Einstein of Western philosophy. As Einstein completely transformed physics, Wittgenstein transformed philosophy. In fact, some scholars argued that by introducing new paradigms and categories for discussion, he ended philosophy as a viable discipline. Like Martin Heidegger, he argued that reality was merely language. If a person could not say it, then it was not real. In other words, philosophy was irrelevant. Only language was relevant. While Western philosophy purported to discuss essential foundations of justice, reality, and ethics, these were, according to Wittgenstein, false problems distracting people from the real issues. Philosophy tried to push people beyond their language. For example, Plato's forms were irrelevant abstractions because no one could really articulate what he meant by a "form." Mankind, Wittgenstein argued, was captured in the reality of language. If he could not speak or describe it then it was not real. This had profound ramifications on Western philosophy and made Wittgenstein one of the early leaders of postmodernism. Postmodernism is a philosophy that argues that there is no objective theory of knowledge and truth.

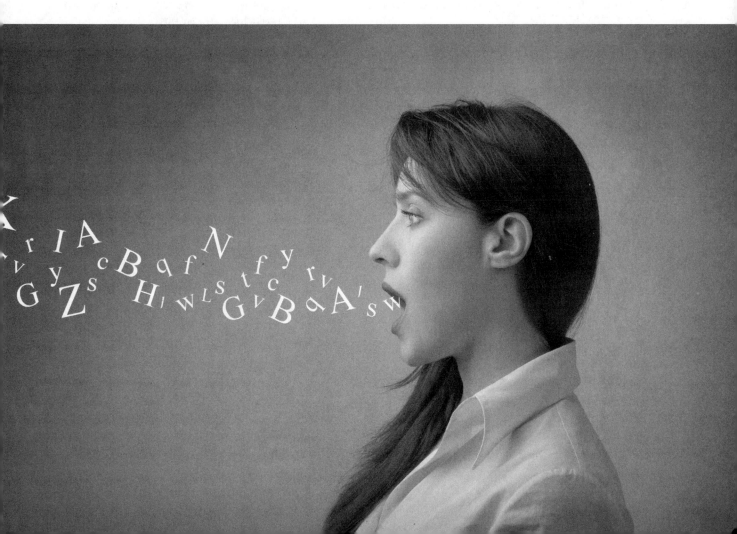

A passage by Ludwig Wittgenstein:

Our language can be seen as an ancient city: a maze of little streets and squares, of old and new houses, and of houses with additions from various periods; and this surrounded by a multitude of new boroughs with straight regular streets and uniform houses.

Bertrand Russell (1872–1970)

Russell (below, PD-US) was an extremely productive writer who rejected all subjectivity. He even disavowed that there was any intrinsic thought or knowledge on which a world view could be built. All reality must be subject to objective logical inquiry. Thus, psychology and other social sciences was suspect. Naturally, all religions, full of speculation and unable to be quantified, were rejected out-of-hand. If an actual event could not be quantified or repeated then it was not real. There was no reality outside of natural science or quantified history.

A passage from *A Free Man's Worship* by Bertrand Russell:

If an actual event could not be quantified or repeated then it was not real. How, in such an alien and inhuman world, can so powerless a creature as Man preserve his aspirations untarnished? A strange mystery it is that Nature, omnipotent but blind, in the revolutions of her secular hurryings through the abysses of space, has brought forth at last a child, subject still to her power, but gifted with sight, with knowledge of good and evil, with the capacity of judging all the works of his unthinking Mother. In spite of Death, the mark and seal of the parental control, Man is yet free, during his brief years, to examine, to criticize, to know, and in imagination to create. To him alone, in the world with which he is acquainted, this freedom belongs; and in this lies his superiority to the resistless forces that control his outward life.

Assignment

A. The Christian agrees that the Word is primary. What problems, then, if any, does the Christian have with Wittgenstein's philosophy?

B. Russell's argument that life is based on empiricism, rationality, quantified truth of any sort, is absurd. Honestly, how does one measure hope? Love? Faith? And what is life without those things?

GLOSSARY

Aeschylus - The earliest and most famous Greek playwrights.

Agrarian - An agrarian economy is based on farming.

Antioch - A thriving Asia Minor Roman city in present-day Turkey.

Andes Mountains - The world's longest continental mountain range. They lie as a continuous chain of highland along the western coast of South America.

Apeiron - Ionian philosophers argued that everything was made from "apeiron," which is not unlike the concept of an "atom" that was discovered in the 21st century.

Appian Way - A famous road that led into Rome.

Aristotelian Empiricism - It argued that reality must be measured and replicated or it was not real. Thus, "love" or "hope" were less real than "water" or "time."

Artemisium - At the sea where the Persians were thoroughly defeated by Greek triremes and ended the Persian threat for a generation.

Bismarck, Otto von - United all of the German states into one nation.

Byzantine Empire - Or Eastern Roman Empire was the Roman Empire during the Middle Ages, centered on the capital of Constantinople, and ruled by emperors in direct succession to the ancient Roman emperors. By the time the Vikings came, it was a shell of its former existence.

Cabot, John - Giovanni Caboto, known in England as John Cabot, was an Italian navigator and explorer whose 1497 discovery of North America was the first European voyage to the continent since the Vikings.

Caravel - A new type of ship that allowed explorers to go great distances in relatively short times.

Catacombs - Underground burial places where early persecuted Christians met to worship God.

Chaldea - The ancient name for the marshy lands in the far south of Mesopotamia, at the head of the Persian Gulf; present-day Iraq and Kuwait.

Charlemagne - King of the Franks (France and Germany) from 768 to his death. His Holy Roman Empire incorporated much of Western and Central Europe.

Constantine - Made Christianity the Roman state religion. He was the last great Roman emperor.

The Constitution of 1791 - The first written constitution of France. One of the basic precepts of the revolution was adopting constitutionality and establishing popular sovereignty, following the example of the United States of America.

Cottage Industry - An industry where goods were manufactured in small homes and craft shops.

Council of Trent - Pope Paul III (1534–1549) initiated the Council of Trent (1545–1563), which rejected specific Protestant positions and upheld the basic structure of the Medieval Catholic Church. For instance, the Council clearly upheld salvation appropriated by grace through faith and works of that faith (not just by faith, as the Protestants insisted).

Cyrus the Great - The first Zoroastrian Persian emperor. He was the founder of the Persian Empire.

Deacons - A recognized office in the early church. It was a calling to serve others, and had no ecclesiological authority. Some church historians think that pastors emerged from this group, not the elders or presbyters.

The Declaration of the Rights of Man - Defined the fundamental rights for French citizens.

Empress Consort Teishi - A 9th-century princess, daughter of a king.

Epistemology - The study of knowledge.

Eschatology - The study of the end times.

Etruscans - Settled in Italy when the Romans arrived.

Feudalism - A political and military system between a feudal aristocracy and his vassals. In its most literal sense, feudalism refers to the Medieval European political system composed of a set of reciprocal legal and military obligations among the warrior nobility, revolving around the three key concepts of lords, vassals, and fiefs.

Fjords - Deep-water bays that extend many miles into the Scandinavian interior.

Gnosticism - A religion that argued that salvation came through knowledge, gnosis, and participation in the spiritual world.

Gupta Empire - An Ancient Indian empire that existed approximately from 320 to 550 CE and covered much of the Indian Subcontinent.

Hippocrates - The father of modern medicine.

Hoplites - A highly effective citizen soldier in the Greek army. The organization of the Greek army was brilliant in its simplicity.

Hussein, Saddam - The president of Iraq from July 16, 1979 until April 9, 2003.

Isolationists - A powerful American movement committed to keeping America out of the new European war. One leading proponent of this position was Charles Lindbergh.

Jōmon - The oldest and first recorded culture in Japanese history. The Jōmon period is the time in Japanese prehistory from about 14,000 BC to 300 BC. The term "Jōmon" refers to the markings made on clay vessels and figures using sticks with cords wrapped around them, which are characteristic of the Jōmon people.

Leonidas - King of Sparta, and his 300 soldiers, momentarily stopped 200,000 Persians from conquering Greek and allowed his nation time to regroup.

Magellan, Ferdinand - A Portuguese explorer who later obtained Spanish nationality in order to serve King Charles I of Spain in search of a westward route to China.

Marathon - The first Persian land threat was turned back at Marathon.

Monasticism - The religious practice in which someone renounces worldly pursuits to embrace spiritual disciplines.

Moravians - The Moravian Church began in late 14th-century Bohemia (modern Czech Republic). It placed a high premium on Christian unity, personal piety, missions, and music.

Mughals - The greatest flourishing of northern Indian culture took place during the reign of the Islamic Mughal monarchs of the 16th and 17th centuries. The Mughals were Central Asian descendents of the great Mongol warriors Ghengis Khan and Timur (Tamerlane), whose hordes of cavalry swept across the Eurasian steppes in the 13th and 14th centuries, conquering everything between Beijing and Budapest.

Nero - An emperor of Rome who blamed the great fire in Rome on the Christians and started a great persecution.

Ontology - The study of the beginning of things.

Pahlavi, Mohammad Rezā Shāh - Shah of Iran, was the emperor of Iran from 1941 until his overthrow by the Iranian Revolution February 1979.

Patricians and Plebians - Roman society was divided into the patricians, aristocrats and landowners, and the plebeians, laborers and farmers.

Peasants' War - A popular revolt that took place in Europe during 1524–1525. It was Europe's largest and most widespread popular uprising prior to the French Revolution of 1789.

Peloponnesian Confederacy - An Athenian-dominated collection of city-states that partnered together for mutually beneficial reasons.

Penultimate truth - Truth that transcends and precedes all other truth.

Pericles - The most famous king of Athens during its most important years, called the Golden Age of Greece.

Petrarch - A Renaissance scholar who greatly advanced the notion of humanism.

Phalanx - A battle formation used by Greek armies.

Plague or Black Death, The - Killed 25 million people—33.3% of the European population between 1347 and 1352.

Robespierre, Maximilien - One of the most controversial figures of the French Revolution. He was a leader in the Reign of Terror, which ended with his arrest and execution in 1794.

Romulus and Remus - Legendary founders of Rome.

Sei Shōnagon - A Japanese author and court lady who served the Empress Teishi/Empress Sadako around the year 1000 during the middle Heian Period, and is best known as the author of *The Pillow Book*.

Seljuk Turks - Islamic militant people who blocked Christian European pilgrims who journeyed to the Holy Land.

Syracuse - A city on the coast of Sicily, which, at that time, was a possession of Athens.

Talmud - Jewish commentaries on the first five books of the Old Testament.

Teutonburg Forest - In the Battle in the Teutonburg Forest Roman commander Publius Varus and 3,000 soldiers were slaughtered by German tribes.

Themistocles - The leader of the Athenian navy who contributed to the victory over the Persians in the Second Persian Wars as much as King Leonidas and his 300 from Sparta.

Thirty Years' War - One of the most destructive conflicts in European history. Initially the war was fought largely as a religious conflict between Protestants and Catholics in the Holy Roman Empire. Gradually, the war developed into a more general conflict involving most of the European powers.

Trireme - A class of warship used by the ancient civilizations of the Mediterranean, especially the Phoenicians.

Vedas - The most sacred books to the Hindus.

Waka - A type of classical Japanese verse. The term was coined during the Heian period, and was used to distinguish Japanese-language poetry from kanshi (poetry written in Chinese by Japanese poets), and later from renga. The term *waka* originally encompassed a number of differing forms, principally tanka "short poem" and chōka "long poem."

Xerxes - King Darius' son, who sought revenge.

Yamato Kings - The earliest Japanese state was ruled by Yamato "great kings"; the Yamato state, which the Japanese chronicles date to 500 AD, that is, the time when a new wave of Korean cultural influence passed through southern Japan, was really a loose hegemony. Yamato is the plain around Osaka; it is the richest agricultural region in Japan.

BIBLIOGRAPHY

Abu-Lughod, Janet. *Before European Hegemony. The World System A.D. 1250-1350.* (New York: Oxford University Press, 1989).

Adams, Brooks. *The Law of Civilization and Decay: An Essay on History.* (New York: Alfred A. Knopf, 1943).

Adams, Robert Mc. *The Evolution of Urban Society, Early Mesopotamia and Prehistoric Mexico.* (Chicago: Aldine 1966).

Adelson, Howard L. *Medieval Commerce.* (Princeton, Van Nostrand, 1962).

Allerdyce, Gilbert. *Toward World History.* American Historians and the Coming of the World History Course. *Journal of World History* Vol. I, No. 1, Spring, pp. 23-76 (1990).

----- . *The Ancient World-Systems versus the Modern World-System.* Review XIV, 3, Summer, pp. 349-385 (1990).

Amin, S., G. Arrighi, A.G. Frank, & I. Wallerstein. *Dynamics of the World Economy.* (New York: Monthly Review Press, and London: Macmillan Press, 1982).

Anderson, B. . *Imagined Communities: Reflections on the Origin and Spread of Nationalism.* (London: Verso, 1983).

Anderson, Perry. *Lineages of the Absolutist State.* (London: New Left Books, 1974).

Ashtor, E. . *A Social and Economic History of the Near East in the Middle Ages.* (London: Collins, 1976).

Baechler, Jean, John A. Hall and Michael Mann, Eds. *Europe and the Rise of Capitalism.* (Oxford: Basil Blackwell, 1988).

Bairoch, Paul. *The Economic Development of the Third World Since 1900.* (London: Methuen, 1975).

Barfield, Thomas. *The Perilous Frontier: Nomadic Empires and China.* (Cambridge, Mass. Basil Blackwell, 1989).

Barth, Frederic (Ed.) . *Ethnic Groups and Boundaries.* (Boston: Little, Brown & Co, 1969).

----- . Fourteen Ninety-Two. *Political Geography* XI,4, July 1992, reprinted in J.M.Blaut et al 1492. *The Debate on Colonialism, Eurocentrism and History.* (Trenton, NJ:Africa World Press, 1992).

Chandler, Tertius 1987. *Four Thousand Years of Urban Growth: An Historical Census.* Lewiston/Queenston: St. David's University Press.

Chaudhuri, K.N. *Trade and Civilisation in the Indian Ocean. An Economic History from the Rise of Islam to 1750.* (Cambridge: Cambridge University Press, 1985).

Cox, Oliver. *The Foundations of Capitalism.* (New York: Monthly Review Press, 1985).

Crawford, Harriet. *Sumer and the Sumerians.* (Cambridge: Cambridge University Press, 1991).

Crosby, Alfred W. *The Ecological Imperialism* (1986).

Diakanoff, Igor M. *Language Contacts in the Caucasus and the Near East.* In T.L. Markey and John A.C. Greppin, Eds. *When Worlds Collide: Indo-Europeans and the Pre-Indo-Europeans.* (Karoma Publishers, 1990).

DiCosmo, Nicola. The Economic Basis of the Conflict between China and the Nomadic Empire of the Hsiung Nu 2nd-1st C. BC. Paper presented at the British International Studies Association meetings, Newcastel, UK, Dece 17-19, 1990.

Dietler, Michael. *Greeks, Etruscans, and Thirsty Barbarians: Early Iron Age Interaction in the Rhone Basin of France. In Centre and Periphery. Comparative Studies in Archaelogy.* (Timothy C. Champion, Ed. London: Unwin Hyman, 1989).

Dobb, Maurice [original 1946] *Studies in the Development of Capitalism.* (London: Routledge & Keagan Paul, 1963).

Eberhard, Wolfram. *A History of China.* (London: Routledge & Keagan Paul. Revised Edition, 1977).

Engle, Shirley H., Ed. *New Perspectives in World History.* (Washington: National Council for the Social Studies, 1964).

Fairbank, John King. *Trade and Diplomacy on the China Coast.* (Stanford: Stanford University Press, 1969).

Farmer, Edward L. Civilization as a Unit of World History: Eurasia and Europe's Place in It. The History Teacher. Vol. 18, No. 3, May, 347-363 (1969).

------- et al. *Comparative History of Civilizations in Asia.* (Reading, Mass: Addison-Weasley, 1977).

Finley, M.I. *The Ancient Economy.* (London: Hogarth Press, Second Edition, 1985).

Fuchs, Eckhardt et al. *Across Cultural Borders.* (London: Rowman & Littlefield Publishers, 2002).

Grayson, Fred. *Cliffs AP World History.* (New Jersey: Wiley Publishing, 2006).

Hall, Timothy. *The Complete Idiot's Guide to World History.* (London: Alpha Books, 2008).

Jacques, Martin. *When China Rules the World.* (New York: Penguin Press, 2009).

Machiavelli, Niccolo. *The Prince.* (New York: Penguin Press, 2005).

McEvedy, Colin. *The New Penguin Atlas of Recent History.* (New York: Penguin Press, 2002).

McEvedy, Colin. *The New Penguin Atlas of Ancient History.* (New York: Penguin Press, 2009).

Roberts, J. M. *Penguin Guide to the 20th Century.* (New York: Penguin Press, 2004).

Stearns, Peter et al. *A World History in Documents.* (New York: New York University Press, 2008).

Stearns, Peter. *World History in Brief.* (New York: Longman, 2010).

Toropov, Brandon. *The Complete Idiot's Guide to World Religions.* (New York: Penguin Press, 2004).

Yohananan, John et al. *A Treasury of Asian Literature.* (New York: Penguin Press, 1994).

Earth, NASA photo

BIBLIOGRAPHY

APPENDIX: TIMELINE

A Timeline of Reconstruction

5000 BC—AD 1800

- People settled along the Nile Delta (c. 5000 BC).
- Amratian Society of Upper Egypt - first signs of civilization (c. 4000–3500 BC).
- Hieroglyphics developed (3200 BC)
- Menes joined Upper and Lower Egypt into one kingdom with the capital at Memphis (3110–2884 BC).
- 1st Dynasty kings buried in first royal tombs at Abydos (3000–2890 BC).
- Papyrus invented (1st Dynasty 2920 –2770 BC).
- Hetepsekhemsy victorious in rivalry for throne; kings' disagreement over gods' (Horus' and Seth) power settled by Khasekhemwy's (who took both titles) rule. Civil war erupted during the end of this dynasty. 2nd Dynasty (2770–2650 BC).
- Dynasty of great peace; King Khufu's Great Pyramid of Giza built 4th Dynasty (2575–2467 BC).
- Khufu (Cheops), Khephren (Chephren), and Menkare pyramids built (2550–2490 BC).
- King Userkaf's temple built for sun god Ra at Abusir (2494–2487 BC).
- High officials chosen from people outside the royal family 5th Dynasty (2465–2323 BC).
- Many records of trading expeditions from this period later discovered. 6th Dynasty (2323–2152 BC).
- Capital moved from Memphis to Herakleopolis in northern Middle Egypt - Upper Egypt controlled by Theban rulers. (2160 BC).
- Collapse of the Old Kingdom 7th and 8th Dynasties (2150–2135 BC).
- Egypt split into the north, ruled from Herakleopolis, and the south, ruled from Thebes 9th and 10th Dynasties (2135–1986 BC).

- Prosperous period 11th Dynasty (2074–1937 BC).
- Capital moved to Thebes; Egypt reunited by Mentuhotep II (2134 –2000 BC).
- Senusret I built temple of Karnak at Thebes (1956–1911 BC).
- Amenemhet moved capital back to Memphis 12th Dynasty (1937–1756 BC).
- Senusret II built Faiyum irrigation scheme (1877–1870 BC).
- Capital once again in Thebes (1650 BC).
- War between Thebes and Asiatic ruler (1560 BC).
- Ahmose victorious; sent the Hyksos (Thebians) out of Egypt 18th Dynasty (1539–1295 BC).
- Thutmose I began military campaigns (1504–1492 BC).
- Amenhotep III (1380 BC).
- Amenhotep IV (Akhenaton) (1367 –1350 BC).
- Tutankhamon (1336–1327 BC).
- Seti I restored many monuments; his temple at Abydos displayed superior carved wall relief 19th Dynasty (1295–1186 BC).
- Capital once again in Thebes (1650 BC).
- Ramses II (1279–1213 BC).
- Rameses III, 20th Dynasty (1186–1069 BC).
- Civil War (1069 BC).
- Civil war, foreign invaders tore Egypt apart. 21st Dynasty (1070–945 BC).
- Conquest of Egypt by Kush under Kashta and then Piankhy (730 BC).
- Assyrian invasion, 25th Dynasty (712–657 BC).
- The Persian Conquest, 27th Dynasty (525–404 BC).

- Amytravios retook Egypt from Persia 28th Dynasty (404–399 BC).
- Alexander the Great invaded Egypt (332 BC).
- Alexandria founded (331 BC).
- Ptolemaic Dynasty (323–30 BC).
- The Temple of Isis built on the island of Philae in the Nile River. (300 BC).
- Queen Cleopatra VII and Mark Antony defeated; Octavian entered Egypt, beginning Roman rule; Egypt did not have another Egyptian ruler for 2000 years (31 BC).
- Thutmose I began military campaigns (1504–1492 BC).
- Egyptian hieroglyphic writing no longer used as people no longer understood its symbols (AD 395–641).
- Egypt conquered by Muslin Arabs (AD 641).
- Rosetta Stone helped Jean Francois Chompollion break hieroglyphic code (AD 1822).
- People settled along the Nile Delta (c. 5000 BC).
- Amratian Society of Upper Egypt - first signs of civilization (c. 4000–3500 BC).
- Hieroglyphics developed (3200 BC).
- Menes joined Upper and Lower Egypt into one kingdom with the capital at Memphis (3110–2884 BC).
- 1st Dynasty kings buried in first royal tombs at Abydos (3000–2890 BC).
- Papyrus invented (1st Dynasty 2920 –2770 BC).
- Hetepsekhemsy victorious in rivalry for throne; kings' disagreement over gods' (Horus' and Seth) power settled by Khasekhemwy's (who took both titles) rule. Civil war erupted during the end of this dynasty. 2nd Dynasty (2770–2650 BC).
- Dynasty of great peace; King Khufu's Great Pyramid of Giza built 4th Dynasty (2575–2467 BC).

- Khufu (Cheops), Khephren (Chephren), and Menkare pyramids built (2550–2490 BC).
- King Userkaf's temple built for sun god Ra at Abusir (2494–2487 BC).
- High officials chosen from people outside the royal family, 5th Dynasty (2465–2323 BC).
- Many records of trading expeditions from this period later discovered, 6th Dynasty (2323–2152 BC).
- Capital moved from Memphis to Herakleopolis in northern Middle Egypt - Upper Egypt controlled by Theban rulers. (2160 BC).
- Collapse of the Old Kingdom, 7th and 8th Dynasties (2150–2135 BC).
- Egypt split into the north, ruled from Herakleopolis, and the south, ruled from Thebes, 9th and 10th Dynasties (2135–1986 BC).
- Prosperous period, 11th Dynasty (2074–1937 BC).
- Capital moved to Thebes; Egypt reunited by Mentuhotep II (2134–2000 BC).
- Senusret I built temple of Karnak at Thebes (1956–1911 BC).
- Amenemhet moved capital back to Memphis 12th Dynasty (1937–1756 BC).

3000 BC — 86 A.D.

- Early Greek cultures (3000–2000 BC)
- Minoan civilization on Crete and movement to peninsula (2500–1200 BC).
- First Greek migration to west coast of Asia minor (1050–750 BC).
- First Olympic Games (776 BC).
- Homer writes the *Iliad* and the *Odyssey* (c. 750–700 BC).
- City-states are formed (c. 750–500 BC).
- First Greek colonies in Sicily (735–700 BC).
- Spartans become a major power (c. 730–710 BC).
- Anaximander dies (540 BC).
- Classical Period (500–323 BC).
- Persian Wars fought (490–479 BC).

- First Persian War: Athenians defeat Persians at Marathon (480 BC).
- First of the Peloponnesian Wars begins between Sparta and Athens (461–446 BC).
- Euripides wrote his first tragic play (441 BC).
- Second of the Peloponnesian Wars between Sparta and Athens fought (431–405 BC).
- Socrates was executed (399 BC).
- Plato founded the Academy (386 BC).
- Aristotle was born (384 BC).
- Philip II became the king of Macedon (359 BC).
- Alexander the Great, son of Philip II, was born (356 BC).
- Alexander the Great era (336–323 BC).
- Hellenistic Period began (323 BC).
- Rome conquered Greece (AD 86).

A Timeline of the Early Church

- Emperor Augustus died (AD 14).
- Jesus was crucified and resurrected (AD 33).
- James, the brother of John, was beheaded (Acts 12:2)(AD 42).
- Barnabas brought Saul to Antioch (Acts 11:25–26)(AD 43).
- Herod Agrippa I, King of Judea and Samaria, died (Acts 12:23)(AD 44).
- Saul (Paul) and Barnabas went on their first missionary journey (Acts 13–14) (AD 47–49).
- The Council at Jerusalem was held (Acts 15), canceling a circumcision requirement for Gentiles (AD 45–50).
- Paul's second missionary journey began (AD 50).
- Paul wrote his epistles to the Thessalonians, from Corinth (AD 51).
- Christians were persecuted during Nero's reign (AD 64).
- Jerusalem was destroyed (AD 70).
- The Coliseum at Rome opened (AD 80).
- Justin Martyr was born (AD 105)(died 165 AD).
- Christians were persecuted during Trajan's reign (98–117 AD).

- Polycarp was burned at the stake in Smyrna (AD 157).
- Around this date, Hippolytus established the date of Christ's birth (Christmas Day) as December 25 (AD 220).
- A private house in the city of Dura-Europas on the Euphrates was adapted for Christian worship (AD 231).
- Gothic people conducted raids in Asia Minor (AD 250).
- Edicts were published demanding outward conformity with paganism; Christians were forbidden to hold worship services, under penalty of death (AD 257).
- Anthony began the first monastic community in Egypt (AD 285).
- Emperor Galerius issued an edict granting Christianity the right to exist and Christians to assemble (AD 311).
- Constantine was converted and issued the Edict of Milan: Christianity was given a legal status equal to paganism (AD 313).
- Constantine required all subjects of the Roman Empire to observe the Lord's day as a day of rest, and also to honor Friday, the day of Christ's death (AD 321).
- Gothic people conducted raids in Asia Minor (AD 250).
- The Council at Nicaea created the Nicene Creed (AD 325).
- St. John Chrysostom was born (AD 347).
- Ulfila, translator of the Bible in Gothic language (the first Scripture translation for a people living outside the Roman Empire), left the Gothic lands when the ruler of the Tervingi, a Gothic tribe, began a persecution of Christians (AD 347-348).
- Siricius became the first bishop of Rome to use the title "pope" (AD 384).
- Ambrose baptized Augustine in Milan (AD 387).
- The Visigoths sacked Rome (AD 410).
- Augustine's *City of God* was published (AD 427).
- The Vandals invaded Northern Africa (AD 429).

- Patrick began his mission to Ireland (AD 432).
- The Vandals captured Carthage (AD 439).
- The Calcedonian Council was held (AD 451).
- The Western Roman Empire fell (AD 476).

A Timeline of Indian Dates

- Indus River Civilization - Development of urban grain-growing civilization on the Indus River (c2300–1750 BC).
- Aryan Migration - Migration into Northwest India by nomadic herding tribes from Iranian plateau (c1750–1000 BC).
- Brahmanism - Early Hinduism characterized by division of society into four classes (c 900 BC).
- Invasion of Alexander the Great Mauryan Empire - Domination of North India by Chandra-gupta, extended to South by grandson, Ashoka (324–200 BC).
- Development/Diffusion of Sanskrit Culture - Major texts of Hindu tradition take shape: Mahabharata, Ramayana, codification of laws, grammar, science, arts; gods Shiva, Vishnu are major figures; spread of Sanskritic culture to South India (250 BC).
- Gupta Dynasty - Guptas dominate North India (320–550).
- Invasions of Huns - Successive invasions of Huns; other Central Asian tribes destroy Gupta Empire (c455–528).
- Islamic Control - Turko-Afghan chieftains establish sultanate at Delhi; dominate North India (1192–1526).
- Mughal Empire - Mughal Empire unifies North and parts of South India under its rule; amalgam of Persian and Indian culture created in its courts and territories (1526–1858).
- European Traders in India - Establishment of trading outposts in India: Dutch (1609); English (1612); French (1674).

- Battle of Plassey - Victory over Nawab of Bengal gives British control of Bengal and begins expansion of British power in India (1757).
- Modern South Asia - Independence from British rule; partition of British India into modern countries of India and Pakistan (East and West). India (1947). Pakistan (1947).

A Timeline of Early China

Ancient China

- Xia (c2100–1800 BC).
- Shang (1700–1027 BC).
- Western Zhou (1027–771 BC).
- Eastern Zhou (770–221 BC).
- Spring and Autumn period (770–475 BC).
- Warring States period (475–221 BC).

Early Imperial China

- Qin (221–207 BC).
- Western Han (206 BC–AD 9).
- Hsing (9–25).
- Eastern Han (25–220).
- Three Kingdoms (220–265).
- Western Chin (265–316).
- Eastern Chin (17–420).
- Southern and Northern Dynasties (420–588).
- Northern Dynasties (386–588).

Classical Imperial China

- Sui (580–618).
- T'ang (618–907).
- Five Dynasties (907–960).
- Ten Kingdoms (907–979).
- Song (960–1279).
- Yuan (1279–1368).
- Ming (1368–1644).
- Qing (1644–1911).

Modern China

- Republic of China (in mainland China) (1911–1949).
- Republic of China (in Taiwan)(1949–).
- People's Republic of China (1949–).

A Timeline of the Middle Ages

- Withdrawal of Roman legions from England (450).
- St. Augustine of Canterbury's mission to Kent begins conversion of Anglo-Saxons to Christianity (597).
- Cædmon's Hymn, earliest poem recorded in English (680).
- Bede completes *Ecclesiastical History of the English People* (731).
- *Beowulf* written (750)
- First Viking raids on England (787).
- Norman Conquest by William I (1066).
- Crusades (1095-1221).
- Future King Henry II marries Eleanor of Aquitaine, bringing vast French territories to the English crown (1152).
- Archbishop Thomas à Becket murdered in Canterbury Cathedral (1170).
- Birth of Saint Francis of Assisi (1182).
- Magna Carta drawn up (1215).
- Dante Alighieri wrote *Divine Comedy* (1304–21)
- Hundred Years' War (1337–1453).
- Black Death kills 25 million Europeans (1348).
- *Sir Gawain and the Green Knight* written (c1375–1400).
- John Wycliffe and his followers begin first complete translation of the Bible into English (1380)
- Chaucer writes *The Canterbury Tales* (1387–89).
- English burn Joan of Arc at the stake at Rouen (1431).
- Wars of the Roses (1455–85).
- Wars of the Roses (1455–85).

Important Dates of World War II
1941

- Japanese attack naval base at Pearl Harbor (Dec. 7).
- Roosevelt gives "Day of Infamy" speech; United States and Britain declare war on Japan (Dec. 8).

1942

- Mass gassing of Jews begins at Auschwitz and Allies forge Declaration of the United Nations (Jan. 1).

- Japanese navy resoundingly defeated at Battle of Midway (June 4).
- Allied invasion of North Africa begins in "Operation Torch" (Nov. 8).

1943

- British forces take Tripoli (Jan. 23).
- Mussolini and the Fascists overthrown (July 25-26).
- New Italian government announces Italy's surrender (Sept. 8).

1944

- D-Day: invasion of Europe begins with Allied landings at Normandy (June 6).
- Paris liberated (Aug. 25).
- German Army launches "Battle of the Bulge" offensive on the Western Front (Dec. 16).

1945

- Battle of the Bulge ends in German defeat (Jan. 16).
- Soviets liberate Auschwitz (Jan. 26).
- Unconditional surrender of all German forces (May 7).
- Victory in Europe (VE) Day (May 8).
- United Nations World Charter signed in San Francisco (June 26).
- First atomic bomb dropped on Hiroshima (Aug. 6).
- Second atomic bomb dropped on Nagasaki (Aug. 9).
- Unconditional surrender of Japanese forces (Aug. 14).
- Victory over Japan (VJ) Day (Aug. 15).

1946

- United Nations meets for first time in London

- Gulf War – 1991
- Rwanda's Civil War – 1994
- Afghanistan War – 2001–Present
- Second Iraq/USA War – 2003–2011

20th and 21st Centuries Wars

- Korean War – 1950–1953
- Vietnam War – 1964–1973
- North Ireland Civil War – 1969–2002
- Khmer Rouge, Cambodia – 1975–1979
- Angolan Civil War – 1976–1993
- Iraq/Iran War – 1980–1988
- Somalia's Civil War – 1988–2004